Up the City of Angels

UP THE CITY

New York

OF ANGELS

by Liza Williams

G. P. Putnam's Sons

This book is for you, and for my son Michael Rubens, and Robert Gold, William Marvin, Clair Brush, Laura Baron, my father and mother, Garry the typesetter, Jerry Hopkins, Bill and Roslyn Targ (who thought it possible and made it so), John Thomas, D. Thomas, A. Ginsberg, K. Whitehorn, A. Powell, the people in it, the people along the road, and the energy source whatever its name.

March, 1971

Contents

Introduction

HOW do you do? I'm supposed to introduce myself, explicitly; that's so that when I have you in my word clutches later on you will have this prior explanation. Well, I am older than I was when I began that sentence, and certainly older than when I began my first sentence which my mother, a sometime nursery school teacher and all-time artist *manqué* told me was "Higa diga digalow." From then on it got complicated; there was a war in Spain, a revolution, and before that Ethiopia and Manchuria, and I remember Hoovertowns though I was very little then; that's how old I am.

I am not very tall; once when standing on a chair to hang a painting I realized that people taller than myself had an entirely different view of my rooms. Perhaps they only saw a line of the tops of picture frames while I stared each picture in the eye.

I am a woman; I found that out recently. In that exploration I made a number of excursions. Much of what I have written describes those trips. I think I am different from you, inside, and wonder what everyone else's world feels like.

I pour out as much as I can to encourage feedback. I got some important feedback from Robert Gold, a master pataphysician, who taught me to laugh at art which was really to love with it.

My father was very melancholy. He was a professor of inorganic chemistry at City College in New York and taught me that there is no such thing as a bigger half. He also repeatedly warned me "not to take any wooden nickels" and signaled me by yelling: "Cheese it, boys, the cop's around the corner." I have a letter he wrote to me three days before he died; he thought I had come to visit him in the hospital, and perhaps I had.

My parents lived with me in Greenwich Village in the thirties and forties. They sent me to expensive progressive private schools where I learned to believe in justice and the divine right of individuality. It was a space-age preparation for a grounded society.

I got expelled from my first college (politely—they still send me alumni fund appeals) for being about to have an abortion while near school property. I went to another college to paint—a lot of now famous artists were my classmates. I went to visit one such classmate recently (when back in New York City), and he said, "Oh I remember you; you were my first model." That's all he said directly to me the whole evening, though we had been close friends.

There were air-raid shelter signs up in the streets of New York in 1951, and McCarthy had cost my father his job and dreams, and I was sick of an old passion and an unfruitful love. I left for Europe with my "brother" Stanley and traveled with him and his collapsed lung and did that for a while, and other things, and then went on a boat to South Africa to get married and eventually have a son, but really to avoid coming back to America.

I came back to America in 1964, crossed the country on a Greyhound bus, poor, $40, sleeping on the bus at night and eating Kraft pimento cheese on Ritz crackers while the miracle of America unfolded under me.

Everything that I see now I see because of what I saw before. This book is supposed to be about California in particular, but the viewer is me and I carry all my baggage with me. I have everything to declare.

Here is an excerpt from a letter I sent to William Targ, my patient editor, explaining the process of putting this collection together. He suggested I include it in this introduction.

DEAR BILL,

I have tried to organize this collection of that wordage and that poetry and that whatever is myself that has poured out over these past five years. The process of putting myself into cohesive form seems like psychoanalysis. I bought this typewriter which writes almost as fast as He transmits through me, and I sit and transmit and think on paper while I continue to consume myself with life, and be consumed. Form, I have to seek form; this is the form; perhaps it will disturb you. I think not, for it is the natural form of it.

I must be able at times to dip back, to refer my readers to my bones, to explain how these eyefingers of mine found the braille of California, and found it through their accumulation of touch, the

years in Paris, New York, London. I did not come here unprepared;
my insights, what insights I have, grew like cabbages from all the
soil I waded through. If I am to have open heart surgery on these
pages, then my case history belongs here, however obliquely.

It has been hard because it has its terrors, and I am alone with my
fears. "You are such a good writer" is what my friends say, "It's
easy," but they do not write nor are they asked to present themselves
cohesed in a time of dissolution and fall apart; things fall apart, the
center will not hold, and I must find the center and the times are
hard, but I am there, and coming up, and coming up means making
it hold together, and I will do it and I do not mean to freak you
with all this but to ask that you understand. And you can see the
spelling problems, but my friends will deal with that, and you can
see the self-doubts, but I will deal with that, am dealing with that,
and meanwhile I have a weekly column to pull from my veins and
a full-time job in a world of corporation capers.

Essentially I feel the energy of it now, and the comprehensive
form—that was the hardest part; all I need is the stamina. So many
people pull at me, want some sort of spark from me, want me to
write about their thing, to save them from intimate emotional disasters, think I am strong. I must draw it all in now, break a pattern
of years, for it was the going out and the being open that let so much
flow in, and from that flow came the material to regurgitate onto
the paper. Now I must sort out all that has gone, been digested,
passed and been assimilated, as though I were to spend days looking
into the mirror and picking out my best features. I am discovering
the architecture of my life, Corbusier, Gaudi, Frank Lloyd Wright—
how they must have trembled over their drawing boards when they
laid the final strokes that would be the impartial imprint of their
psychotic fantasy lives! So I have chosen the columns, and written
introductions to the sections, and it will be a book of some sort,
even if only you and I know that and they all think it riven and
crazed and poetic. It is only the journal of a trip through life; to
see one's life, as the TV show demonstrated, is cause for tears. Love,

LIZA

The sections have titles intended to spread their image over the
groupings of columns. I have indicated the dates when the columns
were written because so many of them speak of a specific time or of
my stage of awareness. Almost all of these columns, pieces, poems,
ravings, effluvia, regurgencies, appeared in the Los Angeles *Free
Press*; the exceptions are so noted. I suggest you read only a little at a
time, sort of meander along with me. I hope it pleasures you, makes

you want to enjoy your life to its fullest capacity. Peace to you, to all of us, and time and quiet and patience and loving feelings, friends and a smooth trip.

Liza Williams
March 29, 1971

Up the City of Angels

TINSEL TOWN is one old lady whose toes, though polished purple, are still worth a suck. How can you tell pure unless you sift the dirt? I love them, the escaped minds that circle the ten or so blocks that constitute Hollywood Boulevard, pushing their households in liberated market carts. There is the Lady in Blue (coffee at Western Avenue, a hamburger on Highland—she patrols her beat even on Sundays). There is The Captain with his navigational library strapped to his back, and Mr. Serape who sleeps on the bus bench in front of the Rexall drugstore at Hollywood and Vine. Hollywood and Vine! (massive boredom) and the gay meat market in front of the Golden Cup on Cherokee, the plaster statue shops, the eternally Going Out Of Business stores, the waterbed shop (formerly wigs), incense and dildoes in the headshops, Mr. Fredericks' cutaway cunt panties, used bookstores featuring fan magazines devoted to peroxide and Garbo, Lebanese pizza merchants, the London Shop (London Shop?!!), Grauman's Chinese cement monument to foot fetishists, Buffalo Bill available for polaroid snapshots (Grauman's is the last place left on earth where you can wear Bermuda shorts and bobby socks and be in fashion), the Greyhound Station, lunchtime secretaries in Lerner's drag, two movies for the price of three, police, Hare Krishna chanters and Jesus Freaks.

Hollywood, Hollywood, Hollywood, Follyglued, it's a permanent Forty-second Street with a tender climate and nowhere to go except off the edge and swim to Japan.

Take a tour, Hollywood, Echo Park, downtown LA (where nobody goes), Westwood, and all the other suburbs that grew from the dream. So here's to you, Hollywood, in Gingerogers, up, up and away! A city of angels? Surely, going up? Definitely.

Every Day's a Holy Day

Can't understand this town. Where is Main Street? Is it the parking lot where the scuttlers slurge from their cars into the seductivity of multiple-choice, oral-satiety joy palaces? Luminous hypnotic trips on soap powder labels, psychedelic visions in the cellophane-meat section. It's all free, free with a wheeled chariot to push, and the baked-bean booty doesn't cost—until at the temple gate they take the collection, vestal murmurings, two for thirty-three, two for forty-seven, the Cabala of odd numbers for even quantities, and stamps. Stamps worth little gilded tin things to hold shiny ceramic things in the decorator-deodorized home is where the debts are. Will cats eat dog food, what is fresh meat, cat food? dog food? Why do bananas have feminine trade names? Thank God cucumbers remain between the watercress and parsley, mutely phallic, though greased. Perhaps one night, while the store empties, I shall hide behind this-week's-special, and having, finally, the whole world of it to myself, live a lifetime on "home-style minestrone," flushing myself on raisin bran, and dressing myself in disposable party-time tablecloths, squirt obscene words, "pure," "fresh," "real," or even "tasty" on the walls with cans of Reddiwip, make love in the vegetable department, and die in the freezer, there to greet the morning congregation with a whole uncut piece of human.

Daily, it is the passing of anonymity that eats the chrome off my car. It is the loathing of the footwalkers for my mobility that pits the jewelry on my car. There must be a thousand, a thousand thousand shops into which I shall never go. Refuge in ten shall please me, the weeping sweat in Ohrbach's is Fairfaxfamiliar, old country style. Klein's on the square sold mink coats for half price, and dresses for a dollar. Better bargains still come from the Goodwill, lovename, or from the miraculous garbage cans of Beverly Hills which have whole alleys to themselves, like it was excreta to be hidden, while in Silverlake and Los Feliz and East Los Angeles the garbage can is outside to testify to the riches that are thrown away, potlatch ghosts haunt the municipality. I know if He didn't love me so much, He wouldn't reward me from the garbage cans with whole households of furniture, with lamps and chairs, bread boxes and bookshelves and old ice-chests so perfect for smoking fish and chicken and pork, with picture frames, with the print of a lady and a dog by the riverside, peaceful in faded brown (that will be IN this year, or if not this year so very IN the next). Once in Echo Park I saw a painting, large, six feet by five feet, propped between tree and garbage pail, but even though it was a jollyclown playing a flute, I did not want it. The next day, driving home past the debris shops on Sunset Boulevard, I saw it standing outside in the sun next to the chairs, gas heaters, baby cribs, for sale. And who could claim the profit? Could the artist demand it back, would the ACLU defend his right to destroy his creation against the right of my fellow grubbers in the free market of the curb and gutter?

America, all your goodies spill out into the street.

February 4, 1966

This Toilet Is Occupied

Fly over Los Angeles, over the marvelously snug canyons, below, acres of flat stoneflung star-spangled-bannered roofs. What an expanse for slogan writers, Captain Max with a spray can of luminous paint strapped to his belly, superwhamo success lives here, air-conditioning lives here, three cars live here, stop the whatever it is lives here; we are arrived in twenty feet of chickenwire, golden letter boxes gleam and blind our eyes, flying hazard, TV antennas sing back at us commercials for silence, there is a whole level of living up above our heads.

Across from my office they have sliced off the nipple of a hill, the land is limp and recovering from its mastectomy. Soon it will be topped with a new hotel, wall-to-wall quicksand carpet, no thirteenth floor, enormous palms and a zoo of colored lights. La Cienega has an oil rig next to a hamburger stand, a block of no-man's-land between the glory restaurants in the shape of dreams, and the shops where the talcum-aesthetic makes the sinuses of the spirit ache. There must be a whole generation that thinks that bathrooms are neoclassic spas, French chateau ballrooms, although at Versailles I believe perfume covered the stench of the body in substitute for cleanliness. What used to say hot and cold has given over to an army of gilded dolphins, the intimate paper sprouts garlands, almost too visually exciting now, we become constipated through our aesthetic frenzy, clutch the plastic greenery, and die of intestinal congestion. Perhaps, there will be, adjacent to this colormatched seraglio, this creamsoap, sunken roman tub anal orgy palace, a small white room, with a seat that remains reminiscently warm, toilet paper on a wire, and a cistern above the toilet with a really rusty, sharp, comforting chain to pull and set off the satisfyingly digestive sound of its gurgling, splunging water.

Someone in England (and America!) has put out a book called the *Good Loo Guide.* A loo is a euphemism for lavatory, or john, or toilet, or can, or craphouse. This little book describes the most comfortable, charming, accessible, pretty, clean, desirable comfort stations in and around London. As in the Micheline Guide Bleu, each dewatering place is awarded meritorious asterisks. I spent part of last summer collecting samples of English lavatory paper, that harsh stern nonabsorbent tissue that has served to remind the English of their national guilt, the daily self-flagellation of what they term their privates. When you reflect that this is the one part of the body that has the least privacy, being poked and prodded throughout most of its adult life, it is a strange world indeed, sir. Having so abused themselves with decades of vengeful wiping, it is hardly unexpected that they abjure each other to keep a stiff upper lip. Here in America, we have a more sympathetic attitude toward our national ass.

February 25, 1966

Love with a See-through Navel

The nonsectarian doughnut domain of the once and for all glazed halo King Cooper be praised. From the streets of banana peels and thousand cauliflowers, of crates of rosy-buttock tomatoes like Eve in green tissue, of spiton polished apples and pale subterranean celery and the wraggletaggle haggle of the fetus hours before dawn, the clang down fronts of the produce province to this squared-off flour room hung with forebearers is one step off the street to turn of the century pride. There the herculean hole cutter, gigantic arm outflung, debowels one hundred and twenty dozen pulsing lumps an hour. No machine with oiledhum precision, with flywheel gratespanned beltlooped cogswirled precision, could match his pounding delicacy. An isolate manmade, craftculled, delicacy factory in the midst of great heaving transports of vegetable.

From Cooper's factory on East Sixth Street, to the twentyfour hours a day shops, next to gas stations, down the sides of parkinglots, little lit places for transients, a steady stream of doughnuts flow; perhaps the only twelve-cent solace left in Los Angeles. Coffee and doughnut and broken conversation with the counterman in apron and cloth.

From all the hotel lobbies near the centers, from long tunnel lobbies filled with bandaged men facing what featured television epic, what satin-smothered fantasywoman, to the hard round stools of Cooper's islands, is but one limp and a socialsecurity dime. Push a finger in and the sugar gives like the remembered breast of woman, the belly of love with a see-through navel. This is a city of plastic paradises wherein one true thing is left, a handmade doughnut.

March 4, 1966

Through a Chromed Eye Darkly

I exhort everyone to listen to the color of light. To rub two fingers together on a clear day, and listen to the air crack between them with the sound of cucumber peels snapping, or when the gauzehaze filters the sun, hear air moan with smog. We choke on that gray sound.

Many years ago this must have been a clear country, the missions standing warm ochre against the watercolor sky, the falling fruit bursting on the clean earth, the smell of slaughtered Indians lying pungent on the wild grass, foretaste of civilization, an appetizer for progress, the main course before the indigestion of our time.

There was a camel route that passed this way. Camels trudging stone from Texas to a pass just beyond the valley, there to die and be remembered in a bronze plaque, some daguerreotypes, a statesponsored wooden building that also houses information on fire prevention. What visions these camels must have brought with them in their slogging hopeful desert search, to die on that hill, run out of water and tents.

On Sunset, near Vine, an old showhouse has a façade of autographs. Look closely, and they all seem to have been painted by the same hand. The names ask you to remember, but for us whizzing by in cars, they remain as blurred as their memory. Inside that building, I once attended a Queen For A Day taping. It was during a time when, unemployed and strange to Los Angeles, I took every ticket and answered every survey, happy to prove my existence by a piece of paper. I offered an exotic but rather cheerful story and was among the twenty finalists to undergo a deeper probing. In my euphoria, brought about by visions of four-burner stoves with eye-level ovens in permanent baked-on decorator color, by a year's supply of supernatural soap powder, by wall to wall carpeting (and if I lived in the Pan Pacific Auditorium would they still honor their offer?), of cartons of electric carving knives, toothbrushes with six interchangeable heads, perhaps survey-proved to be the measure of the modern American family, with all these goodies to have and hold, to provide a FUN time for me and mine, I lost my discretion and told my happy tale. I was rejected in favor of a lady whose baby had died. She wanted a set of translated Bibles for her husband. We atheists have a hard time on earth.

Another afternoon I went to the Hollywood cemetery to see the monuments; someone occupied a cement tomb on an island in a manufactured lake. I asked about it, but the only people there were the gardeners; they came from Czechoslovakia and their information was unintelligible. The grass there is lovely, though, and you can sit on Tyrone Power. Across the street from the cemetery is an auto repair called the Body Shop. I think I would like to be delivered there instead; I have a fancy for closed eyes edged in chrome.

When my father came from New York to visit, I took him to Forest Lawn. It is a cheap outing and they have a tomb in one of the buildings that belongs to Chief Silver Cloud. His name is written in silver inlaid in marble. There is also a mockup of Michelangelo's "David." It has a box next to it with a button. If you push the button a voice comes from heaven and tells you how they had this embalmed copy specially made. My father thought I was hinting at something, so I took him to the Farmers Market, where he bought me some purpleripe cherries. He only comes here once a year.

I have always believed that it brings good fortune to eat the first cherries of the year, and that you find lovers if you hide behind bushes in public parks and read poetry aloud, and that there is a lot of money lying in the gutters, so watch your feet.

On Western there is a shop hung with sunbleached newspaper clippings, pale photographs, old postcards. I knocked on the door and a faded man peered out of the slight opening. I told him I wanted to buy some of the postcards. He told me he kept the shop in tribute to his relative killed in the war, that he changed the display every two weeks, that he never sold anything; he slammed the door with a whispering hiss.

This town is full of monuments and cemeteries. Are there really souls under the names on Hollywood Boulevard? Under the writing on the wall on Sunset? Is Chief Silver Cloud really behind marble? I think people who sense their own dying build monuments.

March 25, 1966

Open Letter to the Ducks on Echo Park Lake

Dear Marrow-boned darling Ducks: your marble eyes wink waterproof. Holders of the ribbon for languid crossings, eaters of flies and golden sprinkled bugs that skim, soft sitters on the lake raft—greetings!

Each morning how the eye is drawn to your resting white shapes there, on the water where one man drowned and another clung to the sinking boat while the Sunday watchers stood on the bank and stared after the hoped-for prize of his body, like Bingo crowds at the fair.

Oh most unusual residents of this city, freeloading off the floating debris, pecking for crusts through half submerged Baggies, fresh and floating between the banana skins and condoms, your garden of treasures lie limp on the banks, and weeds make for your home a waving entrance.

Did he see you, the drowning man, your white shadows floating above him, playing iceberg to his Titanic body as you serenely lay claim to that water domain?

He went to rent a boat—and died on a Sunday afternoon, bloated with Coca-Cola and tacos, nicotined lips sipping the cool water to overflow, down to the bottom of that lake.

The papers say they were motorcyclists. Is that all? Were they and their dreams put only to the turning of wheels? Or can we assume, because we know that they fell through that liquid skin, on that warm day, before the farrow-eyed crowd, that they had had enough of tar and took to water? That they paid their dollar and in their leaky boat sailed across their span of time to turn one man's bones to chalk?

How speed was denied her feast of skin and bone, how lakeland took his body softly down, how he lay there for a time invisible to the grappling men in uniform, how he was raised from the lake and shone for a moment as the sun reflected from his watery caul; all this history, my ducks, is within the world your shallow sitting body sails.

At eight fifteen every weekday morning, when the boat house has not yet opened, and you, complacent ducks, sitting on your raft of wood, are the only inhabitants of that public park, I drive by your world of water, and its deceptive calm reminds me that stripped of their histories, all faces are placid and meaningless.

May, 1966

Hey Superman, Where Is Thy Sting

The comic-book men are right, everyone has a balloon projecting from his mouth containing the ultimate message. I discovered this last night, lying in bed; I saw the people in the streets, their messages neatly placed within the issuing circles.

I saw in MacArthur Park, the old and folded, spread across the inflexible benches, obliterating the waterview with massed dark suits, or slowly crumbling along the cement. And from each a balloon, an enormous balloon containing ten-year roominghouse anxieties, spittle splattered names of women who had passed in beauty during their Midwest years before the exodus to sun and scratched linoleum. The ponded ducks too, once the subject of a war of love, bore stamped upon their oiled surface in legal script the message, Municipal Duck, Do Not Cook.

I saw the Fairfax newsstand man, one foot adangle over the curb,

from his mouth flowing bossanova bright and flashing the words—
Lesbianlovelies stropping goldiedyke prettyface pantielace hotrod
homeysam coedfire flame consume. His phantom face painless and
peeled, his stomach a spongy mass of fourth-class postage.

I saw them on Hill and Spring. They were all proclaiming the same
thing, Paperbag paperbag paperbag, the Greek chorus of the department stores, victims of public transports.

I saw them outside the recruiting station, their hearts neonized.
From their kissey mouths messages of peanutbutter patriotism. Their
words embroidered by a hundred volunteer mothers, those drag-
dugged harpies of the Suburban Ism League. The whole thing spelled
out in glittering lights programmed to play the message and include
the latest scores for games and wars.

I saw them kooking down the Strip, their foureyes ablaze with dull
dreaming, their attenuated hair swirling like oil slick along their
leathered shoulders, gothic-faced and primed with time to spill and no
noise loud enough to still the sound of their warhead hearts ticking.
Saw them under their slogans of touch-me-not and feel-me-up. They
spangled and glittered down the street to their misspelled music.

I remembered that once I had seen them pass the boatbound hours
deckwalking. Two old men, their hands knotted behind their backs,
pacing off their no-man's-land, passportless and preserved in time,
printed neatly in the script of Goethe . . . I am a German and a Jew.

I see myself, the words tumbling out within the circle like the
washing in the windowed laundromat, the meaning and the meaningless tangled in the scum water and the bleach, the sudsing effluvia of
my life measured out in twenty-five cents worth of time.

I turn my head, but my balloon remains out of sight; you will have
to read it for me.

May, 1966

Out on the Streets with Crazy Mary and the Vortexes

Now comes the blanched body of the pure believer, neat Dacron
slax, blue-bound book in thin-bone fingers, slowly to the leatherette

stool of the luncheon counter in the Self-Realization Center at the east end of Hollywood. Ancient handmaidens in Woolworth nylon saris, beatific gold-capped smiles placing wrong dishes from an absence of mind, incense at the pay counter neat in packages next to blur-printed tracts with photographs of old longhaired smiling guru man, blond deal tables with orange plastic mats in curlicue designs. Now—meditate upon the cactus in glazed pot filled with aniline dyed stones from no earth, nirvana for all, 11 A.M. lunch of soybean cake in the east end of Hollywood.

Outside the buses' stench, the anonymity of suffering in the boxed canyon of hospitals, federal compassion for day trippers whose twenty-four hours have stretched to infirmity, bordered by ice-cream parlors and a seller of maybe genuine ethnic relics where bone bead eyes stare back at you, historically stoned.

Go the other way, through the gritty entrance to the park, atop whose half-limbed hill Frank Lloyd Wright templehouse smears its crumble cement along slatted seats; there art classes, too expensive for the unemployed, too daytime for the worker, make puddles of color in matching small Inca square, or see displayed photograph by retired amateur professionals collecting ribbons from candidates, reproductions of Holy Madonnas made from birdseed hang in gilt frames. Down again and round the corner, past splursh of carwash, hissing water dragon, kept by dull yellow expatriates from Mexico, emitting glistening missile motors to zap off into the smog.

Vermont Avenue in schizoid waltz spins belly dancers between the supper tables across from the Thrifty Drugstore, open for bargains and blue chip stamps and the pill. Up the street eat pastry in Sarno's, old Italy taste, with New World prices. Outside the men from the bleak hotels, walking their ghost companions up Vermont past the stone mansion of The Bank of America, splatter their breath against the rising slope.

Once walking on Los Feliz, doing a barefoot circle along the dust path to the observatory and back, rushing through the fun-button automated scientific display, dripping ice cream down sun warm legs, I slid back down to Los Feliz and stood, ankle deep, in a Grecian pond at the entrance to a development that said ready for occupancy and lay unlandscaped behind a wall. I stood in the electric nature of the pool facing the cars plowing through the Sunday afternoon slug grind of aimless city cruising, and sang songs to the empty houses and the depopulated streets. I was Trevi fountain, a water garden, Venus risng from the cloister houses, naiad and nymph, and tired of the city.

Up Vermont! Rise New England state! Shed leaves of amber and purple splotch, raspberry stains on elbows, prickle food injuries comorted on old stump of tree, and between the folded flesh a view of receding horizons, mystic house retreats, supplied with pans of sugar and hand-knitted shawls.

Up Vermont! And to Los Feliz, and down the winding sheet of tar o the fountain isolate on a triangle of cement, like Circe in a cradle of thorns. Great effulgent fountain spraying color! Sitting at night, on he municipal temple benches, eyes fixated and brought to purposeful unfocus, the colored water flowing through between the sound of tires urning and the certainty of disaster, of the awkward explanation, of he reason for sitting, dilated and visioned, like a monument in a city park at night with no visible means of support.

The East End of Hollywood. Zen Macrobiotic Restaurant, mystic bookshop with incense and cat stench, Tarot cards in stylistic woodblock patterns, one Pre-Raphaelite, coveted by Yeats, and we know where he was! dancing there in Ireland to Crazy Mary and the Vortexes, some rock group of the poet's mind, playing to the Zodiac's intestinal beat.

The East End of Hollywood, and up Vermont, Los Feliz and the fountain, my home in the hills . . . and this trip never stopping, round the diamond tarmac of vision.

July 15, 1966

Take Forever

At the Ontra Cafeteria on Vine, just above Hollywood Boulevard, next door to the Hollywood Palace where the burlesque shows are filmed and the fans line up at 7 P.M. in the smoggy light of almost night, clutching their tickets and dream of being spotted in the audience, the tables fill. The Ontra has no stancheon with tickets that pop to the ringing of a bell into your hand, little tickets like tram tickets that the counterman punched as you took your choice of baked halibut or chicken fried steak on the special. I wonder what has happened to those belled machines? Now you go in with the same euphoria as grips you at the supermarket and they don't whisper money till, tray loaded with food, you are stopped at the checker counter.

Everyone at that Ontra is over sixty-five and all are stars, every one a star. If their names are not outside in the cement sidewalk being smoothed to oblivion by indifferent feet, it is only that the break never came, but they continue to pose. A million copies of the trade papers congest the Ontra's garbage between the fishbones and the Kleenex smelling of lilac toilet water. Faces swivel from table to table, a hundred red wrinkled lips purse in salute to the henna-haired director, still wearing his cap backwards, as he squeezes between the formica tops and plastic roses carrying his cheesecake and coffee That's Franco, the woman at the next table says to her friend, and crosses her sagging pink mesh-clad ankles over each other, a piece of paper stuck on the end of her baby blue spiked heel rustling as she moves.

They are stars dreaming in the daylight over creole turkey and garlic bread. They are stars in the daylight fixed in the horizons of each other's vision. She's looking older, she's looking older but I remember when, I do remember as if it were yesterday, and the yesterdays calliope into a fusion of drying sauces on the rims of small plates and the bits of uneaten bread.

Walking is slow there, whether it is hobble or drag, slouch or arthritic curve, slow across the great carpeted stage, with little nods and jerks of head, with delicate waving of fingers and attention to the hair that loosens itself from pins and nets and the tight sausage rolls of style unchanging. Stars, more stars than the blurred images spliced to commercials that pop out at random as you absently switch the dial. What is on, I forgot to buy the *TV Guide,* Ralph Williams seems to be everywhere, caressing the cars, his dog, somebody's dog, lying on the motor. Where are the white gloves and the silver phantoms, in the living rooms the stars have died, but in the Ontra Cafeteria they glow forever, sitting row on row, up against the Mediterranean walls of plaster and the almost-Fillmore poster advertising the special cut in prices from 4 to 6 P.M., crossing the space of their stage to be rewarded, if not by applause, at least by some sort of recognition and a chicken fried steak.

They huddle and bow, they align their chairs in order of seniority, they intercept each other with small bits of information about people I thought already dead. He's gone to Palm Springs, they say, gone for two weeks with Sam; he says it's to look over a script but you know what I think. They nod, grateful for the news that never reaches the pages of the trades, wondering if, when they do exit finally, they will have a bold face notice in the obits. They read, looking to see who's made the grave, in style. That must be a kind of triumph, to find a friend in print, even if for the final time.

Up the street the line grows longer, families from Tarzana and Texas come to see the stars at the Hollywood Palace, come to applaud a hometown boy because he is dancing, third row center, on the big television stage. Up the street they crane their necks as the extras flow in the side door, as the big cars stop, as the stars get out. While just behind them, stored in the Ontra Cafeteria, the permanent cast of Hollywood settles in for the serious business and the rewards of glamor, and a chicken fried steak.

December, 1966

Things That Go Bang in the Night

Driving along the multiplying freeways, surrounded by graveyard ivy, standardized nature permanently dull green and dusty, I am comforted by the thought that in all the houses whose images are blurred by speed, becoming one house of endless proportion and deadly commonplace, people are screwing.

At night, flying through the plaster miles from delicate point to delicate point, flowing in a harangue of enameled metal, each a kingdom to itself, more alone than in space among the dead planets, raging along the concrete artery, I am saved from despair by knowing that out there in the stucco wasteland, locked in deodorized arms, splayed across the flower-bordered sheets, with the sound of plumbing for birdsong, people are screwing.

There is love in West Covina, like a blanket of joy. Escaped from the abandoned hotdog stand, the shut shop, empty dance hall, the powder parlor, the credit dentist from nine to five and later on Tuesdays, there are people lying bed-locked, people sucking pleasure from the suburban night, within their rooms, lit by the blue ghost of soundless television romance, people are screwing.

It is the moisture of love that clouds my windshield, a pale human smog of desire that distorts my vision of off-ramp signs and roadside business. Trapped between the chickenwire divisions with their indented notations of disaster, my nostrils clog with the perfume of love, the scent of the evening is the odor of people screwing.

There is love in Anaheim. Within the shadow of the paper mountain, bodies slide into each other, after the park is closed and the last polite direction given, up the cement branches the Swiss Family Robinson balls on the oaktree bed. In the world of the future the giant computers heave with programmed lust, the monorail seeks its other rod, and in the telephone palace the wires cross, their hum turning to moan, right under the barbered mustache of the father of Mickey Mouse, the wind-up people are screwing.

There is love in Venice. In paper rooms on the edge of the tissue-time of the aged, old flesh finds its sagging brother gently. Touching the central heat of life, the rejected years drop from the graying sheets, whisper along the alleys of girls in flower from central Europe, nose whiskers and eyedrops, grape-green phlegm, murmuring along Ocean Boulevard and Rose Avenue down to the littered sea, the old people dream of screwing.

There is love in City Hall. Bunched against the marble inlay, wrapped around the iron-bound stairs, beneath the sullen carpeting in the soundless rooms, the memos dance. The dear sirs and ladies, the gentlemen and chairmen of the board, residue of the carbon paper day crumpled with their errors, lie in baskets, waiting the hand's tip, the burning without protest. The statistics, imperfect at best, are wild at night, the round holes of nine and six sprout nipples and X remains a virgin with her legs crossed, unpronounceable. If there were people in City Hall, their shadows have escaped, and there is only this paperscape copy of people screwing.

There is love in Hamburgers. Brides of adolescence take vows of mustard and relish underneath McDonald's Golden Arches. From Hamburger Hamlet flows the Piccalilly peasant bent on glutinous orgasm of sesame seed rolls forever fresh, and Cert-destroyed onion breath to kiss away the dreams of meat in the mountain night, redolent on sticks, the fire reflecting the fur and teeth of lovers, shaggy and covered with the brine of flood. In every cave of memory, repeated in the persimmon-pink of Naugahyde and plastic spoon as teeth bite the sagging bun, through the dead mind seeps the knowledge that people are screwing.

There is love between the destinations. Sitting on the moving platform, jetting down the road, the radio crying for forgiveness of smell and hair, for pimple-faces and the names of young ladies about to graduate grammar school, for angst of fear and enemies approaching, for non-stop talk back and songs whose beat structures the lack of melody, for the anonymous whine of desperate peddlers of patriotism, and disaster sooths who fly above in butterfly machines counting bodies and collisions, seeing the endless red lights of departing dynasties bound for where I have just fled from; the bumper stickers like the voice of evangelism pronouncing the new name of God, I look through the haze of days of plenty and hear, half throttled by the machinery, the sound of people screwing.

July 8, 1966

Hometown Heroes

Ralph Williams is wearing a silk suit tonight, he is sitting behind a desk, speaking sincerely, and a little slower than usual, but that's all right, because I remember him out there on the lot, his thick hand caressing the enamel hip of the car, purveying metal-love to me with those incredible computer lips. White-wall-tires-twenty-thousand-miles-or-six-months-all-brand-new-interior-heating-automatic-brakes-automatic-steering, and he is speaking just to me! He is reassuringly there, just as the sun goes off and some unknown tortured extra from the 1940's collapses against the desk and my stomach clenches with anxiety, he comes on again, and it's all normal and he offers me a guarantee and that's not all, he offers me himself, porcine and confident and it's all OK and I know I'm in Southern California and safe for another day.

They can't take my heroes from me, they can't take my familiars, that couple, larger than life and softened by the light, walking with the swans in Forest Lawn rejoicing that everything has been taken care of, that couple of middle age, tranquil in the face of death. It wasn't a tragedy, just a parent, some elderly faceless mother buried without anguish near the swans. I too can be happy when . . .

In the post office there are histories on the wall. Sally Jo Bennett alias S. Jane Bent alias Sarah Bernard alias Mary Frank . . . Mary Frank, that was a departure from the mnemonic of initials; when did she decide to try that name? Was she stranded somewhere with the cops hot on her trail and suddenly she thought, maybe Mary Frank will confuse them, but it seems it didn't, though she is still around, stealing money orders from envelopes, holding the paper up to the light on some crumbly staircase, that's all right, Mrs. Lopez, she yells down the hall, don't you trouble yourself, I'll bring the mail up to you (with something missing hee hee), and Mary, alias Sarah, alias S. Jane, alias Sally Jo, is richer by seven dollars sent from Minnesota.

I don't know who anybody is in this town, people on the street, people in the store, one Safeway is like the next and I have no neighbors, but I am not without community heroes. There is the woman on the supermarket window, photographed holding a check for a thousand dollars, she won it with a little stamp, she won it with a little tab, she opened the lucky envelope and there was E-3, the missing number, the one we all wanted. I stared at her. Did she suffer disbelief, as I do, clutching the envelope, opening it, saying to myself, maybe this time and being ashamed of hope, or burying it deep under the eggs and "specials" until I get home where the little card is waiting for its E-3. But she opened it and there it was, worth a thousand dollars. What did she do, did she rush out to Ralph Williams and buy a car, did she go to Forest Lawn and take care of before-need, did she dye her hair, buy new shoes, or did she rush back to the market and buy more groceries, hoping for another envelope of fortune? I am stuck with her face, Mrs. G. Hauser of 5467 Mirador Drive, Encino, where is that? Should I send her a begging letter, all famous rich people get begging letters, I even got a begging letter once, and I'm not very famous and certainly not rich.

When they remove Sally J. from the post office does it mean that they have caught her, is it all over, the thrill of the envelopes supplanted by the drab of jail, or have they given up, as I give up on the Lucky Bingo, the Fortune Envelope, the Dial-a-Dollar, is it all over, and only Ralph Williams left believing in love and success and the eternal desirability of a white wall tire?

January 19, 1967

˜he City

The basic agriculture of cities is the garbage at the curbside, the ˌotsam papers and shredded butts that bloom on that pavement, the ˌsty water that sits in layers over tar and cement and on run-rainy ˌays, shining for a moment from the configurations of the oil slick, ˌnds off swirling rainbows. But this harvest is mainly out of sight, ˌalking from car to door and door to car, rushing to some predeter-ˌined point, we create our own ghettos, populate them with who we ˌish to see.

I went to Main Street one evening, main street in downtown Los ˌngeles. The street begins and ends upon itself. The slop clothed men ˌnd sex cinemas, the erotic bookshops and pawnshops are its vegeta-ˌon. I stopped to have my picture taken by a twenty-five-cent ma-ˌhine, the kind that audibly digests the images and spews them back ˌhrough a slit mound like some mechanical excretion. Behind the ma-ˌhine were cubicles, made of whitewashed half partitions, like the ˌubicles used for disrobing before an examination, or those doorless ˌoilets in public parks where no funny business is allowed. In these ˌttle stalls of love, men stood, hands in pockets, watching the ten-ˌent cinema contact. The proprietor, with an apronful of change, ˌtared at his rows of books and chewing gum. It was silent, very si-ˌnt, a place of personal worship. Walking at night through this shuf-ˌling city mob, who have gotten as far as the Pacific from God knows ˌhere, were stranded on the cement with nowhere to go but up and ˌown the pawnshop street and alleys of urination smell, I felt conspic-ˌous, an alien from the land of plenty, remote as the moon used to ˌe.

One shoeshine shop had an oil painting of Kennedy on the back-ˌall, the shine man stared at me as I looked at the painting, he saw ˌy sandals and looked away. I wonder if I should have picked up the ˌwo shoes I had seen earlier in the entrance to the Farmer's and Mer-ˌhants' bank, one each in the bottom halves of shoe boxes, unshined, ˌorn, without laces. Were they laid there as a gift to the finder, or ˌvas it that, having brought their owner this far, they would be left ˌach in its cardboard coffin while he escaped forever into some unmarked oblivion? We walked on, past the pawnshops with their or chestrated windows, a lifetime of guitars, a galaxy of trap sets, the drum tops catching dust, the absent fingers tapping elsewhere, per haps on the rutted window sills of the Salvation Army hostel. Dow away, the Greyhound dislodged its quota of contenders, I had come from its indifferent womb just a little over four years ago and, looking out at this gray street and seeing the cityrutted faces of the old men had wondered, is this Los Angeles? Old men? All men who wander i torn clothing with yellow eyes and beer dreams are old men, thei hair sagging around their folding faces, petrified and blank, thei breathing one enormous smothered sigh.

On Main Street, there are bars where the sound of music falls into the street and dies in the sludge of dirt. Inside, figures silhouette against the red light stand motionless absorbing space. Only the tat too parlor was busy, full of people leaning on the partition that separ ated them from the tattoo man and his living tablet. See the ma being decorated, see the man finding out who he is in the morning rolling over on the gray sheet and the yellow stained mattress, starin at his arm and saying, it is me, for here it is written I love Agnes. I watched from the doorway, seeing the framed designs hanging on the wall, like the cross-stitch mottos of New England, why not God Bless This Home? I moved on down this street which I had forgotten among the palms and pools of my Los Angeles.

You can buy a buckle for your belt in the leather shop on Main Street that is made in the form of a naked lady, or small purses made of leaves of leather that close in on each other like the secrecy of a bud. You can buy a leather belt with a center of braided horsehair for ten dollars, the note attached to it says "Made in the Pen." Which Pen? The pen of this street, perhaps, where the hotels are motionless and swallow up the customers. Here is everything, here is total life street, lust in the movies, whipping, sucking and biting, daubed in nip ples on the posters like pock marks, here too the real flesh of the greatest star in America now at the burlesque house, but it is two dollars to enter, and no one on this street appeared to have two dol lars, even for the greatest star. The man in the ticket booth was half hidden by Baby Ruth bars, and he too, like the other faces on this street, looked back at me with indifference. Nothing will change.

Perhaps this street is a refuge for the pure, a place to buy their pound of printed flesh in another world. The bums and derelicts are paid props, the beer taverns and the slop streets, the sagging frie

hicken in the windows painted gold by the lighting, the tired Mexi-
an women in slacks and sleeveless tops who slide past eyeing the
nen or looking with bland eyes at the dog who, crossing with the
ights, his nose parallel to the street, headed toward the oasis of Japan
Town. Perhaps they are all provided by Mayor Yorty. Maybe Mrs.
Chandler came to see him one day and said, "Sam, we have the
Music Center now, the Museum at the Tar Pit, all the culture we can
ever use. But how about the satisfaction of the baser tastes? Done
with discretion, of course. Suppose we get a bunch of bums and no-
accounts and let them loose on Main Street. We could franchise
smutty books and magazines and show sordid movies and our boys
would have a place to go instead of doing it on the front lawn, as the
saying goes." And so the park commission got the word and they
filled the street with ragged men, cementing the parks to ensure the
steady supply, provided the bookshops and sex cinemas, the tacoman
and the dirty chicken restaurants, and it was all part of the great city
plan, the urban renewal, the marvel of twentieth-century catering.
That must be what happened, for just a little distance off, and clearly
visible, the lights of the Department of Water and Power Building
stand as a beacon to progress, and surely Sam knows this street is just
around the corner.

November, 1967

Look Back in Nylon

You're an old friend, or are you? Times have changed, we aren't
what we used to be, but it was nice, and I am glad to see you for the
sake of memory. What have you been doing? But I don't listen to
your answer, my eyes are marking your bookshelf, oh God, *Reader's
Digest* novels. My, my, what a nice doggie, here doggie, what's his
name? Frisky? That's a nice name for him, he is, isn't he, frisky I
mean.

Why did I come here, you called me, that's why, haven't seen you
for so long you said. And I haven't seen you since I walked out the
office door and promised to keep in touch. Well, well, and what is
Miss Farkiss doing now, still counting paper clips? You tell me the

news, the gossip. I seem to know the names, but I can't connect them to the faces. Doris, Doris who? Oh that Doris, really, she seemed so inhibited. Well I mean that time I told the joke about the two nun, who, but I stop, because I am beginning to feel you didn't like the joke either.

My God, how long till dinner, maybe you're a good cook, maybe you've made some exotic thing from a Sunset magazine recipe, like Tuna Casserole, with olives or steak fried chicken with Shake and Bake. Yum Yum. Your kid is shouting for you, don't you hear him, that is your kid, isn't it, the one in the other room crouched before the TV set. He wants a Coke. Good, you're out of the room and I can scratch my hip where my girdle is choking me, my flesh all compounded into this sausage shape just to please you (and hold up my stockings). I have a run, but if I keep my legs crossed maybe you wouldn't notice it, my right leg is going to sleep, I should have worn my slacks. I'm a coward. What the hell do I care what you think anyway.

I'll be right back, I yell, and go to the bathroom. It's all lavender, or is the word "mauve," mau-vah, vhy-yo-let, lih-lahk, even the electric toothbrush matches. What color is your electric knife, sorry, I mean I notice how fashionably you've done the Dee-Cohrrr, and in the kitchen too, how lovely, a brown fridge, doesn't show the finger marks does it, oh, I see, it's California ranch style, silly of me. Me? Oh we live quite modestly, I mean, we rent. (The fridge door has a broken handle and we hold it closed with an ingenious invention made of a rubberband and a piece of cork.)

Oh I agree, it is nice to own your own home, and out here, where are we! I think I spent half the day on the freeway and only found your house because the number matched the one you gave me. Nice neighbors? Oh, that's swell. Swell, when did I use that word last, swell date, Fred, your mom's swell, or did I hear that on the late movie, I think I'm going crazy. Why not go crazy, light up a joint, lie on the floor, turn on KRLA and wiggle my feet, tell her about the naked painted body party, about sitting in the front row of the movies stoned out of my head trying to reach up and touch Omar Sharif? Why not? Because I'm a coward. I'll just sit here and discuss Huntley Brinkley and fashions and the problems of teen-agers and whom to vote for (better be tactful there) and . . . well anything, it's all so cozy and nice, and she is an old friend, isn't she?

February 2, 1968

Psalms Based on Personal Advertisements—
Back Pages Free Press

I am a beautiful antique cog and I want you to groove with me. I will eat your axle grease, chew your thumbnail sketch, three pistons a pleasure and dig watchbands, watch, I am a Doctor, very respectable, seek people with hideous diseases to examine, write including specimen, all returned, it all comes back in the mid hours or cocktail hours what cocktails I have to tell.

I am a white thing lonesome in Altadena, please, will all others go with me, love nature, climb trees for matinee, my wife understands me and is looking for a dwarf.

Forget fingers, try this flagpole made of sponge, comes complete with flag and every star a tickler, and every stripe turns black and blue; all included for the one low price of and comes in plain brown or post office ambiguous. No phone numbers, put a stamp on it, send it off through the membrane red orifice of the postbox. Warm the slot before depositing. In Hollywood the postboxes dribble down the curb.

Just arrived seek Momma slapped my hand at home where are you Bennie we miss you call Gloria Sandy and Poopsie.

Off loading crate of girls, going cheap This Week Only some uneven tits rejects of model for fifty dollars an hour for stage scream and rape.

I only read that stuff in the bathroom, it helps me shit.

Frankie Snapp, call Aunt Velma, you hear me Frankie Snapp, stop that lollygagging about the town while Velma, dressed in velvet, violets, voile, voluminous, veiling watches you make a fool of yourself.

PrettygirlsPrettygirlsPrettygirlsPrettygirlsPrettygirlsPrettygirlsPrettygirlsPrettygirlsPrettygirlsPrettygirlsTittycurlsPrttygirls.

Beth Gould, call Rex James and if he's not home try Aunt Velma.

I want all my mail to go to Laurel Canyon while I hang out at Topley's watching discreet couples do their thing in beer mugs, finger in the beer dear, come here dear, you alone or together because Friday night is couples only and their permutations, oh lovely oh blissful oh isn't love grand I never knew it could be like this like this like this.

Fat ladies, petite girls, thin gay guys, bodybuilders, straights, somebody out there loves you, just send a photo, just drop by, the house is clean and the bed is sighing empty and my loins are charged by the line and my mouth kisses you all over.

Discreet lover, only advertises in newspaper all profound perversions all goodlooking having fun time in Las Vegas, Lost Vagaries, lonesome boy with alternating current seeks socket.

It's disgustingdisgustingshouldbebannedit'sdisgustingwhatifthekids.
. . .

When you grow up you will meet him/her. He/she will look into your eyes and you will know that that is it. He/she is the one for you and you will love one another forever and live in an all electric house and have twopointthree children and spend money and buy things and lie together under flat stones and your children will mourn you and the garage will be full of cars and everyone will be happy and that's marriage.

Attention girls eighteen to twenty-one, two handsome bachelors, three friendly businessmen, photographers, movie executives with Mustangs, beautiful ac/dc blonde with well hung husband and beach pad, who need love girls, who needs love, what makes the world go round. Love makes the world go round, suck, suck, suck.

June 23, 1968

Touring Echo Park

Echo Park, known in the thirties as Red Gulch, twines its way up a crease in the not Hollywood hills but downtown almost. The rent is cheaper, the residents more permanent, a year in the same house is not extraordinary, and the house passed on to friends in a new urban system of inheritance so that people come to visit you and say, Gosh, I know this place, didn't . . . used to live here? Echo Park Lake has the world's largest lily leaves, grotesquely large, frightening, a place to sequester bodies of babies and lovers chopped up in the night time and hauled down to the lake in cardboard boxes taken from outside the we-never-close Pioneer Market on the corner of Sunset and Echo Park. Never close that market where the aisles are wide enough for

one thin maybe middle-sized person and they are crowded and pushing along shove and haul with squeaky pushcart wheels and masses of
flesh hauling great armfuls of strange Latin American vegetables, cel-
entro all perfume, and Japanese eggplants and guava paste and bins
of beans and nuts and rice and pigs' feet and to make *menudo,*
spongy tripe, white and pale as an invalid.

Outside, if there is ever to be an outside again, if you can get
through the squeeze aisle past the piles of flesh and products, there is
the splattered asphalt of the parking lot and the Pioneer Takeout service of greaseburgers and Spanish pizzas and liquor store hangerout-
ers, leaning sinister against the walls, their eyes threatening, and the
stone freaks eating spongy buns and fries, wandering around looking
for their cars at four in the morning or getting lost in the market
buying coconut ice cream and banana cream pies, eaten before they
defrost.

Echo Park has its slum line, bordering the road itself, clutching at
the low levels; the disinherited stalk the avenue, the kids drag like wet
paper through the streets, the gangs decorate the white garage walls
with thin attenuated gangscrawl. Beware. Up the side streets, past the
now closed dream of a teen center wall battered and window
smashed, up the side streets which fling up the hillsides, the other
people live. The not Laurel Canyon, not Beverly Glen, not Venice
people, although at one time or another they will move out to one of
those places, or out from, coming to Echo Park, if they can find/
inherit a house, and hide a bye in the slope feeling somehow a little
superior, a little more with it in a quiet way. Not that it's not happening in Echo Park, but it is happening inside, see, not out on the street
with sports cars and meeting at the canyon grocery where the prices
are higher but you are seen and get to see, but happening in the living
room in front of the hi fi playing Big Pink and you are smoking a
joint but that's not anything special and you are maybe reading some
poetry, that's pretty far out, it's still linear in Echo Park and lots of
people over thirty-five and more aging every day.

Up Sunset it is going on too, up on Micheltorena and Effie and
Maltman, all along in that undefined section some call the Los Feliz
area and other people just designate by waving their hands and pointing toward the Silverlake off ramp of the Hollywood Freeway, is there
any other? and explaining it is near . . . near what? It didn't
used to be near anything unless you count Channel Seven and its
anomaly of a studio just off Sunset where it is still Sunset before it

becomes by a flick of the cement Hollywood Boulevard. Near the
Akron perhaps, the Akron full of the gay people from Hyperion
where the baths are, and the restaurant, and near to all those bars,
goodness, so many bars, but it's a quiet sort of life not at all like the
Hollywood cruising, but houses and steady couples and regular clien-
tele and homey, domestic even. Yes, near the Akron, and Channel
Seven, and now near a row of shops which have in desperation given
the area a name that can be recognized, though hesitantly, you can tell
from the name, not claiming a positive place, but more like saying,
well, not where you'd expect, they call it The Other End of Sunset,
forgiving you for thinking in terms of 8,000 and 9,000, hoping you
will believe them, explore it, and find them there, clinging to the
roadside, wedged between the old-fashioned shoes on display in the
front window, wedged in there, the antique clothes shop where the
freaky boppers get their tablecloths and lace and tat fur and shimmy
satin and squeal and simp among the boys trying on velvet, for God's
sake isn't it you, but exactly.

Serious stuff there too, clay and leather and good wool and artful
handweaving, even weaving lessons at the row of looms, and spaced
along the street where the Army Surplus Store tries to keep up by
hanging medallions on their surplus shirts and the dying stationery
store sells last year's posters or tries to and a scruffy window is all that
remains of the drugstore by the bus stop, except that someone has
written quite neatly across its windows in white paint the "exploitive"
profits made by Chrysler last year, among all this: bits and pieces of
this generation and the one before and before that, almost back to the
Stone Age like the saw repair shop with religious mottoes, among this
are the new antique shops and the gallery cum store where the flat
bright color paintings of the flat bright color people, feathers and
faces, spaces and silence, the boredom of acid, the blankness of cool,
stare from the wall at their matching watchers.

It's not all Other End; there are little wisps of offshoots, all the way
along to Western where the Russian shops are and the Russian
church and the shop that proclaims "Victory through Vegetables."
Creeping up Hollywood, past the German delicatessen; there must be
Germans about, past the decorator shop that's never open, the
second-hand roses begin to bloom, behind the Akron on Fountain, a
mass of them, tangled and sweet along the street, rocking chairs and
velvet, mirrors, campaign buttons, cut glass and mahogany, a new
"in" place at every corner, all the way along to the hospital row and

even past it to the repertory theater, the whole area is expanding, it's coming to its own, it's where it is, or about to be happening.

Uncle Wiggly's Pickle Farm didn't make it in the Ukrainian Cultural Center topped by its art nouveau theater sign on Melrose, but the Scorpio One, formerly Mother Neptune's, is spouting poetry readings and fantastic windows of unique and wonderful design which are echoed up the street at Gebo's Eye and Open City, the latter two with potted trees outside on the sidewalk and sunflowers, a little bit of Paris or Greenwich Village or Somewhere Else for God's sake civilized and quaint. And the Afro shop and the students from City College where they have experimental classes and do topless things and argue right out loud in their ordinary nonintellectual clothes, they flow around and live in the houses where you can see peace posters through the windows and walk around, lots of hair and beards and old cars to drive as they visit in the houses and old-time large room apartments of wherever it is that starts somewhere around Vermont or Western and triumphs on the hillsides of Echo Park.

There's no MacDougal or Haight or Telegraph or San Michel or King's Road or . . . but so what, so no pastry shops to sit in or places to get seen in, not exactly, though the newsstand at Echo Park and Sunset sold the *Free Press* before a lot heard of it and the Jade Garden on Hoover has the best Chinese food in the whole goddam world, and there are two good potters just down the street from there and lots of your friends live just up the hill or over the hill or near the taxidermist or near the laundromat or near the Safeway or . . . and the roads climb the hills and circle down again and the streets start and stop dead against reservoirs and fields of grass, you should smell it when they burn it in the summer, and there is always the Burrito King at Alvarado and Sunset, the Burrito King who keeps strange hours but makes kingly burritos, *machaca* burritos, *quesadillas,* and if you want to sit down there is Baragons down a bit toward town, and past all that the park, Elysian Park, with trees, real trees, and a baseball stadium that no one I know has ever been to, and beyond that, at night, if you have a room with a view, facing downtown Los Angeles, the ever-golden blessing of the lights of the Water and Power Building caressing the dark.

October 2, 1968

Vanity Fair

He wrote to me: I am an agent with a lot of ideas and think you would be interested. I would appreciate your phoning me to discuss them, or make an appointment, Yours sincerely, A. Wendell Thruggs. I phoned him; he answered his own phone. We talked; was I interested in writing for television make lotsamoney? I could consider that. Did I want to see my name in lights? I hadn't really thought about that, but now that he mentions the possibility it sounds intriguing, perhaps a small billboard on the Strip to start with? (A chocolate mousse pie named The Liza? A Liza poster, my face on the wall, a Lizabout, a new kind of patented couch?) I should come to his office, he would like to talk to me further—in greater depth—he could squeeze me in between his conferences and clients (OK Phyllis, but you better call me back on that, sure Bob, we'll forward your mail by helicopter, No, Tennessee, your script doesn't quite make it). I said I would get there (his office) after work, and supper, say about eight, would that be OK, did he stay in his office so late? Sure baby, for me, this one time he'd do it.

I ate a hamburger, leaving out the onion, let's not offend, and had a cup and a half of coffee, I was nervous, better have a little sugar, if I get on TV I'll have to diet anyway, makes you look ten pounds heavier, twenty maybe, and do something about an image, get a special-appearance dress. It was only seven thirty, and though I am never late for appointments, never, I do think it's equally gauche, if not more, to be early, there is a fine point, a five minute waltz of time, five before, five after, hope I'm not too early, smile smile, sorry if I'm late, smile smile, so I decided to use the time by walking to his office. Fountain near Curson, the street is widened, cars pock it with lights, red, white, they glow by. The houses squat behind palms and colored spotlights, the lights set just so, just so that the reflection of the palms darkens the glittered plaster. I remember a radio commercial that said to knock on the walls when buying a home—look for genuine lath and plaster. Haven't heard that commercial for a long time, maybe too many people knocked on walls, and their fists sagged through, right into the modern kitchen, right out into the smog. For rent, bachelor, heated pool, garage, one bedroom, furnished, colored TV cable, wall-to-wall carpets, drapes, maid service, singles only, all electric, built-ins, doorman. I looked through windows as I walked by, wondering where the office building was among this conglomeration of apartments. It was there, right there, behind its own palms, own colored lights, own *For Rent* signs, it was an apartment building.

Hugh Hefner, I have read, in any number of publications, not just *Playboy,* Never Goes Out Of His Mansion. Maybe it was going to be one of those offices—A. Wendell Thruggs, front room reception, a slim smart scary girl in mod boots taking my name, saying over the intercom, Mr. Thrugggggssss, a Liza Williams to see you. (I hate that—A—Liza Williams to see you, how many Liza Williams are there, or Nancy Smiths, or even John Does, I've never met a John Doe, never heard of anyone who has.) I would have to sit there on the leather and steel sofa and read *Image* or *Printer's Ink* or *Realités* or *Time* or *Bazaar,* all up to date issues, no dentist office this, and the secretary would eye me and pretend to be doing something important and private like sending Dean Martin his salary, and I would try to look like I wasn't used to being kept waiting, as though I would rise up and stalk out at any moment, and then the door would open and this handsome man who looked just like Cesar Romero, Paul Newman, Steve McQueen, Jerry Hopkins, this amazing man, full of solicitous cool, almost sincere, very flattering—so glad to finally meet you I've admired you for such a long time—would take me by the hand and lead me back into his Bigelow office cum living room, a real painting over the sofa, a tray of drinks on the genuine Italian provincial cabinet fitted with TV, the drapes parted showing this amazing view down La Cienega or over the ocean, but this was Fountain, so maybe the curtains would be closed.

I look at the mailboxes inset in the lobby wall, they were of a shiny brass color (or was it supposed to be gold-colored like those monstrosities on posts in Truesdale Estates that are gold-plated) and had little framed spaces for the name card to fit. Half were empty, and some were handwritten, Mr. and Mrs. J. Garcia, Miss L. Hamilton, Patti Mercy, and some were printed, part of a business card, so that you could read the firm's name too, where it had been scratched out, if you really got up close and peered, one said A-1 Loan Co. I found A. Wendell Thruggs' name, it was typewritten.

His office was in apartment 3-G. I started up the stairs, the stairway was narrow, it turned a corner halfway up and ended on a balcony which ran alongside the building. The doors were all painted, a little flakey, and had numbers and those tiny secret peekhole enlarging mirror devices, so that you knew that after you rang, and stood there, someone could sneak up on the other side and peek out at you and see if they wanted to let you in. 3-G was up another flight, and at the end of the balcony. I could smell all the cooking as I walked along, the kitchen windows opened onto the walkway, as did the bathrooms. I saw a sink full of dishes and a man eating baked beans from the can and reading *Variety*; he hadn't pulled his off-white drapes closed, and I could see him sitting there at the formica table, under the bright ceiling bulb, eating beans with a spoon, out of the can. A Wendell Thruggs had his name on a card on the door, held on with gold-colored Christmas tape, and a sign that said A. WENDELL THRUGGS AGENCY, INC., THEATRICAL AND LITERARY AGENT TO THE STARS. His garbage can was outside his door, just like all the other doors there, a neat can outside with the apartment number painted on it. The lid for his can was missing, and I could see that it was almost full, there was an empty Nescafé jar and a selection of TV dinner boxes, mostly enchilada dinners. I stood there without knocking, staring into the garbage can.

The door opened, he stuck his head out, his Edward Everett Horton head, his Three Stooges' head, his mouth opened, can I help you, he asked, are looking for me, are you Miss Williams? I'm sorry if I disturbed you, I said, so sorry, I was looking for—Patti Mercy's apartment! I guess I read the wrong number on the mailbox. I was still babbling as I scuttled back along the balcony, past the man eating beans from a can, down the stairs, and out into the Hollywood night.

October 25, 1968

Where Do We Go?

Where do we go for anywhere in this city? Where do we go for central joy, like Times Square at midnight on New Year's Eve? We go to the Thrifty Drugstore, open twenty-four hours a day, and play with the plastic bargains, or read the magazines and marvel at the perpetual Jackie on the cover, never interviewed but always top copy. Where do we go to celebrate in this blobtown, amorphous city, melted metropolis? We skit along the freeway oblivious to the containers of existence on either side, the endless Bo-peep houses in their rhythm of ugh pink and yich blue, the cement office blocks, pastrami stands, hot dog houses, we zip along the freeway to one house in particular, a friend, a party, we are vagrants in our own land with no visible means of support except the directions memorized, turn left at the 76 sign and right at the dry cleaners.

Bea Lillie, according to a story in the LA *Times,* asked (while on the *Queen Mary*), "When does this place get there?" We are there, though where we are is privately devised. This city is a game of stops, separated by nothingland, by stretches of streets which will never be familiar. There is no here, here, only there, here. One friend lives there, another there, and there is where you can buy the best cheesecake. The Movie is playing there, but the Restaurant is over there, miles of city, like miles of desert, separate goals from each other.

Describe me this place, tell me this city, where is downtown, oh I know, and aptly named, very downtown. But downtown is not where the town is, though that's where it used to be, downtown is everywhere there is a parking lot and a laundromat/giftshop/barber/supermarket/dress store—that's where downtown is now.

There are areas. Beverly Hills, sprawled on gold, and Bel Air, sprawled on purer gold. There is Laurel Canyon doing its Thing in the street and behind doors, contemporary *à la* pot, and La Cienega contemporary *à la mode,* and Echo Park, *au courant à la* poverty. Everyone says Venice and there is Venice, surely Venice, decaying wooden houses and new developments and European Heartache memories by the sea. Artists, that's where the artists live, though I doubt it, being in the street with paint on your pants doesn't make art, artists live in trees everywhere like monkeys, making mockery and joy.

There is the Other End, which at last names the place that bumps and grinds from Vermont and Hoover and Franklin, and Sunset and Silverlake in residential spirals and has views of houses with views, and views of lakes, and garages with views and streets with curves and trees with tired branches. The Other End has a Renaissance now, boutiques and antiques and frantics and fanatics and romantics and homosexuals, who may be also any of the above. It's cheaper than Echo Park, which is cheaper than Laurel Canyon, which is cheaper than Beverly Glen Canyon, though Beverly Glen Canyon is nearer to UCLA where some things happen. Everything is cheaper than Truesdale Estates unless you're speaking of taste, in which case nothing is cheaper than Truesdale Estates.

Pasadena has junk shops and junk shops and junk shops. Glendale is near Pasadena and has Nazis and junk shops. Eagle Rock is near Glendale and has Nazis.

Griffith Park has trees and rapes, depending on who you are—if you're out for a picnic it has trees, if you're a cop it has rapes.

This place, or collection, or unhomogenized urban nonrenewal is what you make-take of it (as long as you have a car). It is a body with cement veins, a universe connected by cement, a sprawling, messed-up old tart with occasional decorations in unusual places. This city doesn't make you—you have to make it.

December 29, 1968

Metropolitan Transports

Morning, on the bus, the skin of everyone next to me, across the aisle, breath, hair, clothing, conversations, tired faces, early morning and there are tired faces, rows of feet in white shoes, maids en route to Beverly Hills. Exact change, clicking into the box, pushing toward the back of the bus, black faces, old gray heads, young tired heads, pun, windows thick with skin grease, someone has tried to rest against the glass, left the pattern of their pores.

The bus jumps to a stop, we pop forward still in motion, the bus is halted, we bang against each other, the seat in front, the walls of metal. Behind someone coughs, thick cough, green cough, it is California cold, California winter, morning's chill. I examine strangers with my eyes, secret staring, catching their pale reflections in the window, as we pass a dark wall their image springs to life, a transient color TV set, they fade as we rush down the street.

Conversations, sometimes intimate, what do they look like, these snatches of existence who tell all behind me? How can I turn to stare, meeting their face surprised at my intrusion? Yesterday morning a young man in front of me, his cheeks falling straight into his collar, fat, with ears flush against the cheek neck fat, hands curled passively on his thick thighs, curiously young hands preceded by a wrist matted with dark reddish hairs. Clean clothes, very neatly cut hair, sitting very still. I wanted to lean forward and say to him, I know all about you, you still live at home with your mother and you masturbate too much. That set me to wondering what too much might be, warts on the hand? Using up the five thousand orgasms everyone is entitled to? My bus stops and off, crowded against other people and warm, then suddenly into the cold wind of Hollywood and Vine.

The night before while waiting for a bus and huddling against the painted wooden bench back (did it advertise a mortuary?), a woman sat behind me using me to shelter from the wind. It's always windy here at Hollywood and Vine, she said. Always. On the bus I sat next to a small child wearing black shoes. His father, or someone, was explaining hexagons to him, drawing on a piece of paper. The child was about three years old and listened patiently. Then he leaned across and taking the pencil from the man drew a wiggly circle on the piece of paper the man was holding, and smiled, and turned to me and said, "I can sing 'Jingle Bells.' "

Oh Metropolitan Transports, Metropolitan Transports Company, oh the company, oh the metropolitan transports, transporting. Very hip now, the bus advertising. Bus cards tell you about Scorpios, they are not entirely trustworthy, watch out for Scorpios. Or the Best Seller Publicity Company advises you to hand your burdens over to Jesus. If you have dropped out of high school and look like one of the four minority types illustrated, re-training is offered. Recipe for pork chops with canned celery soup sauce. Photograph of polite bus driver of the month, letter recommending your choice of polite bus driver solicited. How many people get off bus (after copying down address) and write letter commending the driver? Who can feel good about a bus ride that costs you thirty cents to go ten or twelve blocks. Who can feel good about a bus ride?

Yet there must be people on those buses who never, or hardly ever, ride in cars. People to whom distance is always measured by waiting time, and crowded push and shove, and little pink pieces of paper for transfers, and then the walk to the final destination. Driving, as most of us do, whizzing along, we remain comfortably ignorant of all the old and poor and tired people huddled on buses, or benches, windy corners, cold walls, dirty windows, thick perspiration air, jouncing and sliding along the streets, lurching and bumping between corners, surrounded by strangers, late, hurried and uncomfortable.

March, 1970

Dope Is the Sex of the Brain

Sunday morning, and rather than lie here, a looney malcontent, I have crept upward from my bed to deal with specifics at the typewriter. The threaded tape runs through my head and immortal phrases drown in the sheets. Reading Michael Zwerin in the *Village Voice* about attending a Wet Dream Film Festival in Holland and he speaks of Wilhelm De Ridder whom I met, albeit soggily, at a party in Venice some weeks ago. It was a long walk by the canal, directions from a man with gout, leg propped up in the blue television light. Gilbert, he said, lives upstairs. One should not meet one's heroes. I had wanted to write Michael Zwerin a letter of grievance because he had been in California and I had wanted to meet him. Could I tell him (as I was assured when later I was in New York and was told) that as with all other mythics, it is best not to meet.

Wilhelm was there to make a film. I publish *Suck,* he said, pronouncing it like "sook." I misunderstood, finally figured it out and said, Ah yes, like *Screw.* It remained hopeless because of the din, fatigue, confusions of language, and nothing happened, though what might have happened remains unclear. Do you think Michael Zwerin would want to receive such a letter.

Driving home one afternoon in Bucky's Volkswagen, it occurred to me that DOPE IS THE SEX OF THE BRAIN. I told him, and later worked out a series of progressions on that theme, or maybe fugues. A few days later, reading Ned Rorem's Paris and New York Diaries, I come across this passage—"I have been spending my first days here then, looking in the mirror at the black eye on this face which, Julien says, in a few years no one will notice any longer in the street, and by that signal I shall know that I have gotten old." Reminding me of my last week's column. And so we are all hooked into that same cosmic grace, yet should avoid each other.

Then again, I wish to please. This makes my every day more pleasant but certainly keeps me from greatness, barring other factors. At
Jerry's party I met a man who told me that when we could finally
communicate with the dolphins, we would ask them about ecology. I
said I would ask them how it feels to be a dolphin. He also told me to
read *Cosmic Power,* written sometime at the turn of the century (the
century turns, a visual purge of Victoria's power, the skirts slipping
off the piano legs, the angels, some two turns ago, having danced off
the head of the pin).

This is a straightforward process between me and you, our bridge
made by these white plastic teeth inscribed with images. I am anxious
to communicate.

Elliot Mintz went back to his childhood on radio, in the hands or
waves of a psychic hypnotizer, and then back to before his birth. He
turned out to have been a coal miner in the Midwest, very unassum-
ing, and so different from my own previous experience, flaming from
the burning gypsy village, drifting through Vienna in a haze of pastry,
drying out over Dover and coming up for air on West Eighth Street
just in time to hear that Roosevelt, who wasn't a Jew after all, had
died. My father and I held hands and cried in front of Whelan's, that
same Whelan's that has now removed the phone booth and the counter for fear of the marching Marrakesh invasion. But most of that is
untrue and I have been unswervingly middle-class since Yiddish.

I want to write to all the people that I had read who turn my mind
around and give it windows. Hello—about that thing you said on
page two—it would take forever and I should be obligated to the
mailman for my ego. A silence, a refusal, so blighting, would confirm
my self-suspected nonexistence. Went to a party the day before
Christmas. The host was in Arkansas, but the room was ghosted by
him, and we, the relatives, while waiting for the will to be read,
seemed to have none of our own. Had a squid of nitrous oxide, felt
the buzz and zing and teetered on the verge of horror recall of New
Jersey abortions and the explanation of the spoon and the sexual
parts of the aborted fetus. This boy, I said, is old enough to be my
number one son.

Some days later I tried to figure out the odds for any one person
being born, taking into account all the sperm and ova from time's beginning, all the love and toilets, all the final fights, and doors opening
and shouts and blood on the sheets and rubbers and Margaret San-
ger's clinics where they asked you how many times a week you had

sexual intercourse and you said five for shame and pride. Statistics being proved, through my own manipulation at an early age, unreliable, the amount of anything, including the chances of being born, are infinite.

Lemmings swarming at Laguna. Someone said, "Festival," and then, losing faith, "George Harrison." The roads were clogged with cars, the field a massacre of bodies, and helicopters zoomed in relief packages bound for Pakistan, diverted to teen-agers who chomped boiled rice as a new religion. I learned last night that Mark Lane has published a new book saying that we are all war criminals. He gave an interview to the TV news. There are two lines of white hair in his beard and he looked rather stolid and secure. I watched him, trying to picture him making love to Jane Fonda, and wondered if he thinks his life has changed for the better ever since that man, allegedly leaning from the Book Depository window, splattered John's brains all over Jackie's clothes.

There is an amount of excitement about the changing of the year, although only we know for certain that a new year is about to begin. Every season I recall the first four days of a new year in Paris, lover turning to the wall, the grayness of the winter morning accompanying me all the way to London where I sat in Paddington Station alone and weeping on downers. That remains my definitive new year, and were it not that love takes me this year to Winterland, I would stay at home with these internal gyrations and avoid the road statistics which seem aimed directly at me. Perhaps this is my last message.

Now that my mind is lying here before me on these pages I have the whole day to deal with in an attempt to reconcile myself. I shall reread this and weep, but to you, the happiest of new years, and some peacefulness to pursue your own particular madness.

December 1, 1970

The Show Goes On

S TEP right up, hoopla hoopla hoopla, it's the world of entertainment and this is the entertainment capital of the world, oh yeah, razzmatazz and money money money. Where once the champagne flowed and people in long dresses tripped into swimming pools stuffed with rubber horses, the young thin and pimpled moguls of the music world smoke joints and fuck groupies. It's just a down home evening in an $8,000 a month pad. Dylan stayed here, that's the rumor, and why not, the view of the smog is great and there is black tile in the bathroom and a million mirrors to dissolve you into a million faces. You wink and the flash blinds you, so pop a pill and sniff some coke and drop some acid and freak out because its the life-style and it's yours for the price of your talent and your nerves.

I got a hot group for you, yeah, but can they play baroque? I got a hot group for you here, yeah, but can they sing like CSN and Y? I got a hot group for you here, yeah, but how long is their hair, history, bank account? I got a hot group for you here, yeah? are they all fags? Dopers? And who do they know?

Hollywood is the marketplace, lots of weird things happen in Hollywood, and some nice things too. You can still go into Schwab's Drug Store and spot a star, maybe only of TV commercials, but a public face nevertheless. These pieces are written as travelogues through this strange place, and represent a few moments of time caught in plastic while the show goes on.

Enfant Terrible

At five in the afternoon.
It was exactly five in the afternoon.
A boy brought the white sheet
At FIVE IN THE AFTERNOON.
The rest was death, and death alone
AT FIVE IN THE AFTERNOON.

(First stanza of "Lament for Sanchez
Mejias" by Federico Garcia Lorca,
New Directions)

It wasn't five in the afternoon in 1935 in a prewar bullring in Spain, it was eight thirty at night in the Los Angeles Forum and the year was 1968. The war wasn't over; the babies of the war generation whose babies sat there had the smell of blood in their plastic plasma. It was the DNA of the soul mixed with the DMT of the media, but it was blood they were after, and it was the young bullfighter who was going to make the passes, his muleta a mike, his banderilleros the preceding acts.

The place smelled of blood and Coca-Cola, the crowd was ready for the orgasm of kill, it was five o'clock in the afternoon or ten o'clock at night, and Franco was still alive in the Spain where he'd murdered Lorca, and we were bombing Guernica, only now it is called the de-militarized zone—easier to say, sounds almost unviolent, like the death of the unbelievable bull, like the hoped for death of the bull-fighter out there to be gored between the sequins and the silk, out there in his beyond our reach, his poster self, his fame disemboweling him before the door to the ring parted and he walked across the space of the arena.

The banderillas were placed, Sweetwater, a Chinese ethnomusi-cologist, Jerry Lee Lewis, all of whom deserve to be spoken of in depth, but this is about Jim Morrison and the Doors and that is what I am writing about so you will have to take the others in the context of the bullring, there but appetizers, there but only to incite the bull, the crowd to lust for blood, to escape for pain, the death to come, to the ceremony of death, to the ultimate crime, killing, slaughter, made a dance, made an art, man against his fate, man against his desire for survival, man choosing to show his disdain for death, against an animal. We were the animals, we were the spectators, and he was, he was, he was the young matador dressed for death in the hide of the bull dyed black, dyed black as the blood is burned black in the sun, the child, the angel of death, the fired della Robbia of innocence, purchased by the Borgias to ward off the evil within, the angelic art of the Renaissance of Italy when slaughter and poison and the artist as captive found no conflict.

He looks like a young Medici, his head back, that throat, that throat of the exquisite muscles holding the face which hardly rises in prominence from the column of throat before it is swallowed in the cherubic curls, the young prince, his heritage the wealth of the spoilers of the Orient, or the spoilers of the now more subtly called Far East. They shouted off the picadors, they crouched in their seats and growled, there in the Orange Julius stand decor of the Forum, they waited for the hero and the death.

He is so innocent, Jim Morrison, so innocent, as a child who tortures the cat to examine pain is innocent; there is only now and the urgency of feeling. He is so innocent, he is the innocent child who is not evil, who is forgiven because he is a child; he is the sexuality of child, the not female, the not male, the sensuosity of child only, the sexuality of child, not man, not woman, not guilty, at times not even able yet to walk, toppling off high stages across the country as though we should have known better than to let him climb up there, or rather, than to have set him up there and said, run, not holding his hand, letting this wild full feeling half crazed with wonderment child free upon the ledge to fall and die for our delight, or be horned to death on the sharp points of our blood-greedy eyes, dressed only in his thin bullskin pants, the child of death, the child in matador's clothing.

"Light My Fire" . . . they yelled for it, light my fire, it was Their Song, light the big fire, play with with the forbidden matches, we aren't even adolescent yet, we want to light the match and burn the bed and the curtains and mummy and daddy and everything and see the beautiful flame we have never touched and only a burned child doesn't play with matches, but we don't want to be old enough to know that yet and he must sing that song for us, he, the baby bull-fighter out there in the purple juice light and we will light our sparklers and he will set it all up in flames and he isn't real because he is a poster or a golden record or an idol or a picture to kiss at night under the covers, a piece of paper, a doll, he is the ultimate Barbie doll, and Barbie speaks when we pull her string, that's what she's supposed to do, and she only says what we want her to say because you see on the other end of the string is a piece of tape, that's why she is our Barbie doll and that's why he is our Jim Morrison and that's why we want him to sing "Light My Fire" and stop Stop STOP all these other strange sentences that the doll didn't say when we bought her, these new words on the tape, she has no right to new words, just do her thing which is our thing because we own her/him/the ticket/ the poster/the record/the idol. He, he is made of plastic, an animated long-playing record refusing us our favorite cut, the cut we want, the arm sliding over our favorite groove, the arm gone wild, the cuts strange, the record different, give her a lobotomy, give him a lobotomy, tear off his toy clothes, let's see what's in there, we don't mean the flesh part or the skin under the sad black bull pants, but where the tape is, you know man, like the heart, the tape, the TAPE man transplanted in there from the golden record, the one we bought, the one we helped to make golden—who knows but ours may have been that copy that made it a million. He is ours and he better get to "Light My Fire" quickly or we are going to throw him out of the crib.

He is the innocent, he is the innocent child, he is the child, he is not good, he is not bad, children are neither. He plays with himself, not fucks, he is neither boy nor girl, he is feeling, he is the child. He is all dressed up for the party, and it's being catered by grownups and they are charging to get in, and they aren't letting us play with our doll, they have got him up there away from us and they are keeping him nine years years old forever, the black bull pants are strangling his balls, never mind, children don't need balls, enough to suck your thumb, or mike, and if you piss on the stage it's defiance like holding your breath until your face goes blue, or yelling, doing your yelling out there in the middle of the living room, only they aren't listening to the yelling but offering him gigantic electric trains that run by remote control, and echo chambers to hear the sound of his own screaming even louder, com'on baby light my fire, and the snakes are crawling and the child is dying up there and it's five o'clock in the morning and the frail of lime is already prepared, and he is there see, he, someone, a man perhaps, someone strapped into the baby carriage by the big dyke governess of musicbusinesspromomedia exploitation and his mother is gone away and left him and if the governess can keep him little for just another year she's got a good thing going, and if we can see him die we can grow up, or die with him, or ignore the whole thing, or kill him ourselves, because we are all children there with our popcorn pockets full of matches and sparklers, com'on baby Light My Fire, com'on baby.

December 20, 1968

Encountering Janis

Walking up Grant Street in San Francisco, that street which bisects the North Beach area famous for bare tits and bare feet. Looking in the Italian grocery store windows, at the psychedelic poster shop, minding my own business which is minding everyone else's thing, a madly rotating eye. Into a dress shop and over to the size fifteen, chagrined but determined to look groovy even if larger than life-size.

Whamooo!!

Who is that freak girl with the wild hair/gestures/eyes/hands/ checkbook? Janis Joplin!! Janis in purple blouse and something vest that barely (is the word here—barely) meets over the cleft. The queen of clefts, musical and chestwise. Trying on clothes right here next to me, maybe available?

Hey—I say—hello, I'm Liza Williams, you know, I write for the *Free Press* and other such things. "Oh yeah," she says, "I know you, you're that strain of consciousness writer, aren't you?" Score one for Janis. Well, what I want is an interview so I tell her this and she says, "Well OK man but you'll have to wait till I get finished here." She has a pile of brilliantly colored clothes stashed on a chair and is tripping over other vests and blouses.

"Look," says the salesgirl, "you'll have to give me proper identification if you want us to take your check." Don't you know who she is? I ask. "Who she is, we know all right who she is," says the salesgirl, "but she moves around so much, we need an address for her." "Oh shit," says Janis. I depart with her promise to meet me outside the door.

I make it up the street to get a bottle of Southern Comfort, that's what she drinks it says in all her publicity and I may need a carrot for what may turn out to be a balkish star. Back to the shop, hands full

Liza by Liza

Janis by Janis

Liza by Janis

Janis by Liza

of purple tissue paper to write on bought at an art shop for a dime (A reporter is always prepared!). I nab Janis in flight up Grant. Hey wait! "Oh man. OK, let's go to the Coffee Experience." So we do. It is a combination bar and coffee shop. "Hi," she says to the bartender who nods glumly back at her. We go into the back room. Here, I say, hauling out the bottle of Southern Comfort, this is for you. "I never drink that crap," she says. "I drink Sweet Sleezys." I thought you only drank Southern Comfort, I say. "Well, I did for two years," she said, "that's how I got this." She stands up and parades around in her ten-foot thick funny fuzz of a fur coat. It's from no animal that I ever saw. I go to the bar and get two Sweet Sleezys, which turn out to be sweet vermouth. The bartender looks resigned; I go back to our table.

Hostility. She hates me! I am just another brain-picker to her, out to make a buck off her brain. Brain drain. Eyes meet eyes. Well, what the hell, I am not going to deal on that level so I take out the purple paper and the green pen and start to draw her picture. I don't say a word and she shifts about talking a mile a minute to the assortment of people who prop themselves against our table and say, "Hey, Janis man," and "Are you Janis Joplin?" and such things.

"Whatcha doin'," she finally asks, noticing me. Drawing you—I say. "Let me see that." I show it to her. "Ugh" she says, "I can do better than that. Here, give me the pen. I was an art student once, you know." And she looks like one, like an art student, like a twenty-four-year-old tired beat-up art student who has an analyst and parents who pray she'll straighten out. "Man, see that boy over there," she says while drawing me, "boy would I like to get him." "Hi there, pretty boy," she says. She is eyeing a long-haired effemi-nate bar boy about eighteen. "Wouldn't I like some of that." She sounds like a truck driver but I don't buy it because no truck driver has a thing about his tits and Janis does have a thing about her tits and one thing tits aren't is masculine. She draws me and it's not too bad, a little too much emphasis on my double chins for my taste. I think my one of you is okay—I say. "I can do a better one of me than you can," she says and starts to draw herself. I look at it when it is finished; it looks exactly like Jim Morrison, which she doesn't. That looks exactly like Jim Morrison, I say. She leans over and scrawls— "Fuck Yeow"—over the drawing.

So we talk a bit and she tells me about her car outside. It is a Porsche, or was before some genius turned it into a psychedelic Sis-tine Chapel. "You should hear the radio I've got, wow! I drive around in that thing playing music real loud and it blows everybody's minds." She loves the car, she especially likes the idea that people can enjoy it too. We go out and look at it. Come back in. Sit down again.

Where do you live—the girl with the false eyelashes who's been sitting next to me wiggling in her chair asks Janis. "I have a house here," she says indicating somewhere outside with a vague wave of her hand. "It's always full of people" she says to me. "When my roommate hears I am coming home she stands up against the wall like Jesus with her arms out waiting to be crucified; she knows she won't get any sleep when I'm home. I don't know if she can stand it. Hey, do you know Frank? He's a speedfreak, I'm gonna get a lot of crystal and shoot him up and then I'm gonna ball him. He's a pretty boy, I sure want a piece of him."

I am starting to rock back and forth now, my arms clutching myself. Whenever I get all overcome with compassion I start to rock as though I could hold the other person in my lap like a baby. Compassion because she is really not a bad looking girl, because she is a girl not a truck driver or a hooker or some dime-a-dance sleezy. She is a girl who can sing a woman's heartache and desire in its fundamental agony, who is all soul and shouting pain and here she sits making a travesty of her femininity. I want to say—pretty— you're the one who is pretty, you're the lovely one, they want to ball you, see, or mutual, but don't do what you are doing.

I am a witch—I say. (I suddenly decided I was one the week before.) "Bullshit," she says, "have you one nipple larger than the other? Because I have and that is the true mark of a witch. Wanna see?" She stands up and starts to take off her vest and blouse. I believe you—I say. "I have nice tits, don't I?" Janis says, leaning backwards. It hurts too much, I want to go. I have to split now—I say. "Me too," she says. We walk outside together, she flashes a grin at the bartender who nods just as glumly as before. "I've been thrown out of here twice" she says. Outside two ladies come up to Janis— Are you Janis Joplin?—they ask. "Yeah," she says. "Is that your car over there?" "Yeah" she says. "Well—your meter's expired; say can we have your autograph?" "Sure" she says. That will be a dime for the meter—I say. The lady gives Janis a dime, Janis gives her the autograph. I walk away, I can feel her standing there trapped in her fuzzy fur, needing someone to say—hey there pretty girl, I'd sure like to have some of you.

December, 1969

Tune in All Day This Song Is Just for You

Hey hey what do you say the rock 'n' roll king is on his way and he's going to shout you down the stoned path to near ear suicide. The louder they shout the harder we come in our soul, it's the ears' bordello and the radio fucks the spinal canals all day.

Loudness! Why such loudness? after that war they crooned us, Stars Fell on Alabama instead of civil rights workers, now Ole Man Ribber is out of business (no loss), and That Old Black Magic has become a White Rabbit, drags you down its swirling hole with cacophonic claws. Lucy may be in the sky but I'm down here on the floor with the volume and my head both turned on high.

I watched an eight-track recording session in a studio on Selma in Hollywood. Five tracks had already been recorded of the "name" group" and the band backing. Three middle-aged men in the soundproof booth, headphone on one ear, hand cupped over the other, shouted onto the remaining tracks, yeah baby yeah. How's that, did I get it up through the nose enough, hey man, is that take gonna make it? They emerged, leaned on the jukebox Ampex, sipped coffee from paper cups, discussed the stock market trends. At twenty-two fifty an hour they are growing fat, these ghost singers of Hollywood.

When the kids rush up and dance on the stage, grab golden hairs, kiss booted feet, it's about as valid as the sex they feel, because it's the sound of three middle-aged men they really love baby.

It's loud makes crowd and alone in the four-door fastback on the dark street when unlined hands cup growing breasts and they wig out to the sound from the car radio, it's somebody's father that's shouting through his nose, it's love is where it's at, yeah yeah.

I saw Donovan at Santa Monica Civic Auditorium listening to Maharishi. Donovan fingered his face with his thin fingers. . . . I must be here, I am feeling skin, familiar face skin, my face skin, I can feel my fingers feeling me, my satin collar, my baby mouth, my soft curls, they are all here. I know my friends are sitting next to me, they walk where I walk, I know their names if I want to talk to them, they let me speak first, doesn't happen often me speaking first, I see my face in the newspaper, I stare at myself staring at myself, I hear myself from passing cars on the freeway, my reality is being over-dubbed, I am a million copies of my own voice, I am my face poster size hanging on walls in cities I have never heard of, touch, my face, mouth, there, eyes, there, nose, there, collar, there, I am here, this is me. His hands move incessantly over his face, tediously mapping out his own reality.

The three middle-aged men go home to various arrangements of women, children, architecture. They stare at the television set where they see four boys playing soundless instruments, see four mouths move across soundless words, hear the sound of their own voices, singing, yeah baby yeah. They stretch their legs, light a cigarette and wonder who they will be next year.

November 3, 1967

Twentieth Zaps Profits Bull's-eyes on Kids

A gentleman from Texas (who shall remain nameless to protect his investment) knows how my mind works. Three days ago when I picked up my mail at the Freep there was, among the assorted communications, one from Texas containing two invitations and a proxy for the Twentieth Century-Fox Stockholders' meeting. He asked me to go as his representative, vote as I saw fit with one stipulation: I wasn't to give anyone a raise. The preceding explains why, early last Tuesday morning, Robert and I parked our car on the grassy stockholders' parking lot at Cheviot Park and embarked on the following adventure:

10:45 A.M. We got out of our car, clutching our golden invitations, wearing ultra-freak, mafiosa felt hats, ribbons, long hair (both of us), flowery clothes (both of us), large grins (both of us). "Are YOU stockholders?" said the parking attendant. We did a dance waving our proxy at him. Robert took his picture in his attendant's uniform, there amongst the parked Cadillacs and Continentals. "Talent scout," I said to him.

10:54 A.M. Disembarked outside sugar pink giant sound stage, after having been driven through set of *Hello, Dolly* (reconstructed 1890's New York, big El Station all green patina, as I remember it many years ago, lacy, lovely, metal and castlelike). Went inside sound stage. Gigantic, three stories tall at least, all padded with burlap. Handed ashtray, signed paper registering our proxy, smiled, wandered down aisle to frontside seat. People stared at us, tried to take our picture, ducked the cameras, waved hands deprecatingly. Sat on wooden seats, many people, stage with twenty-nine men in two tidy rows facing us, all with name plates, Spyros Skouras, Darryl F., others, all wearing dark suits, etc. serious distant.

11:00 A.M. Meeting commenced. D. Zanuck, small man, mustache, began recitation, net profits $4,700,000-fifty-seven cents a share/$7,729,000 first quarter before taxes, highest since '62 reorganization. Audience quiet, swiveling heads looking at food table at back of room, coffee urns covered with plastic bags. Zanuck: *Valley of the Dolls* exceeded film revenue of *Peyton Place*. *Planet of the Apes* box office Smash. $14,174,000 grossed by *Sound of Music*. Bible playing the drive-ins this summer. *Dolittle* in 579 top world theaters. Largest stockholder gathering ever. Thanks to everyone. Introduces son Richard D. Zanuck (thirty-three years old, balding) as a real go-getter. Richard speaks. New York home office/LA plant, no time-lag like other studios, no political influence between coasts, fully employed buildings inside and out (they use outside for locations: the plumbing building looks like a church/barn depending on whether there is hay in the windows or not). Only goal is to maintain leadership in industry. Future blockbusting flicks include *Star,* with the same team as *S. of M.* Cleveland and Denver loved *Star* at preview. *Boston Strangler* with Tony Curtis (comedy?), two Frank Sinatra flicks, *Prudence and the Pill,* a "modern story" featuring (modern?) stars, Deborah Kerr and David Niven. And that takes care of films, now to TV. World's largest producers of prime-time shows, seven and a half hours weekly, nine series (whoopie) blah blah blah. Had we noticed the large neon sign outside that says: "Think Twentieth?" put up four years ago, many thought it a joke, but those now laugh out of other side of checkbook for all think Twentieth, and that's why everything is so groovy.

11:36 A.M. Board of directors introduced, William Randolph Hearst, Jr. everyone applauds, General James Van Fleet, everyone applauds, other people, more applause, Mrs. Zanuck, applause. Now for question period. From A. D. Murphy: What are total rentals to date on *Dolittle?* Answer: The answer is confidential. (Ah ha, I better listen carefully, after all I am here in a responsible position.) Mrs.

F. Friedman: Are profits only consideration in corporation or do they ever consider quality or the situation in the world? (Art?) Zanuck: We try to use best judgment, try to make pictures not only profitable but helpful (have I missed the social protest content of *Peyton Place, Valley of the Dolls, Sound of Music, Dolittle?*). Zanuck: Made *Snakepit,* changed loonybin laws in twenty-two states, made *Pinkie, No Way Out, Oxbow Incident,* against racial violence (groovy—but twenty years ago!). Try to make films of benefit to humanity, "This is a human corporation." More blah blah blah money questions. Truman Rambush asks to speak, is recognized. He is from Indianapolis, gray-haired, dark suit. Begins to read from prepared speech after announcing that he is well known in Indianapolis and has lots of pals. Starts haranguing Zanuck. No prepared speeches, says D.F.Z. T.R. continues in booming voice, making quotes, being angry, something to do with money policy for rentals. Zanuck says ask question or sit down, Rambush continues to speak, Zanuck tries to shut him up, T.R. goes on, quoting obscure magazine articles, shouting, Zanuck: you're out of order, Audience: sit down, T.R. still shouting, hostess (starlet?) holding phone which stockholders use to speak through mike, looks very nervous, T.R. very determined, Zanuck flustered, Board of Directors, men on platform uptight, audience yelling now: throw him out, buy him out (sounds like the place may riot). T.R. has no following, Zanuck has the crowd clapping, finally someone grabs mike/phone to ask questions and Rambush sits. More blah blah blah. Well-dressed spade asks company policy on hiring black people. Zanuck says he prepared for that question and reads long answer from piece of paper (Twentieth has always had open door policy on hiring). Later, we see the same well-dressed spade talking to executives during lunch (company Tom?).

12:30 P.M. Everyone starving, nudgy in seats, the present board is renominated and seconded with no alternatives proposed (I wonder what I should do), am also hungry, get up to go to back of room to get in food line, so does half of the audience, voting (?) continues without me, or most of the others (have I been remiss in my proxy duties?), get in line, they refuse to serve the prepared food until the meeting is adjourned, meeting going on behind me. Man standing in line next to me suddenly shouts "second" to close the nominations, then says in normal voice, "I'm hungry." Meeting over, lunch counter opens, am given cardboard box containing potato chips, half a ham sandwich, a chicken sandwich, a banana, a cellophane tasting prownie, a thingee of mustard, paper napkin, and toothpick. Go out-side, sit down in sunlight near portable toilets, eat lunch, then join group for the studio tour.

The only question/answer from the audience that sticks in my mind (the preceding was re-created from notes) came from Bruce Gold (who appeared to be about twelve years old, and identified himself as a stockholder). B.G.: "Are all the TV shows going to be for adults, or would some programs be for children?" Zanuck: "It seems to me that they are all aimed at children now!"

May 31, 1968

Sage Age Rocks Rock

Mr. Wunsch is out to lunch, permanently. And why? Because Youth Wants Truth is IN and Mr. Wunsch, last year's boy genius, is growing older, but not fast enough. It's the Age of the Sage, and that means the over sixty-fives are the Now generation, now. The brain drain has already depleted the retirement communities of leaders for Contemporary Literature and Creative Writing classes, leaving the hobby field in the hands of Woodwork, of Needlepoint, and such like.

Well, you read it here first, the news today is—Old. Over at the circular Capitol Records building a lot of chuckling is going on. It's their turn to laugh, erased are the years when their record-shaped ref-uge on Vine was the White Elephant of the industry (with lower ranks consigned to the windowless points of wedge-shaped suites). Now it's their turn, for what is more suitable to the wheelchair execu-tives than a circular building? Think French chateaux with its round tower containing a ramp circling the outside so the carriage could de-posit its nobles at the top. Think Capitol with its new OBG's (Oldies But Goodies) circling round and round in their wheelchairs, palsied hands pushing at the motor button as they swirl upwards on the spiral of success.

Are you lost? Well I will recapitulate, or rather, using Mr. Wunsch, tell you what's happening. Remember the slogan "Youth Wants Truth"? Taking it from there let's visit with Mr. Wunsch at his Hour of Truth.

Scene: Office with window, carpet, bulletin board with press releases on groups in psychedelic lackgrammar, "the outofsight sound of the Acidikes, three girls and a boy(?) sing Freak for Fiends, if you haven't picked up on it now, you don't know a square from a cube (sugar) etc. . . ." ad nauseam. Poster from Krassner—"Fuck Communism," letter from Apple signed in illegible scrawl, order blank from Midwest for two copies of far-out group, photo of Mr. Wunsch with arm around Dylan, etc. etc. Door opens, in comes middle-aged man with cigar, sits on Wunsch's desk. Well Bob, . . . Well . . . says Mr. Wunsch, clutching his leather lapels closed and putting on his with-it look (a jaded but eager twenty-two-year-old smile, his Liverpool accent clotting like buttermilk). Let me level with you, says cigar. (Wunsch begins to rise from crouching position but changes mind and sits down.) It's like this, you yourself said, "Youth Wants Truth" and it makes me think. Wunsch begins to cower, he knows Thinking is Out, Feeling and Loving are In, or were, and he was all feeling and all loving and young, young Young. Yes, says cigar, Truth, and who knows the truth, who amongst us can say he knows the truth? Is it a question? Wunsch parlays with a—Who Indeed? Exactly, says cigar, you are with me (but for how long Wunsch begins to wonder) so I'm sure you have come to the same conclusion, it's Age that's Sage. Ah, says Wunsch, trying to squeeze his face into the semblance of age, frowning wrinkles on forehead, hollow cheeks, drawing lips over teeth as to make them disappear. That wouldn't do, says cigar, for if Youth Wants Truth, they aren't going to buy your wrinkles, baby, are they?

It's been a pleasure working with you, Wunsch says, tearing up his Fuck Communism poster (he was brought up strict Church of England and hated the damnable thing ever since he forced himself to tack it up as indicative of his position). Look here, Wunsch, says cigar, it's going to be tough for you, you started at the top and now, well boy, let's face it (cigar really likes to face things) you're off the edge, and you're not the only one, A & M let Sprouse go and I hear that MGM is trying to buy out Gritz-Michael's contract, the streets are going to be crawling with hasbeens of tender age (cigar is a frustrated writer) and you've really been doing your thing, I mean you've really contributed your talent (the change has taken place already) and we are not ungrateful so, well, it looks like the shipping department for you, my boy, and maybe, if we all survive, you'll mature enough for us to use you again.

Thanks a lot, says Wunsch, but I think I'll go back to college, I was getting a crack in my spine from crouching over this desk anyway, and besides I have long had a fascination for Oriental Archaeology and . . . That's a good fellow, says cigar.

And so Wunsch is out to lunch, permanently, and the gray beards are ordering specially designed wheelchairs with built-in bars featuring His and Her Hemlock glasses, and Youth will get the Truth at last. Isn't it all groovy, oops, I mean, splendid?

January 24, 1969

Rockconcert

The lights are flashing it's YOUR acid trip baby it's high-eye and flip it's happening now in color at 360 degrees and we are here/now where it's at and where it was never like this before. Outside the cool air, the cool air that is breathable, free nostril air. Inside is ribcage-rubbish breath, is everyone exhale at once, warm, wet, the air under a blanket when you pull it up and over your head to shut out the mystery night stalker or to kiss secret parts it depends on how old you are. Inside this place is young, all young, so young that there is no young, a generation that dies when it goes outside the door where the cold cops are, Margo from Shangri-la getting it for final at twenty with no wrinkles.

Outside on the sidewalk someone begging for money. Hey, have you got any spare money? It is a beggar from Benares wearing Indian clothes from Zeidler and Zeidler. Inside the melon of sound, inside the womb of sound, bloodclots of sound tubes of sound up your nose, pumping humping smears of sound chasing the 260 degrees of coily oily swirly pearly light coiling over everything, walls, doors, exit signs, bales of hair.

It's the same place always, blast and boil inside getting deaf and numb. Watch the band, see him stand there only the fingers move, see him, how he frets and flips at the end of his electric umbilicus, see him, more sexy than possible, he sucks the microphone. Suck the microphone, suck the song, suck the breath out of hundreds of newly nippled chests and make them pant and sigh and clutch, they clutch themselves, no one touches.

The Oldfolks are waltzing! They are waltzing away the starlit air-conditioned night to the soft sounds of Favel and his Magic Trio from Vienna who play every Saturday night for your dining and dancing pleasure there in the dimly lit restaurant near the corner by the bus stop. Oldfolks are touching! Touching and whispering into ears and hearing aids how lovely you are tonight, how lovely you always are to me. They hold each other's hands, press suited chest to corseted breast and sweet it is, sweet romance at any age, the dinner was good, the steak tender to the teeth, the sauce a little rich but for special occasion and it's Saturday night, candlelight, roses and remembrance.

Lights blaze, hotdog stands overflow with bright orange-colored imitation orange drink that swishes round the plastic bubble dome and paper cups and slops over the counter's edge. Mustard lips make yellow smiles, mustard breath, colors the hot air all the way into the boys' toilet and the girls' toilet where they line up to pee and comb hair looking in the mirror and maybe squeezing a little pimple. On stage, another band. Bang goes the drummer and bang the guitarist slowly falling down the stage in snakes in silk pants and open-throated shirt showing his my God how sexy neck wish I could suck on his jugular vein and all the nice girls turn vampire.

Collective fantasy starts with poster obscurity lettering announcing absurdity name, face, place, date, price. Every occasion a marathon, between the live bands too loud recordings, silence is dangerous here in the lightswirl, the lung death, the ear blast, the crowded push and nowhere to sit. Watch the amazing clothes, watch the dolly-freaker lesbian dancers in torn lace dresses and frizzy hair flop on the floor floozily, the round eyes of fifteen-year-old boys, the paid guards who look the other way, the little girls with big curls and empty faces, the heads breathing up their sleeves, the dancers who only want to move, the managers who hope, the people selling hotdogs, the lonesome looking for love, the bands themselves all covered with spermy dreams sometimes actually making music who go out there catatonic or frenzied, their amps on speed, creating whatever it is that is rockconcert.

September 6, 1968

Pop Goes the Chiseler

OK you readers out there in the Midwest, start crying because this
is how it is here in glamorous Hollywood, this is how the Beautiful
People of the media swing. Early Sunday morning (early?) 9:30 A.M.
we are driving up Sunset Boulevard past the not-been-to-sleep-at-
all Saturday night leftovers, on our way to our champagne, chartered
bus tour to Tijuana to cover the First Annual Tijuana Pop Festival.
We (members of the press) are guests of a promo house; they have
provided bus/sandwiches/champagne/members of the band/barman/
driver/smiles/etc. We arrived at the office of Promopop (pseudonym)
to find door locked, no people. Have we missed the bus? Couple
show up, he famous magazine writer, thin (skinny) friendly, young
(very) and girlfriend in what she tells me is Psychedelic Country and
Western shirt. They sit on the stairs and wait with us, lots of fascinating gossip/shop talk which I don't understand. Promopop lady arrives, charming, dippidy-doo curls and lots of eyelashes. We go into
office, all apologetic, tried to contact us, bus scheduled to leave at
9:30 now going at 11. We scroonch into seats, Robert and I try to
decipher trade magazines, couple gossips, Miss Promopop makes
coffee, is genuinely solicitous. More people arrive, vests, suede,
colors, small men and large women, lots of chit chat, time is passing
me by, outside the Strip is deserted, the up-all-nights gone to bed, and
the gone-to-sleeps not up yet. Around 11:30 the bus arrives, it is a
giant silver Trailways bus, we get into it. Start drinking champagne
and orange juice, "That's what Elizabeth Taylor drinks," OK, that's
OK, puts us all in the same boat. An hour later we move off, the
three members of the Big Name Band on board, huddled in the back
of the bus speaking in North of England accents and hoarding their
chicks, who are blond, young, silent.

Everyone getting drunk as suburbia en extenso flows by, oh golly
gee there's an orange tree, we nod and exchange seats, much whiplash
from trying to see everyone at once. Speak to a girl who has lived in
midst of pop music scene since age nineteen. She is delightful, fresh
and full of enthusiasm, tells marvelous sordid tales and recounts better times: Family Dog, Pigpen, Acid Tests, rooms full of people shoot-

ing up, busts, murders, pregnancies, loves, music, rainbows, dancing, friends, police, thievery, lovers, she is right in there sopping it all up. The managers of the group wear suits, with shirts matching ties, very elegant, continental looking, suave. I am having a great time, talking to people I have never encountered before, watching California whiz by, eating ham and cheese sandwiches.

Three P.M. we are at the border. Everyone drunk, have to abandon our nice silver bus and foot it across past all those ominous uniformed border types. The advertisement in the paper said the police were going to refrain from mauling us until midnight if we were going to the Pop Festival, we got across without incident. Our Mexican bus was waiting, we got on, the champagne and sandwiches left in the United States, along with the bus driver. The Mexican bus hurtled us past the kind of cardboard and despair hovels I remember in South Africa; they matched the grayness of the earth, of the faces staring back. This obviously wasn't the main road for tourists, no quaint rickety *muchachos* selling red-flocked plaster bulls, the same bulls whose chalky plaster bodies are piled on the roofs of the houses near the border, presumably to dry in the sun, like bleached pumpkins. Five miles past the hovels we come to the bullring by the sea. I had seen this ring four years ago, before it was open. It stood next to the sand, a rising spined circle of cement, and below the ground staked out for the promenade, the beach, the faded blue paint of the little food stand that also sold religious postcards. It is different now, there are clubs with neon signs and bastardized names, El Moonlight, and prices translated into American dollars: Beer twenty-five cents. The boardwalk has not been completed, there are fancy cement access steps down to the beach level, and uncultivated rubble-strewn lots on either side.

Our bus headed for the large double wooden doors of the bullring, we are VIP's and the driver is determined to take us right inside. There was a bright new Mustang parked a little too close to the entrance, but we drove on until the bus began to scrape the paint off the car. We stop, we all look out the window, the policeman who has ridden his cycle in front of us all the way from the border, commandeered some eyebooglers to help. They pick up the car from the rear and shove it aside. The driver drives forward again. Scrape. He backs up. They pick up the front of the Mustang and move it over. A unique solution that cracks everyone up, because we are perfectly able to walk the two feet into the bullring.

Once inside the ring's courtyard, we are informed by one of the promoters that everything is a disaster. Seems he has gotten all the permission he needed and has bribed everyone he thought he had to bribe, and then, just three days before the event, the mayor of Tijuana feared all the long-haired people were Communists or some other fantasy and the bribe process had to start all over again, and meanwhile the San Diego radio stations have thought the thing cancelled and so, and then, and thus, and so, and . . . we go inside; there are about 3,000 people there.

The bullring is very nice, it is a scooped out melon of cement, tiers of seats going almost straight up and a dirt ring in the center. A band is playing, kids are trying to sell popcorn, men are lugging buckets containing ice and Seven-Up. I don't see Coke or orange crush or root beer, only indigenous Mexicans drink apparently Seven-Up. The taco men can't get us to buy because we are all afraid of getting sick if we eat/drink anything. Everyone has a fearful story to tell of *touris-tas* or other gastric horrors, besides we are promised an exquisite meal afterward in Tijuana at some exclusive good restaurant.

We wander around, my bottom is numb from so much sitting; it is late afternoon and we have been parked in various seats since 9:30 A.M. I watch the Mexican people watch the American people. One elderly Mexican vendor stands amazed in front of a black American who, dressed in a mirror-cloth Indian shirt, is gyrating and dancing frantically to the driving rhythm of the C.T.A. Mostly, though, the audience is teen-age and hard to differentiate whether Mexican or American. I keep thinking that it isn't the music that is what is happening here, but the interchange between the young people of these two countries. Not that anyone speaks to strangers or that this is a Love-In, but the young Mexican and American kids are able to watch each other, sit side by side, share a common experience. This seems to me to be one way of overcoming artificial barriers between humans; a sharing of experience demonstrates the universality of humanity.

Some hours later: the sky much darker, our spirits sagging from the inundation of mostly flat sound from the lead singer of the Yellow Payges, who despite our knowledgeable critique of "lousy" has the crowd dancing and clapping and really enthusiastic, our buttocks exhausted, hungry, chilly, fed up, bored, we wait for Eric Burdon and the Animals to perform. The Iron Butterfly has apparently arrived, and finding out they might not get paid, has flown away or turned into moth paperweights or whatever Iron Butterflies do. There are various announcements about the Animals, and our curly-headed Promopop went off to find out what was happening.

What was happening. The Animals were there or they weren't there, they were going on in twenty minutes or they weren't going on at all, the amplifiers were missing as were daylight, patience, and good humor. The angry rumbling of voices murmuring, "Rhubarb, rhubarb, rhubarb, rhubarb," gets loud, so our little party rises as one man and creeps off in the dark to our bus. But we can't escape, because the bus driver is missing. OK, small sorties to find the driver, all the time the grumbling in the arena and visions of our bus being overturned by revolutionary mobs of rock 'n' roll enthusiasts. Some of us prefer to remain calm, I opt for rumors and hysteria, choosing to make the most of any situation.

The bus driver is found but refuses to drive. Money, he wants lots of money. Meanwhile it becomes necessary to remove the Animals clandestinely from the arena. They are to be secreted onto our bus and we will all escape. Then the negotiations with the bus driver were joined by the policeman who was our escort when we arrived. Finally we drive out the gates, away from the ravenous Romans, safe, or almost. Seems there is a landslide which has closed the main road while we were sitting safely in the bullring. The bus driver makes a miraculous U-turn on a one-lane section and our policeman rises to the occasion and leads us, his light blazing, along the wrong side of the road, all the way back to the border and the safety of America, for which service he is, of course, handsomely rewarded.

The ride home is uneventful, probably because everyone on the bus drinks a little wine and falls asleep. And that, my dear friends out there in media wasteland, is how the spirit crumbles.

October 18, 1968

Kiss

You want some coffee? Abilene, get your fucking fingers out of that! She leaned over and swatted at the child, swatted at the air really, in the direction of the child, at the space between us, where we sat on the couch made of a mattress on top of a door over two traveling trunks, leather traveling trunks with faded labels that sunk and sagged under our weight, made the couch lapse against the wall, slide away from the wall when we leaned back, the pillows falling between the wall and the mattress. I kept reaching back to pull up a pillow and my hand would touch a baby's bottle, the pillow, a crumpled piece of paper, an accumulation of things temporarily lost, casually retrieved by accident. You want coffee, she asked, leaning farther back, not looking as though she were ever going to get up to make it if I said yes, or as if she knew that, as usual, I would get up and go into the small tumbled kitchen, push aside the pan of beans, dried scum around the edge that half-hid the grease-clogged burner, search for a pot to make the coffee in, finally wash a pot, put the water on to boil, look for a cup, emptying out its debris of cigarette ends sogged with coffee grit, and make the coffee for us. I was never consciously angry but did a lot of banging at the cupboard doors trying to shut them over the torn packages of cereal, open boxes of cocoa, piles of spilled sugar, salt, pepper, anonymous gritty things, stuck to the shelves, stains, syrup, melted candy, pieces of bread as hard as wood, the leftovers of leftovers that must have been their diet.

I'll make it, I said, and got up, stepping over the now-crawling Abilene who bit me on the foot as I walked by. Smitty phoned me, she shouted, though the kitchen area was only separated from the other room by a plywood partition, no door, just the space for a door. He called me last night, said he wasn't coming back, so why call? I said, he makes me crazy, Abilene stop that, so I said why call, you cruddy bastard, if you're not coming back do you think I CARE? I don't care if he never comes back, creep, he's uptown with some girl he met at Larry's party, did you see her, Barbara something or other, works in an advertising agency—"Oh are you Smitty, I've heard about you, you're supposed to be a marvelous painter, are you?" looking at him with big Murine eyes (as though she didn't know I was standing there at all). "I'd like to see your paintings, can I?" He took her name and phone, all that shit, said he'd call her, and that's where he is I bet, Oh, Smitty, you're so exciting, Oh, Smitty, I've always wanted to meet a real artist, Oh, Smitty, and I'm a week behind in the rent, the baby-sitter said she'll quit if I don't pay her, Abilene, ah shit, Abilene. I heard her get up and the baby yell, she yelled back, I'm going to put him to bed, he's driving me crazy, and she took the boy into the bedroom and slammed the door, but I could still hear their voices coming through the wood, now goddamn it go to sleep, and his howling, and her voice lowering into cajolement, and his howling and her screaming again and his howling and the door opening and being slammed again over the sound of his high yawling.

I brought in the coffee. She was sitting on the couch, smoking. He'll shut up in a minute, she said, he's just tired. We drank the coffee, the child's voice gasping into stillness so that the sound became our swallowing and the noises from the street below, the buses lurching to a halt, the cars' impatient honking, trapped there behind the spewing exhausts of the buses, trapped in the dull dark dank of the summer street, trapped in the metal of the car, in the despondence of driving between the torn walls and the high rises, playing games with the red lights, the green, slurging along the hot sticky tar.

What will I do if he doesn't come back, what, I don't know what to do. My folks live in New Jersey; I could take Abilene to them. I don't think they'd like it; neighbors, they're ashamed. The sentence stopped, she remembering I think, that I believed, or that she hoped that I believed, that Abilene was her son by a Texas marriage. I mean they'd take him, my mother's old, she's worked all the time, the Depression and all that stuff, my father couldn't get work for years, and there were so many of us it doesn't seem fair. I thought we'd be OK this year (she moved the cup along her lower lip as she talked, almost sucking at it) I had it all fixed when I was at school the baby-sitter and Smitty to help with the rent, he's still on the GI; we managed. She stopped speaking, her voice neither rising nor falling, just ceased as though she had come to the end of whatever it was that she understood, could say; she could find no more information to transmit.

He'll come back, I'm sure he'll come back, Carol. I tried to sound sure, thinking of his little cowboy boots astraddle my feet, pinning me as he kissed me in the hallway one night when I left their apartment. I'll see Liz down the stairs, he had said, after not speaking to me, not one word the whole evening, just sitting in a corner near the light, drawing pictures of horses, using black ink and the stub end of a brush on gray shirt cardboards, which he scrounged from the Chinese laundry around the corner. We had walked down the stairs, Smitty just behind me, his wooden heels clicking on the steps. I turned at the bottom to say, it's OK, I can see now. (The hall lights didn't work, and it was only as you got to the front door that a haze of streetlight, filtering through the pane of glass above the doorknob, lighted the faded brick pattern of the hall linoleum, so that suddenly you knew where you were stepping, having descended on trust, as though into the mouth of a whale.) It's OK now, I said, and he grabbed me and kissed me, his wiry red mustache catching in my nostrils, his teeth scraping my lip, his breath warm and unscented, benign, unflavored either by drink or food, bland, undelightful. I had pulled away and laughed, a special laugh that neither committed me to taking him seriously or to mocking him, or so I hoped that laugh sounded to him casual, perhaps friendly, not at all unused to being kissed by my friend's lovers, knowing it was no indication of a breach of trust, that it didn't put me on his side with a secret I couldn't tell her, sharing some knowledge of her with him through his lips, making us partners beyond her reach.

After that, I'd always ask, "and will Smitty be there, working I mean, I always feel like, you know, our talk disturbs him," and if she'd say, don't be silly, I'd persist and only visit when I'd know he'd not be there. Not be there, with his eyes perhaps watching me, maybe waiting to signal to me, as he sat very silently, moving his reddish freckled hand across the gray board, forever drawing the same black plunging horses set against a low, vanishing horizon.

December 9, 1968

Gathering Moss

"The Leading Stone Has Quit Rolling!" So said the headline of the London *Daily Mail* the day after the wedding, and what a wedding it was! The flight to St.-Tropez takes a few hours, all of which were spent in bubbles of champagne and orange juice. "Mick's a lovely fellow," said the PR man, a swizzle down the aisle, making sure that all of this contingent of the yellow press was properly gilded for the occasion. We landed in a skid of anticipation, just in time to see the orange sun fall behind the palms and blue of the shimmering Mediterranean. Beyond the quay the yachts bobbled and twirled at their moorings, tiny figures dressed in Pucci pink and sailor whites raised tiny glasses which shone crystal sparkles of light under the million-dollar sunset.

I was given a room overlooking the harbor, gulls perched on my balcony rails; lovely young hotel pages in satin trousers knocked at my door with flowers and baskets of fruit. The maid, a flutter of starched white crinoline and black bombé silk skirts, ran my bath and poured sweetly scented oils into the throbbing water whirled by my own Jacuzzi. St.-Tropez, St.-Tropez, and the wedding, would I ever forget it? I lay back in the tender embrace of my warm bath and toasted the lucky couple with a glass of chilly local wine, delicate and with full fruity aroma.

The wedding was to be at the mayor's place at 9 P.M. There was time to change into my Mr. Freedom hot pants and crocheted top made of intricately twisted Oriental string in a star pattern. I put on my Chelsea Cobbler boots; the snakeskin glowed in the soft light from the crystal chandelier which sent prismatic rainbows along the damask walls of my suite. On my newly layered hair by Raoul St. Angulo I wore an ostrich feather hat, little tendrils of fluff made their way downwards toward my Mary Quant yellow eyeshadow. I was ready for the social occasion which, I am sure, will be in the memory book of all of us, whether we were among the lucky hundreds to be invited or not.

In the hotel lobby the other journalists grouped themselves for the ride across the square in the hired carriages whose horses, all white stallions, bore plumes and roses on their necks, each one a winner. I was lucky enough to sit with Dalstrom Retardo and Michaela Ognasti of the Lebanese Rock and Roll Press Syndicate, from whom I have heard that the best Red hash can be obtained for small favors. "Ah," I said, "I do love your trousers," and indeed Dalstrom was geared up to perfection, all embroidery and ribbon sewn onto the finest of pale antelope skin. They told me, between puffs from their glass hookah (so cleverly collapsible and carried in a fine silver mesh pouch attached to Michaela's waist cinch of puma heads), that they thought it was lovely that all of us could be together from so many parts of the world for this happy moment when our star wed. We got quite full of merriment (and hash) by the time we made our way through the rabble-filled square to the mayor's home.

Mick himself greeted us at the door. What a charming gesture! I was sure he had many things on his mind; the responsibilities of leading a revolution are not light ones after all. We kissed on both cheeks as is the custom in France (How quickly this young man has adapted to his exile!), and he pointed the way to us through the great halls toward the crowded parlor where we, the invited, would be able to share in his moment of bliss. And what a splendid assembly it was; promotion men with little boxes of souvenirs for each guest; a golden zipper, so charmingly reminding us of Mr. J.'s latest musical offering; and neatly typed bios of his fabulous career and handsome photographs of the couple smiling in front of the Imperial Palace in Tokyo (reportedly where they are to spend their honeymoon).

The ceremony began; unfortunately I wasn't able to see much of it, being stuck behind the giant backs of the top men of the people's industry who had come to see the top man of the people's industry marry the top girl. But I could hear the sonorous voice of the mayor intoning in perfect French, that language which is one of the disputes of the Common Market, the British opting for English and the French afeared that their lovely language will fall into disuse. But I digress. The eternal vows cement a union of two souls in bliss. We all raised our silver goblets in toast as the ceremony ended and three pages dived off the balcony that overlooked the deep blue water like swallows returning to Capistrano.

Everyone who was anyone was there! It was so egalitarian: princes, queens, moguls, titans, thieves (but only those who steal fine art from private museums—after all art belongs to the people), hired assassins (so very *in* this season), darling dress designers and darlings in designed dresses, Europe's most famous hairdresser, his bald pate covered with chalk; Poland's top refugee ballet dancers, second-generation White Russian exiles wearing medals of caviar encased in plexiglass on purple ribbons, heads of state, and many heads just in a state. Mr. J. draws the absolute devotion of the masses; he is our voice, our songbird, our beacon of the future. Always the role of the artist, *n'est-ce pas*?

I was quite fatigued by the time I returned to my suite; we had danced for hours on the parapets and run naked and glistening with laughter into the warm sea and had eaten great quantities of the local food—pheasant under glass, macaroons stuffed with nightingales, grapes coated with brandy and sealed with sugar to which, the rumor had it, Mr. Owsley had contributed the seasoning. I was quite content at dawn to fall asleep under my canopy and rest for the flight home. There I would sit down and record for all you—you who could not be there—this lovely occasion when the king of rock and roll took a queen. Ah, isn't our culture grand!

May 21, 1971

Melanie: Songs of Life

She sits there, her flesh in dimples, holding a slice of raw squash on her fork, waving it in time as she tries to remember the words to the song I had asked her about. You see, she says, dripping a little salad dressing on her lap from the waving squash, I never write down the words, just sing them over and over until I know them. But I persist, there in the outdoor patio of H.E.L.P. (vegetarian restaurant) facing my own plate of fruit salad, feeling like an inquisitor facing a victim over the food. (A lousy position for both of us, very unnatural, especially as I felt I had a lot in common with this girl who made from her own life the material for her art, who shared, without reserve, her feelings with her audience.) Try and remember the words, I said again. Oh well, she dimpled, and wiggled in her chair, oh well, let's see (the squash still waving and shedding oil).

> . . . They say get out and sell them
> But selling's not my aim
> I'll sing the life I'm living
> And try to ease the pain . . .

Yes, those were the words I had heard at the Troubadour the night I went to hear Melanie, those, and a constant refrain through all her songs of the word "Mama." You use the word "Mama" a lot, I said. Oh oh, you noticed that! She squidged her head around, smiled, laughed a little. She might as well eat all the bread too I thought, she will never look thin, she will just look human, very human female girlish somewhat plump and maybe neurotic a little like everybody else and not hiding it under a glaze of Image or What I Want You To See Me As. Yes, Mama, well, she was very close to her mother, pause, very close, and well, it seemed the logical person to address her questions to, someone close, someone you are close to.

I eat a slice of melon. Melanie eats some raw turnip and a piece of raw mushroom and smiles some more. I have to keep asking you things, I say, I guess I feel uncomfortable because she is so natural that this whole formality of question and answer is bugging me it's bugging her too and she has just come from another interview an hour before. Tell me how you started? (That sounds like a corny question but it is necessary because it often reveals so much, such as, I started because I wanted to be a star vs. I started because I always loved music.) More squirming about, she'd so much rather just eat than answer stranger's questions when all she had to say was in her songs really. She didn't say that, I just felt that.

Actually, Melanie's story, like her songs, is very tender, touching, lonely, friendly, naïve, lonely. She sang for a year or so one night a week in New Jersey at a beer bar that looked like a ski lodge. She sang mostly Beatles and Rolling Stone songs then, and some university type folk songs. She also sang a few of her own songs. When she wasn't doing that she was sitting in Whelan's drugstore or the Port Authority Building in Manhattan, her guitar and overnight bag (toothbrush, deodorant, pajamas, and hairbrush) by her side, drinking coffee and reading the "trades" looking for the opening she needed. She always drank coffee as that looked more legitimate than a Coke, you could sit there, and she did, for hours and hours, and months and months.

Months later, gallons of coffee later, she saw an advertisement for a girl to play Barbara Allen in *Dark of the Moon*. She had never heard of the play but liked the name and set off to audition. While looking for the room number for the audition (she got the part), she met two music publishers who asked her to audition for them. She did that too and they signed her to a publishing contract. Happy happy Melanie, now she was going to get somewhere, now she was going to get her songs published, good-bye to Whelan's and good-bye to the Port Authority Building and good-bye Alpine Ski Lodge Beer Bar. But it didn't work out like that, because even though they published her, and some songs were recorded, they wouldn't give her any money. I went to them, she said, and asked them for money for carfare and they just laughed at me. It was awful. She was broke and lonely, most of her friends were theater people, she had met them in acting school, but she wasn't doing anything and couldn't hang around with them because the biggest bring down for theater people is someone out of work.

Peter Schekeryk to the rescue! He was an independent producer, he got her out of her publishing contract, he reassured her, he made her more confident. You see, Melanie said, when I went to see people I would just say—Here are all my dreams—and they would look at me and think, what a freak! But Peter polished her up a bit and Melanie's astrologer saw the letter *C* in her future and Peter had done a record for Columbia so Melanie went to Columbia Records. I asked them to listen, she said, and to let me make an album. They listened, but they said no, that I should use more instruments, that I should be more commercial and besides no one knew her anyway. Melanie started to cry and the Columbia man said—don't get emotional in front of me, I am the president of Columbia Records!

After that she had somehow gotten to Neil Bogard of Buddah Records and he had said he didn't care how long it took and she could have whatever she wanted and they would make albums for her. As a matter of fact they were on such warm terms that they forgot to sign the contract until the album was already made! Then she was sent on a European tour, lived a while in England doing college concerts. She went to Amsterdam and was on the TV and pulled a little plastic bag of Dutch dirt out of her handbag to show the audience, explaining that she had it because the soil of Holland was so beautiful. They looked at her a little strangely but they must have liked her, and her bag of dirt, because she was getting a gold record in Holland.

Well, she came back to the States, and did a Fillmore, and went back to Europe twice more and now she was just finishing at the Troubadour. But, said Melanie, that's the last time I will do a club, because I don't want to interfere with people, I mean if they want to eat and talk, why should they have to listen to me! So she was just going to do concerts and recordings and something about a movie and a TV show with Johnny Cash and, yes, she had a new album just finished. It was more or less a documentary of her life because although she had a lot of other songs it didn't seem reasonable to her to go into past feelings just to make an album.

So our lunch was over, I told her how much I had enjoyed meeting her and how much I enjoyed her performance and how pleased I was to have been able to talk to her. How I felt she really shared herself with her audience and how much I appreciated that, and that was why I had asked to do this interview. And I also told her how exactly like I had thought she would be, she was.

> They say get out and sell them
> But selling's not my aim
> I'll sing the life I'm living
> And try to ease the pain
> Of all the ones around me

No matter who they are
They stand behind my curtain
And hope I'll be a star.
—Melanie

June 13, 1969

Hoyt's Ax(ton)

The Michael Pollard grin stretches across the Rod Steiger face; are you listening, the eyes ask, the mouth returns to the serious business of singing. Hoyt Axton's voice is all his own, his own voice with his own self to sing, a self born in 1938 Oklahoma, a little child in the wilderness of post-Depression America.

"Did you know," he asks me, holding up a copy of a 1934 *Time* magazine, "did you know how many people there were in 1934 who didn't make enough money to pay taxes? And at the same time there were millionaires, billionaires, some had money and most had poverty."

"I shouldn't have bought this sports car" says Hoyt's little son, careening around the carved antique furniture on two wheels of his tricycle, going from huge utility room to huge sunlit room zip, making happy sounds in the view-filled Laurel Canyon house where Hoyt lives with his lustrously beautiful wife Katherine and their three children.

It is a long way from Oklahoma to the Hollywood Hills, a way that took Hoyt Axton across the country in beat-up cars, that had him strumming guitar in the Navy, that had him whistling away his childhood loneliness as he sat beside his father in the truck crossing the states while his father did his thing as a professional sportsman. Hoyt's parents married and divorced each other three times. His mother had a doctorate in literature, his father played a stable of sports, and for his own amusement sang Jimmy Rodger's songs and the traditional songs of rural/urban America. "I was born," Hoyt says, "the year Bessie Smith died, that must mean something."

At sixteen, Hoyt was writing what he now calls "bad cowboy songs." Later, to pass the time while he was in the Navy, he started to play the guitar. "I got out of the Navy in '61," he says, "and found myself in Los Angeles with five dollars and six cents and a battered Plymouth with no radio. I made off for New York, it took me thirty-one days and a lot of singing at filling stations for gas, but I made it across the country. When I got to New York I lived for a time in a boxcar in the backyard of a tenement in the Bowery, it was a pretty strange scene." Hoyt hung around New York for a while, and on a trip south to the Ashville Folk Festival met Bascomb Lamar Lunsford (who wrote "Good Old Mt. Dew" as a protest song and had sung it on the steps of the local courthouse, thereby influencing the jury to acquittal on a moonshine case!). "Bascomb was a great guy," says Hoyt, "but mostly we just sat around talking about the goddamn Commies!"

Sequential events, however, don't tell you much about a person's life unless they are making some sort of regulated progress toward a given point. For an artist, the progress is often more diffuse: side-tracks which later blossom, periods of inactivity, and trips to obscure places. Mainly just a peripatetic ingathering of the materials of life from which they fashion their art, especially if their art is socially committed, and Hoyt Axton's art is exactly that. Suffice to lump together random experiences: Hoyt in Mexico filming a "lousy" movie, Hoyt in San Francisco singing in coffee houses, Hoyt at the Troubadour, Hoyt doing TV shows in Hollywood for the bread (thinking that if he ever got to do a film with Alec Guinness he might take acting seriously), Hoyt listening to classical music, Hoyt listening to jazz, and traditional blues, and rock, and urban sounds like Caterina Valente who he thinks is the greatest singer, or maybe it's Freddie Neil. Hoyt soaking up America, the wilderness which is vanishing and the urban sprawl. Hoyt thinking about the meaning of life, watching some of his friends go mad on hard dope, thinking about student unrest, taking his world seriously, using his music to voice his feelings.

Hoyt's first big hit was "Greenback Dollar." It was recorded by the Kingston Trio and sold a lot of records. This is how he came to write it. "One day," says Hoyt, wanting to make sure he shares the credit where due, because he is a modest man in the way all honest people are modest, "I was sitting in a laundromat with Barry McGuire and Dicky Davis (former Buffalo Springfield manager) talking and singing, we were there together to combine our wash and save money. We were sitting on the tables and this kid comes up to us and says 'Hey man I've got a song.' So he proceeds to sing it to us. It's called 'Free

Man,' and it is forty-five minutes long! We have our guitars with us so we sing it too and afterward I ask Barry if he wants the song. He didn't, so sometime later I fooled around with it and rewrote it into 'Greenback Dollar.' When the Kingston Trio decided to record it, I had to locate that kid. I finally found him and split the royalties with him 50/50. Hey, did you know," he adds, "that they are using my song 'God Damn the Pusher' in *Easy Rider*?" (*Easy Rider* is the Peter Fonda movie that is likely to be the overground-underground classic film of 1969.) "Yeah, that song is what I think about hard dope. I didn't sing it on the stage for a long while, just sang it around the house. I guess I didn't sing that song on stage because it didn't feel right for a while, then it felt right and I began to perform it. I just do the best I can, I don't have much discipline or knowledge, just balls. But in the past three or four years I've changed a lot, trying to make up for all that time of ignorance."

Hoyt calls it ignorance, but it is more likely an open approach to life, a spontaneous ingestion of life which flows in and flows out, only it comes out in song where much of it must go in as pain. Pain because Hoyt is a feeling man and a man of love, in a time when those words are overused and becoming trite, he restores to them their essential humanistic meaning. "What I believe in," he says, "is what's on that plaque over our bed." I go and look and read the plaque, it says—*See-Feel-Be-Love*. "Listen," he says, "I used to be what you might call a conservative militant but I got to rethinking and I met Stan Borman (ex-KHJ-TV commentator who resigned in protest when the station tried to censor his viewpoint) and we talked a lot and I realized that these kids who are anti-establishment are really involved in doing a constructive thing for their country. Sometimes it goes too far, I mean, I don't believe in anarchy." He looks at me for a moment very seriously, then adds, "Maybe you better add a tra la la to that, as a matter of fact you better add a tra la la to everything.

"Let me tell you about a good time," says Hoyt. "Brownie and Sonny were at the Troubadour and Lightnin' was at the Ashgrove and we all got together and decided to go to a club called the Xanadu. We drove out there together, stopping to pick up half pints. They got drunk up real fast and we'd have to stop and buy more. We eventually got there, it was a nice place, people sitting around playing chess and checkers and just being easy. Brownie and Lightnin' sat down on these straight chairs facing each other and began to play. Lightnin' played country spade and Brownie played urban. Brownie made some mistakes, but Lightnin' sat there and just flowed on guitar. Boy, the music that came out of that, that was a special thing!"

A special thing, music that talks, music that talks man to man, mankind to mankind, that's why Hoyt is especially fond of playing to college audiences. "Those kids in college are sober and responsible, they are the ones who are going to be influential, they are working intellectually." Then Hoyt picks up his guitar and starts to tell me about himself through his songs, and I hear some words—"I've been a long time getting up here/where the vision is clear . . . There are reasons for the songs I sing . . . I'm tired of plastic people/with their neon souls aglow . . ." After he has finished singing, including a duet of "Twinkle Twinkle Little Star" with his young daughter and a lingering rendition of a song about the wide spaces of Colorado and the Rocky Mountains remarking on the need to preserve the natural lands of this beautiful country, he pauses, then adds "becoming is fear and we all have to think about that one—it kinda blows my mind."

So Hoyt Axton, product of America, voice of his time, a bulky huge man with a huge voice that is tender, gravelly, howling and gentle, full of energy and sound, fingers pulling moans and yells from his guitar, creating theater with his music, is going to continue adding his voice and his meaningful songs to the voices of the present generation who take the preservation of life, the preservation of the land, and the preservation of the love of man for man seriously.

August 22, 1969

The Pureshit Revolution

Part I: The Pureshit Revolution

Goose Lake, the 380-acre site of a three-day pop festival, is in Jackson, Michigan. It is a green countryside about 40 miles from Ann Arbor where the Blues Festival (scheduled the same weekend) draws a crowd of about 10,000. More than 200,000 are at Goose Lake; they have come from Detroit, Chicago, Cleveland, Toledo, and the neighboring states to hear such imported stuff as Small Faces, Jethro Tull, 10 Years After, and their American star counterparts, plus a bucketful of Michigan bands all sizzling with "high energy" sound—much of it unidentifiable—guitars whining like generators, singers who yell unintelligible lyrics, and pounding drum solos. Most of it is a drag.

The press corpse (sic!), isolated from the public by an eight-foot wooden wall (under constant attack by "them"), alternately sit in their tent smoking dope or on chairs by the wall, keeping one eye on the stage in front of them and one on the wall behind where occasional faces pop up to get a look at the "stars."

Beyond the wall, which fronts a pit by the stage full of press and hopeful groupies ("if I can just meet him maybe he'll take me to England—Joe Cocker pays his girls $300 a week to travel with him"!) stretch acres of Sears-Fellini, grass, acid ("pure—it's pure"), speed (with a kit to use, if you left yours behind), balloons of nitrous oxide (two tokes full—twenty-five cents), Mescaline ("pure—organic"), THC, hot dogs, pizza, Coke, ice cream, and sloth. Bullhorns and hand-lettered signs tout the dope business—lids, tokes, organic, pure, cheap, now!

At the back of the audience area are large tents, one for dope bummers ("Don't go in there; they just lay guilt on you"), free food (the supply ran out Saturday, the second day), and one for "movement" people—White Panthers, Chicago militants, lots of babies, etc.

It is crowded everywhere, perhaps a fifth listening to the music, much of which (when outside the bowl-like area that fronts the stage) hangs in the air like a desperate scream. A mile or so away there is swimming, nude or not, in the brownswamp lake and the comfort of thousands of cars to wander among or crash next to.

Around all this rises a metal link fence, around and around, encircling the thousands. Through its gates pass the people—once inside there is no way out unless you leave permanently, or by ambulance. The pathways that circumscribe the quaintly hip named areas—"Tokealot," "Layalot," and "Tripalot" are reminiscent of my dreams of Calcutta. Stoned people nudge along in the dust and debris to the sounds of the dopechanters and the sparechange freaks. Eyes are cold, dead, and secretive; water runs from the drinking fountains and turns the paths to mud; people lie about glazed and sated with uppers and downers, freakers, flashers, zoomers, bombers, and fatigue.

In the woman's toilet are rows of exposed seats over the great trough of shit. You squat there watching pale city girls curl their hair and shave their legs ankle deep in water. Someone said people fuck there at night, in the slime in front of the black hole-eyes of the toilets.

Outside, the crowds move on, waveringly, slide down the plastic slide laid across a bull-dozed dirt hill, stare toward the music, watch as someone leaps from a high tower near the stage in an attempt at what, flight? Escape? No one dances anywhere.

The printed program warns against "bloodsuckers" in the swimming hole named "Golum Swamp," but the real bloodsuckers are invisible; they are flying overhead in helicopters looking at their investment, or waiting outside the fence to bust people.

"It's great to be free" is the usual comment given to the reporters when they ask the kids why they are there. "I can walk around at night without being hassled; I don't have to brush my teeth; I can dope all I want," seemingly unaware of the metal fences that enclose them, hold them in a giant concentration camp away from the nation they claim as their own.

It must be a test run of the final solution! Lock the kids and crazies up; give them dope and circuses; pacify. The war outside goes on; Michigan halts the bill to reduce marijuana possession to a misdemeanor and John Sinclair, busted for two joints, is away in an old-style prison, misses the fun of this minimum security bash.

But not his party—The White Panthers. They are there with their band "UP" trying to sock it to the people. "UP" is loud and almost unintelligible; what words they want to say in their music are impossible to understand. If the band is to alert people, using rock as an educational medium, it fails. There is a failure to communicate; the crowd remains apathetic. The people's music must be something the people relate to, or it is only music, and, as musicians, they seem strident and inept.

For that matter, what are they doing at Goose Lake at all? One reason might be because they had been given the Festival Program concession (and they need the money badly to survive, to try and free their leaders). But back in their home community of Ann Arbor the real "people's music" (historically speaking), the black music, goes its usual low-priced, low-paying way. Only 10,000 blues fans came to honor the black musicians, and it is rare that these musicians get such a gig. (Sunday night at the Blues Festival Johnny Winter appeared unannounced to jam—he was *really* playing for the people!) I would have thought the White Panthers would have been among the first to support the black musicians. To point out the exploitation system that has ripped-off the black culture and sold it back to us *à la* Rod Stewart, a prancing white-suited decadent English "star" whose soulful agonies consisted of mauling the mike stand and wiping his blond hair from his eyes with delicate upper-class gestures. (Unfortunately the crowd loved him.)

What an opportunity it could have been for the White Panthers to reach a captive (literally) audience of 200,000. They could have followed the example of the San Francisco Communication Company which, in the Flower Power era way back in 1967-68, were cranking the mimeograph handle daily; taking to the community the latest political and community news. The Panthers might well have asked in leaflets, "Is this how *you* want to live? Are you enjoying this festival? Why aren't you at the Blues Festival? Do you see now how the people's culture is being ripped off?" And so on, and so on.

If I am hard on the White Panthers, it is because they are in the vanguard of the people's movement. Their paper, *Sun Dance* (first beautiful issue just out and available for fifty cents from 1520 Hill, Ann Arbor, Michigan), deals with the politics of music, their imprisoned leader, John Sinclair, has just published a "right on" article on "Liberation Music" in the current issue of *Jazz and Pop* (August, 1970). They have taken on the tremendous task of trying to educate and liberate the youth who they rightly see as the only hope for change. Their task is made more difficult as their leaders are decimated, turned into political prisoners. It is important that they find efficacious ways to communicate their ideas to young people. (Sadly most of the young people at Goose Lake seemed to mimic the lifestyle alienation of their parents. True, they substituted dope for alcohol, but apparently only to achieve the same stupor. Their parents watch TV passively; they watch the rock stars in much the same way, or lie down next to their cars as though they feared it might be Armageddon and they wanted to take their one status symbol—the car —with them.)

Part II: When the Goose Hit the Fan

No one danced! No one wore flowers! The clean green new tents from Sears, pinioned near the cars that brought them, gathered dust. The bikers stood next to the fence holes that had been made by kids trying to get in free (the three days cost $15) and demanded $5 a head to come through. On Friday (the first day) five women sat beside a pretty display of Women's Lib literature they had hung on a makeshift wall next to one of the pathways. By Saturday there was no trace of them; mud and softdrink cans, soggy paper, an abandoned shoe, watermelon rinds, and dope had replaced them.

Out in the "Goosenest" in front of the stage, people clustered in groups, sat in the dust and debris, staring toward the blaring music or shuffling about. Overhead the helicopter dipped and churned and the fences stood all around all around, and the fences stood all around.

What can be the reason to promote 200,000 people at a time into a confined space? Instant slum, overcrowding, all the disadvantages of a ghetto—re-created folks, for your listening pleasure! The idea of a music festival in the country is the conception of tranquillity, cleanliness, flowers, woods, space, celebration, all the things which are unavailable to us in our urban environments where our space is pinched in direct ratio to real estate values. We go to the country to be free, to breathe clean air, hear good music, and get high in a natural environment.

The same people who crowd us into urban slums crowd us into giant "festivals," take our rent at the door and to hell with the plumbing. Not only have they usurped our life-style and sold it back to us, they have duped us by selling us an inferior product with built-in obsolescence.

Part III: Wither Will We Wander?

Is it possible to have a festival for people? Yes, you can put on your own festival, start in your living room, play the kazoo, go to your park, take your tambourine.

What about hearing the big "stars?" You are the big star, people just do the best they can. Is there a criteria? It's what you enjoy and *participate* in. Enjoy your own music; enjoy your local bands; relate to their music. But how do I see the "stars"? Look up—or if you have to have the hype—watch them on TV; that way you can go to the toilet or dance or make love to the music or get high with some degree of comfort.

You mean festivals are over? No, only rip-offs; not everything called a festival is one. So what should we do? Liberate your music. Take it back to the people it came from; insist on controlling it. It was your music; it is your music; start over. Don't buy a ticket to anything where there are more than 50,000 people outdoors or 10,000 enclosed. Boycott the hype festivals. Support "unknown" bands who play in your local clubs. Support the bands who play in the park for free because they want to make music rather than dollars. Enjoy the music *you* like. Don't buy the star system; it's as plastic as the stuff it is marketed on.

Part IV: Chorus

People: It's your music; take it over! If it is their version, don't dance to it. Free music is the voice of free people. You are not free in a concentration camp, no matter how famous the bands, how available the dope. Don't forget that outside the wall the war against youth goes on. Tear down the walls! Power to the people's music!

August 14, 1970

Monday Night, Troubadour Bar, Time—Now

Crowded, but everyone counts, and is busy counting. Eyes make long-distance lunges over shoulders, hands clasped in the calisthenics of the new grip-something about fingers on pulse, boy scouts' honor, testing the direction of the wind. It's a matriarchal society, the Moma is a dark spark virago in the guise of waitress. "I hate people," she says. Smiles ache across faces; they beg their drinks. "Can't you see I'm busy," she grits the words from clenched teeth and recapitulates their youth; no love but an alcohol titty if they behave. We love you, Moma, the chorus builds, boys make out best and girls try, it's a battle for acceptance all the way.

The self-proclaimed "most important DJ in Hollywood," aging perceptibly, his Flower Power a wilted daisy, goes paranoid over his position—describes a clerical error as a "grave injustice perpetrated against me" and "wouldn't say fuck up to a lady." A pitifully chauvinistic male, one can only stare in wonderment, God help us if he leads the kiddies' crusade; he's drowning in his own green wax paper.

And what about the Monkee deep in despair, yanked from a deserved facelessness, and set to dancing for one season and two renewals. He is canceled now and adrift in beer, hoping to be discovered for his real self (as yet undetermined). He leans on the table trading mournful moments with the host of last year's bomb hip show all dressed in white, a deserted bride, eyes still clear, curls so loose and tender on his head, if only they can get it all together then maybe they can do something big. What's the fad, rave, movement of the moment? Slip them the info and they will run with it, speed it along, sell it to the cornflake company and try for thirteen weeks.

She is there again, omnipresent Moma, shoving the customers aside and making them kiss for service. So many shit-grins you could fertilize a pasture, if there was anything around but cement and instant fame. Outside (on the curbside) the young ones plan strategies—get in the door and make it! Talk to a road manager, talk to someone, they know they have got to start somewhere. They can't just come in and sit at Her table, though She is there tonight in feathers and lace and fur (just like in the photos!), Her lava face instantly recognizable, nonchalant and defiantly the Queen. Hats off to Her, She is all art and blood and knows the game from the back alley to the Klieg lights, commands Her team, and makes a goal each time out. But they can't just walk over and sit with Her, aside from trying to maintain their cool, Her friends stare everyone down, hold onto their chairs like linesmen, if She is going to break and run, they are the ones who will be close behind.

The bar holds elbows and glasses, behind the bar is a mirror on which eyes meet and jump, there are moments of kindness but you have to be on your toes to catch them. From the back of the room it is a horizon of hair, fringe, rippled asunder as Moma plows through carrying her drinks on a tray, looking for her next victim.

Well—there is no room for compassion here, or pity, it's a voluntary slaughter, it is self-induced agony, and it rubs off and it corrupts. What is going on? It is Hoot Night at the Troubadour, and the kids who want to perform have been lining up in the alley since the A.M. to get a turn to sing and play for the "heavies" of The Industry. They are inside the club now belting it out in their "big chance," but a swinging door separates them from the bar and most of the "heavies" never hear them. The "heavies" are in the bar, playing chart numbers and doing their masochistic obeisance to Moma, trying to score a hit, a job, a chance to jive and shuck for one more week, until it's Monday night again and the bar fills up and the positions are rated and they find out if they have made it, or even survived. Hey Moma, give us a drink, Moma Moma, call me by my name.

August 30, 1970

All Those Stars Dying

Yes and I was bopping down the street and past the barber shop; inside they were rolling hair doughnuts, hoping for an upsurge in business, the red line of success thrusting across all those thin blue lines and off the margin so that all the aunts and uncles would be knocking at the plate-glass door that said, TEN BARBERS NO WAITING, asking for handouts, and they would sit there in their swiveling pneumatic chairs with the door locked and say how much better it had been before they were rich and all anybody wanted them for was their money.

Lots of those chairs are refugees in living rooms, face the TV and get sat on by people holding beers or smoking dope. You flick the handle and the chair goes over the clouds; you give a push with your foot and the rest relaxes so your ankle can swim out as in a pool of water and nothing for it to battle. They have silver armrests topped by little leather pads in the shape of an elbow. In the silver part are words, MADE IN CINCINNATI, and stuff like that. The headrest has finally fulfilled its name, but what about the ten barbers? It's they who are waiting now, on mortuary benches at bus stops or down at the racetrack window elbowing Bukowski away so they can get the winning ticket. The doors still say, TEN BARBERS NO WAITING, but the marble is spidery with a layer of dust over its natural veins and those thin bottles filled with lugubrious green stuff that they shook out over the pompadours are pouring vinegar on Hollywood salads at this very moment.

I tell you the barbers aren't going to Miami anymore to clutch girlies rising out of cakes while their friends spray them with bullets from machine guns. Their wives don't smell of lilac anymore or push fat daughters through Irish weddings looking for the unmarried best-man to offer him an apprenticeship on Elm Street where there is one chair unattended in the back, piled high with sports sections, unused since cousin Alfred crumpled right there, his hand still on the lever just like Casey Jones, crumpled and fell, his face going white as talcum, fell into the shreds of hair, the snow of clippings on the floor, leaving his customer stranded four feet up and waiting. They turned off Alfred's light, stacked his bottles, and whispered about how he looked at that moment into sudsy ears for five weeks after, top story on the block.

Of course there was the day the dirigible caught fire. It burst into flames without the benefit of TV but the broadcaster's horror was a spoken visual—my God, it's on fire—and all over America (still spelled with a *c*) they could visualize the bodies turning crispy as they fell into the New Jersey marshes. It was a better time then for horror, sort of a one-at-a-time sportsmanship thing about it then. Twenty crispies out of a dirigible were so much more fun than a trench full of bodies. Kept the barber chairs buzzing for a month or more—that proves it, air flight ain't ever going to make it, if God wanted us to fly around under the belly of a balloon he would of put a can of beans in our hair—sort of a sick barber joke. Everything has its vogue and now we are stuck with needles.

I mean all those stars dying. If it had been TB, we would be wearing those little red double cross pins and licking stamps right this minute and writing articles about not sleeping in damp places and how we got to have our lungs examined regularly. They would start painting swirlies on the mobile X-ray vans and someone would write a song. But shooting up and out leaves us breathless. Everyone rushes into print with evaluations, like He and She and Him again contributed this thing and it had nothing to do with us that they popped their veins and fell over. Well, just another crispie on the news going snap crackle and pop into the arm or under the tongue. (Do you have to tie your tongue off when you shoot under it or do you get a friend to hold it, staring you in the eye and holding your tongue, perhaps between two pieces of blotter, just the tip, a quivering captive, while you slip the point laden with sleep into the tunnel of blue.) Weirdness is in the streets and no one notices it much because there are how many deaths on the road and how many in Asia and so what if the pelicans' eggs are soft and our motels full of corpses dressed in tiedye and fringe.

If it was the electric razor that killed the straight blade and weakened Uncle Arthur's arm, and if it was the aeroplanes that made the rockstars lose their identity, and the TV that took the smell out of death, and air-conditioning that saves the executives from smog, isn't it all part of some plan? Tell that to the kids who die and see if it compensates them for a thousand missed malteds.

Anyway I am forced to note flux and change and to mark all these things with simile metaphor in the process of digestion. One thing I seem to learn as I go on toward my own conclusion is that there are so many ways to die.

Eras have their own way and people and stars and war victims and pilots and barbers and revolutionaries. They cut Che's hands off his corpse for further fingerprints. I read that in this week's *Time*. I remember the ghost story about cutting off the old woman's hands to get at her rings. That's the stuff they tell you over campfires when you are a kid putting the grizzly firmly in your head. Once you know a thing, you can figure it out on your own morality meter.

Well, Janis and Jimi and Al have gone away and we all knowingly say to each other—Drugs. If they are going to die, we want it to be in a fashionable way, good to the last drop. We don't go to barber shops to talk about it anymore, but there are still a lot of dark rooms in the city.

October 16, 1970

Stoneground

An attempt to translate a week of ecstasy into print so that I can share my joy with you.

It's all come back again, the high and fly of it, the move and groove of it, the old passion and the lust for sound, as though it were 1967 and the Byrds were playing at the Trip and the kids were on The Strip and it was *our music* and *our bands* and we rushed around telling each other. The rock 'n' roll gypsies came to town last week to takes us all away with music and their name is—Stoneground!

What a week it was! What a first cry for a newborn year! (What will I do now that the band's left town?) All week, every night, I've been at the Bitter End (aptly named: Mourners' benches to sit on, crappy sound system, badly promoted) listening to Stoneground, grinding in my seat, dancing on my haunches (no dance floor and a band like that which rockets you up in dynamite flow of rhythm), totally running wild with the music. Real music! They have given me back my ears! All day I heard their sound in my head, saw them in my eyes, kept waiting for nine o'clock when I could shoot them straight up my spine, I'm an addict, I'm hooked, my brain is full of tracks. Rock and Raunch, Fuckrock, Rock 'n' Roll, Rock a star come cotton me throat honey and gaul. Rock me the tensions of your absence and the sudden rush and fall, oh sing it soul with a crash of crack throat thigh bleed bleat of pain—oh sing it with the morning get up agony and the all day continuance. Yeah, let it scald the air and lift the floor and leave me dance in the thickened blood world of sound, oh yeah, I care, I care, I care to feel that rush up and grab it there in the tar freeway tears and scream the blues oh yeah.

Lydia, oh get 'em up Pearl and peak and naughty. Oh naughty Lydia, smile your song teeth up and look that mike is there and you're on, Lydia, and the bombs and rockets are full of vaseline—every mother's daughter right up on the stage disgracing the family, I'll clap along to your funky song, Lydia, little red hot chile Lydia, you are out late and your mother's on the wind and just pull your panties down one more time and I'll take a peek can't hurt you and you're up there singing your song and death will never get you.

Comes he up hips and haunches too demon beautiful and calls through the weeds to make a sliding landscape. It sucks me down into its troglodyte pool while the band rushes to rescue and his dark eyes roll before he devours me.

Truckstop lover gypsy
park your big Mac truck over here.
See how the moon is shining
The highway ribbons on endlessly
But I've time for a cup of coffee with you.

with your pierce eyes of golden glowing
slow over at my rest stop.
I've got a lot of landscape for your knowing
And I'm showing you all my hopes.

Go good away swift rider
Only redhearts lights mark your leaving trail
But I've got another pot of coffee brewing
And I'll bide my time with sewing
Until your big Mac truck
comes back into view.

Touch me, no, cellophane—whispered response, silk slide over tenuous bone and inside the ragings of fire. Beckoning flame to your moth destinies, we hang suspended on your whim, touch, but oh lightly, our suffering flutters.

Voices, voices, pleading for the labors of women in hump of arch bend and longing night with shadow pillows never come and the song drifts in and pulls up the covers.

Came from the burger parlor in my fastback cut black laid back funkmobile to turn your crank and tell you my only words. Listen to my motor roll, let my fan belt turn, I pluck it right into your little lace exhaust!

(OK, enough of your euphoria, a little information please, Liza, a pause of rational explanation, after all, we weren't there.)

Ten people bursting with joy and madness, playing with music's original intention, to give us the feel of it, the body call, the bone rattle, the blood boil, the heart weep, the skin crawl, Magic! And who are they, these psychedelicized minstrels? For they are minstrels indeed, having fallen together for the Caravan of Love (or whatever it was called) that rooked and grooled its way across the states last summer with catering by Wavy Gravy being filmed by Warner Brothers and ended up in England where they had the British climbing the white cliffs for joy.

The movie was over but the band played on, and on and on. You may have read about them in *Rolling Stone* and the *Village Voice* and *Fusion,* and some people say they are the best band around, I don't know, all I know is that they are the only live band I have heard for a long long time that can get me off in that good old way.

Stoneground's leader is Sal Valentino. Sal of the insinuating deep and dangerous voice, the pure devil, the black angel, once leading the Beau Brummels, always spinning with music, haunting and driving his dark passions through your bones. His counterpart lady, Deirdre La Porte (the butterfly lady of my legends), fragile and burning spirit, made of tender steel, bird moth and Scorpio whose passage is swift and crafty, whose world is full of jasmine and musk. Lynn Hughes, just in from the highways, living in the back of a truck, moves it to you with crystal knives, cuts you up and spits you out and puts you all together again with the glue of her dark-blue lusts. Lydia Phillips, the runaway darkling childwoman raised by wolves in a city forest, howling at the daylight with night-time brave eyes and a little girl smile. Luther Bildt, madman and recluse, talking guitar and a throat full of gravel and always a bulldozer heart pushing through. Michael Mau beating his drums in a race with time and laughter, John Blakely standing there, a redwood forest giving shade and strength on rhythm guitar. Inscrutable Peter Sears at the piano, echoes of Bartok and Barrelhouse, Tim Barnes tied to his lead guitar, howling and strung out on music, singing with an uncontained urgency. Annie Sampson, giantess, mother earth, looking to ball the heavens, starting out deep and pulling out her soul to blind the day.

Sometime in the future, when they've finished editing the film, you will get to see them, because it's all over at the Bitter End, Stoneground is on the road again, or recording up in Mill Valley singing to the redwoods. But they'll be back, they have got to come back, only the next time I hope it is in some big place where thousands of people can rise up and stomp and clap and dance and freak and share the joy (if there is any justice it will happen, 'cause it ain't right to keep a good band down!).

January, 1971

New Year with the Dead

Bill Graham moved in a sideway crablope from the front of the stage to the midway point of amplifiers, picked up two empty beer cans and a crushed cup and put them in the trash barrel. Then he put his finger to his forehead at the exact spot where his wires crossed and completed his anxieties by shortcircuiting himself. He was the prime mover attached by his army; it was New Year's Eve at Winterland and the Grateful Dead were catering. Don't eat anything—I'd been advised—don't drink anything either, not even beer, unless you wipe the can. They doctor the edges!

Backstage: long interleading rooms ending in the one with the sloped ceiling and the toilets. Two men were sniffing coke; we watched them, disguised our watching with a sophisticated cool. The tall, elegant man turned toward us, held out the small delicately inlaid wooden bottle, the tiny golden spoon with its pile of pale dreams. We bent low and drew it into our nostrils. So many people, Deirdre, butterfly lady, and I flew through the spiraling nest, across the empty theater floor and up to the balcony where the sound of men being devoured by a buzz saw came loudly through the men's room door. Two men came out. My God, I said! Who's being dismembered in here? They looked at me and moved past. "It's the juicer," the girl next to me said, and pointed toward the organic food concession.

We leaped and flew in front of the giant mirror in the ladies' room. Deirdre's butterfly was captured by a stork and she said I looked very very small. Robert was in the slope room with Sal and the band—Stoneground. They were to have opened the show at 8:30, were now suddenly scheduled to play after the Dead at 2:30 A.M. next year. They were wound up with nowhere to fly.

The costumed people who paraded the fur-lined halls were dressed in velvet with Rhinestone messages. "Beware—I am the new life." They sparkled and radiated around the giant fires. "All the queens are here," the bishop told me as he wiped his venison fingers on his marmoset hem; "it's the final first reunion of a continuing resurrection, nothing said." He crossed himself. "Janis and Jimi are with the angels now." He paused, and then, "Weren't they always!" I evaporated him with a wave of my fingers and went to find out what was happening in the trenches.

There were TV cameras on stage, eating up the life for a two-city quadraphonic simulcast. The cameraman did a tap dance zoom. A blond girl in the front of the audience turned on her hair which flung round and round until she rose straight to the ceiling, where she remained for the rest of the concert. I saw lots of famous people; their faces rose and swelled in front of me. I knew them all though their names remain mystery. We stood together by the food trays, waiting. I wiped the top of a Coke can I drew up from a deep pool of water and ice. The woman next to me nursed her tie-dye baby. I held the baby in an eye lock, its pupils grew and grew and were of an amazing blue; they were the earth seen from the moon on which I stood. "Food will come," said the woman in silken flames pasting velvet on her arms. People undulated in the dim green tunnel, searching faces, smiling smiling, all an intensity to be relived.

I pasted my Fillmore West bumpersticker stage pass around my upper thigh. I sat on the backstage bleachers, the probe beams of the spotlights shuttering my eyes, then swung away to allow me the audience which twirled under the strobe light with the rhythm of sea anemones. I moved again through lace and leather, feather, silk and fur. Food, haunch of beef and dangerous looking sweetmeats, baked potatoes, smiling faces pressing toward me a forest of skin, opening mouths, golden, golden, radiance, an organic Fellini.

It is almost midnight; Bill Graham ushers in three people from a

Haddasah meeting, mother? father? sister? Guides them to a box or stage where they sit brave and composed, not every son can be a doctor. Two men in white togas are hoisted to the top of the stage or little hoist seats and sway above us. The giant screen over the stage shows a clockface where before the projected permutations of dye and oil and water billowed and glowed. A burst of light! Another! We held our breath, the strobe light bounced shatters of light from the giant turning mirror ball, drums! Firecrackers! The men are descending from their high ride, throwing flower petals on the audience. They have leaped into the aisle in front; they are freaking out! Spurting champagne on the audience, they are taking off their clothes! They are naked and glistening with wine; they are holding their arms up. They are in spasm! The band is driving death away! It's 1971!

Earlier, a naked man had leaped onstage from the audience and into the waiting arms of two guards and Bill Graham. "It's all organic!" he shrieked as they carried him past. "I am the Messiah, we are all the Messiah," and then as he vanished through the crowd forever, "It's all organic from now on!"

Back in the tunnel I hold an envelope in my hand; everyone is holding an envelope. (No one saw who handed them out.) I open the envelope; inside is a beautiful card with a glowing colored mandala. At the center of the mandala, neatly stuck on with Scotch tape, an orange tab—"Merry Christmas, Happy New Year, from the Sunshine Family!"

The slope room is hissing, Keasy! I rush to the tank, we all rush, sucked into its spewing nozzle. The man with the suede jacket gets the nipple deep within his mouth, binds his arms round the tank and hangs there. We wait, torn between compassion and greed, has he OD'd? He slips to the floor, another mouth sucks; bodies glide down, the floor is strewn, a baby sleeps under a shelf, an empty bottle by his face, his face, the faces on the floor, it all slips away.

Sitting high on a shelf with the Light man, looking down on the floor at the pie man, and the rock band, it's Stoneground! Deirdre is dancing with a fancy man, the ladies are singing with the rock band, the band is playing like a demon, and I think I'm flying but I'm only dreaming, but it's all right, ma—'cause it's 1971.

January 8, 1971

Culture Comics

I first started writing for the Free Press in 1966; it was launched from the basement of a coffee bar called the Fifth Estate in the midst of the then-volatile Sunset Strip. It was a pretty makeshift organization, partially run by Garry, the typesetter, who slept somewhere under the machines. Evenings in the little basement office we would stand around pasting up the paper, drawing fillers and trying not to be put on a bummer by the Sheriffs in gold helmets, guns, bullets, and handcuffs who would trample in through the door, then stand there, hand at the ready, staring at us dangerous commiefreakpinkofaggot-hippiedopers. Anyway, the point of this is that Garry, after I had written ten a few pieces (at the instigation of Clair Brush to whom this book is also dedicated!), suggested that I become a regular columnist. OK, I said (not thinking of the terrible toil and anguish of writing a column a week forever), as long as you don't edit me and I can write whatever I want. Sure, he said, and so it has been, and that is why there is such a range of stuff in this collection, and why you are here confronted with a section of criticism and comment on the cultural scene.

This liberty to speak has been a tremendous gift to me and also a responsibility. I think that criticism should be as constructive as possible. If the subject of your scrutiny is honest and sincere and there is no big exploitative hype connected with it, yet it stinks, it is best ignored. It's when they try to sell it to you that the critic is free to indulge in splenetic frenzies, and of course, splenetic frenzies are the most fun to write!

Although I poke a lot of fun at the party for Donovan at Tommy Smothers' house, it was, after all, the best of the decadent do's! I keep hoping that there will be another! I think it was Paul Krassner who was quoted as saying "decadence is the most comfortable form of life." Perhaps it is, in transience, but having lived in South Africa where if you are white, decadence is forced on you, I can tell you it isn't that comfortable in the long run, unless you find a numbed soul comfortable.

There is an underground newspaper in Baltimore named *Harry*. They have the typical calendar section at the back of the paper listing the typical underground social events: Women's Lib meetings, Spiritual Enlightenment seminars, Natural Health lectures, Anti-War protests, 1926 Russian experimental films, and so on and so on. They entitle the section "Nothing Ever Happens In Baltimore." Well, a lot of the same Nothing happens in Los Angeles . . . Ah—there's good news tonight.

Done with Taste—The Beard

What was going to happen?

The newsmen interviewed everyone; was it going to have that scene, you know, where he does "that" to her on stage? It will be artfully done, they were assured, done with taste (no pun). Someone interviewed the father of the producer who had put it on at Fullerton State College some months ago. Was he ashamed of his son? No, he wasn't ashamed of his son. The next item on the news was about the rape of two little girls in Pasadena and then a bit on a man who had been found guilty of murdering his wife and her lover in their bed. This same news program had a month or so ago filmed a reenactment, a police-boy and a police-girl, lying together on the actual deathbed, just as the lovers were lying when they had curdled into death. But that was life, or death, and therefore news not pornography. This was to be art, and much more dangerous.

Opening night and the street outside the theater was clotted with cameramen, first nighters, famous faces frozen into TV smiles, lines, groups, flashing lights, everyone smiling liberally their liberal smile, cool, we were all glamorously cool. It was good theater on the sidewalk and we weren't sure what to expect inside, except that at some point, he would do "that" to her, tastefully (no pun).

More cameras in the lobby, more lights, more smiles. Well well Jim Morrison, well well Otto Preminger, well well The Mommas, well well the Poppas, well well Les Crane & Tina, well well everyone. We nudged our way inside. You could tell it was an important night; everyone twitched about face hunting, seat taking, aisle cramming, program waving.

First item, a light/sound montage. Multi-projection, very loud music, Bach, Missa Luba, rock, pictures of animals in cages, pictures of 1930 stars in makeup, more animals, flowers, soldiers, more music, swirl pattern, colors, sound, shadows, birds flying, a film of a dancer almost visible behind the other images, Goldwyn girls, Negroes, animals, sound. It was beautiful, poetic, conceived, and received much applause. Then onto the stage, bare except for a large hand-shaped couch, stalked Billy the Kid and Jean Harlow. They pranced, they danced, they sulked, they shouted all the four-letter words loudly, softly, hissed them, kissed them, sneered them, loved them, over and over, the same lines with changing inflection, the movements slid around the stage, they posed, they leaned, they sat, they froze, they melted, on and on, over and over, grace, humor, lust, tedium, lust, boredom, tedium, the words became familiar, lost their potency, fuck you fuck you fuck you, a modern mantra. It continued, we sat, it continued, we sat, it continued, we sat, and finally, he did "that" to her (with taste, no pun). It was over, the lights were out and up again, and no policeman with plaster face had leaped onto the stage and pried him from between her open legs shouting naughty! or dirty! or shame! We got up and moved to the lobby. In the lobby the newsmen were everywhere, the lights were everywhere, a frightened girl was wandering around with a tray on which were three half-full champagne glasses. A voice called out over the din—open the doors somebody and let some fucking air in. We smiled and fled through the opened door.

Outside more people, looking inside, and people coming out, looking serious and mature. There's the police, someone said, pointing to the two men writing out a warrant while leaning on the cashier's box. A woman who had come out just behind me, a neat tidy middle-aged woman, said to the man next to her, did you hear what he said in the lobby? No, the man said, who said what? Well, the woman said, he said—open the door and let some F . . . ing air in, just like that, he said F . . . ing, right out loud.

1967

The Craft Is Ebbing

Let's hear it for pornography (a deep throaty sigh will do) because what has more socially redeeming value than a good come anyway? Why all this rushing to court to defend sexual art on its social or artistic merits? Can't we defend it on the grounds of pleasure, for art gives pleasure, and pleasure is redeeming, and usually social. Why not art whose highest achievement is to make you wet your pants? I hereby announce the Org awards, a rubber-coated phallus erectus to be given yearly for the most exciting work of sexual art in the opinion of a panel of judges made up of lay men (and women). The first Annual Org awards, which will be carried on closed circuit television, will be held in the Twin Pines Motel, Rosehip, Nevada, sometime in the spring.

I can remember reading Krafft-Ebing when I was in high school. My friend Barbara's mother had a copy and we would go over to her house after school and, fortified with a package of Hydrox cookies and glasses of milk, sit down to read it aloud to each other. We took turns, reading about such things as the Hungarian soldier who got his rocks off by drinking the water he had used to boil his fellow soldiers' socks (which he surreptitiously collected at night from steel lockers). K-E had a lot of goodies; he had real necrophiliacs who kept their beloveds in dirt pits under the floorboards until suitably ripe, folks that liked to drink piss (including a French fellow who placed bread in urinals, retrieving it later—deliciously soaked, and a multitude of other wholehearted and imaginative sexual endeavors. It made us realize the variety and scope of pleasures open to us (apart from Hydrox cookies and glasses of milk). It didn't, however, turn us into socksoup drinkers or corpse-suckers, so I am hard put to understand the citizens' groups to protect our youth who want to keep sex off the newsstands.

Unfortunately there weren't any garter magazines around when I was a kid so I never knew the pleasure of black underwear, and now, years later, I just don't have the figure for it. But the other day I was reading Dr. Eichenlaub's *Guide to Married Sexual Pleasure* or *Married Love* or *Heightened Physical Awareness* or whatever coy title the book has, and I came across an item which he specifies for "celebrations." It has to do with cramming a fistful of ice cubes on your husband's balls at the moment of orgasm, I wonder what K-E, that fairytale hero of my youth, would have thought of that? Good try, Eichenlaub, but you don't get in the running for the Org because you couch (if I may be forgiven the pun) your smut in medical terms, and the whole point of Org is to bring sex out in the open where it belongs. (See recent Love-Ins and decrees [reactionary] about young women having to wear panties.)

The Beard doesn't make it either, because for all the four-letter words and the quasi-cunnilingus at the end (and this time no pun is intended) there is nothing to tickle your fancy (euphemism). Candy Barr is OK, but the print I saw the drab, or maybe the people were drab, gray ghosts fornicating without desire, sort of mechanical, I thought, though a step in the right direction. What we at Org want to see is sex presented sexily, rutting with style, beautiful people fucking beautifully, novels without a lot of historical trappings (usually inaccurate) which you have to speedread until you come to the pages that sock it to you, and I know that most people agree, because if you will go to any library and look at the pages, and analyze which are the dirtiest (not in content but in thumb marks) you will see, that we all want to be titillated.

I look forward to the day when there will be a section in every bookshop marked Prurient Interest with quotes on the book jackets like "Made me reach climax"—the New York *Times,* "Induces satisfactory orgasm"—Wilhelm Reich, "Came all over myself"—Lawrence Lipton, and so on. Meanwhile I guess we have to settle for translations from the French, nonabridged, including every word of the original, kindly issued for our pleasure by those progressive worthies at Grove Press.

March 15, 1968

Park Homofilms

The Park Theater on Alvarado near MacArthur Park has been showing programs of homosexual films for some months now. The first of such films I saw were at an early morning show which they advertised for fifty cents, a bargain compared to their usual five dollars admission charge. Of that show, I remember a hazy assortment of genitalia and one very good film called *Jason. Jason,* however, was a monologue recounting a life-style, no nudity. Last Tuesday I attended a press showing of the current show at the Park, a group of seven films all made by Pat Rocco.

What am I doing at homosexual films? Why not, especially as Mr. Rocco informed me his intentions were artistic, and besides, I should be able to get a kick from looking at nude men. "Should" is the important word, for although there is a well-defined art of titillation dependent on beaver splits, etc., directed at men, and now there is homofilm again directed at men, there doesn't seem to be any specially created sexual exposure art for women. We are left to project ourselves into the passions of men, peering over their shoulders as they read *Playboy,* watching the trade cruise Hollywood Boulevard or the naked giants fall out of Las Vegas ceilings on sequined swings. Where, for instance, is the Carol Doda for women, called perhaps Carlos Dildo, with a twenty-inch silicone-boosted schlong?

Homosexual films, at least this group by Mr. Rocco, are acted entirely by variations of adolescent Doris Day's and Rock Hudson's, who are themselves, I begin to suspect, both creations of Mr. Rocco's counterparts in the legit industry. The films feature a collection of shiny-eyed wet-lipped small-assed teen-aged, passionate tender silky-haired muscled smooth-skinned small-hipped, long-tooled kids.

Basically, they meet, they look, they lust, they tender, they kiss, they strip, they eye each other's equipment, and I use this word advisedly, because instead of the genitals being the means of consummating a relationship, they seem, in most of these films at least, to be for the most part, the most part. Instance: in *Early to Bed* a naked guy sees through his window another guy standing in the street, he gives him a big look, and the outside guy comes in, through the opened door, and finds the first guy sprawled on a couch with one leg over the back, so that his penis and testicles are front-stage center. This seems to me—and I certainly have nothing against peni and testi—to be somewhat unromantic, unappetizing, and reminiscent of delicatessen marketing. In some of the other films the approach is much more romantic, but again, the goal seems pretty meaty. One exception might be *Dusk Glow* wherein a boy with eyeglasses reads a book of poems (unmistakably Rod McKuen) in the country, falls down beside a waterfall that has "beckoned" him, has a vision of dancing through the wheat with this nymphy-eyed boy who appears from the waterfall, the whole episode reminding me of *Le Bonheur* in its colors and use of leaves and flowers and romanticized landscape. The boy then wakes to find the spirit gone, and his previously weak eyesight cured. It's a fairy tale, indeed.

But have you noticed that all of this is on the level of adolescent romance, of nymphs and permanent youth, of sweet, hardly bearded skin, of silken hair and blushing cheeks, of swimming eyes, of flat tummies and rounded buttock, of the perfect schoolboy lover, the one that must have existed when that particular form of sexuality took hold and rooted, the sexuality of the pre-heterosexual teenager.

Pat Rocco's films are tidily made and visually interesting; he uses double exposure and stop frame and the color is often lyrical. These are not sleazy gray-spotted Tijuana flickies, but the beginning, I suppose, of what may grow into a serious cinema of the homosexual— and why not? I would much prefer to see more serious attempts to portray the sexual/emotional relationships between men, including love scenes, but presented with the same insight as the art films of the heterosexual world. On the other hand, if the intent is purely titillatory, these films will no doubt have the patrons of the Park Theater standing up to applaud and, at the same time, wiping a tear from their eye: for it's pretty sentimental stuff, and what wet dreams are made of.

October 18, 1968

Getting Head

I enjoyed it, I want to say that straight off, had a good time, the film, the opening, the searchlights, the Big Stars, Elliot Mintz in ankh and Mexican shirt standing on a platform squealing through the loud-speaker—"Wow! Here comes someone we've all been waiting for— but I won't tell you, just give you a hint, his name begins with M . . ." and Robert and I running down Hollywood Boulevard trying to guess, Mickey Rooney? Mickie Shapiro? Melvin Belli? Maria Callas? Mike Mansfield? and then Elliot telling it like it is as

usual, "Here he is folks, MIKE Nesmith!!! Hello Mike, step up here
how's things, watscher planznow?" Whatever he answered wa
drowned out by the sidewalk screamers' yell-in. Whoopie. And, Here
folks comes Nat Freedland, step up here Nat, you all know Nat, Na
is one of the groovy columnists for the groovy *Free Press,* well
Nat. . . ."

So, seeing a space, Robert and Alan (our friend) and I dodge in
the line and sneak by Elliot on his stand and there we are, under the
marquee, it says, Premiere of *Head,* up above us. I'm not stoned at all
the lights are bright, I am leaning all over some man in a glistening
silk blue jacket asking who's that who's that, while he nicely tells me
that that is in fact Sal Mineo. Now Sal Mineo in the actual flesh looks
more like someone who is second runner-up in the Sal Mineo look-
alike contest. He has approximately the right sort of look, but his
eyes are not tearing and he's not so dark and sweetly poetic, he looks
quite nice, I like him. He gets by after doing his Elliot Mintz micro-
phonespotlight thing and is replaced by Rudi Gernreich who is with a
lady all in black, including black earrings, and a redheaded girl who,
for some reason I don't get to find out, is posing all scroonched up in
a metal shopping cart, perhaps she is the general release retail shop
model of the other lady in the black earrings. Meanwhile Gene
Youngblood, that earnest movie reviewer of "underground" films, is
slipping up the entrance aisle with his pretty escort and I am holler-
ing, Hey there Gene Youngblood, but he doesn't answer me, just
hurries inside, sort of as though he wishes to be anonymous. Robert
meanwhile is trying to take photos of Peter Tork who has been cor-
nered halfway up the entrance by a lot of hand shakers; he is bearded
and long-haired and is not so clearly a Monkee at all. Get his picture,
I yell, get him get him! my motive being a certain twelve-year-old in
Massachusetts who doesn't know better and collects monkeeyana. We
should get inside now, says Alan, always composed, the film is going
to start. I hate to leave the entrance, it is all I ever dreamed it would
be! searchlights! stars! limousines by the millions! all piled one atop
the other like those gigantic scrap piles you see along the highway or
poetically in French sociologically-oriented travel films about the decadence of the USA; but, we go in.

Inside we amble down to the front rows where we sit near Mr
Echerson from the *Herald Examiner* who loves to accuse me of being
"sensitive and poetic" as though that would explain why he is earning
money and I'm not. "You don't look sensitive tonight," he says to me,

probably because I am whirling about in my seat looking at everyone and getting all excited as soon as I recognize a face or see some bit of clothing that strikes me as Fantasy! Hollywood! Glamscam! Frumcious! Owdasite! Wowser!

The film begins. It is luscious in color and loose in plot. Plot? I don't think there is a plot unless it is that there hasn't been an In flick with a plot since the Beatles' *Hard Day's Night,* and that in itself is a plot. I wouldn't review the film because I think I am somewhat jaded having seen a lot of the technical innovations before as done by the UCLA students and other underground filmmakers and so am not knocked off my seat by solarizations, etc. But I am sure that for people who don't get to go to "art" movies all the time, which must be the majority of moviegoers, it is certainly going to be a significant "art" experience. It is better, I think, than Shucktalkwah and You Are What We Can Get You To Swallow, and if it isn't "Magnificent," as Dennis Hopper yelled so loudly at the end, prancing about at the top of the aisle, making his pitch, it is certainly worth a few dollars at the box office to the kids on their night out.

One girl at the preview came in late in a silver dress; it had red and green lightbulbs in it that flashed, and a battery-operated heart that blinked on and off, a nice touch I thought.

I enjoyed myself so much that the next day I set about trying to get my name on the invitational lists for openings.

November 29, 1968

Midnight Movies

Passage of time, noted by comparison. Someone wrote, or said, that when you notice that all the policemen are younger than you, you know you are getting older. It is hard to remember time itself, that is why, I suppose, games of nostalgia are so comforting. When someone else remembers the same penny candy, sticky and fluorescent in its little tin with its own little spoon, we know that time has passed for them as well. In some ways things are getting better all the time, in other ways not. We whine in our memories for the good old days, forgetting the bad parts.

Things change so radically in a city, so much more than in the country where the changes are seasonal, leaves, dry branches and leaves again. In the city buildings which were like walls fall away and are replaced with tarred lots full of cars; where did they all park yesterday? New restaurants open and are suddenly full of people; where did they eat last week? I often think of the Cinema Theater, of how it used to be three, or was it four years ago. The midnight movies, a line outside all the way down the block past the O Sòle Mio pizza restaurant where the owner painted on the window, THIS RESTAURANT FEATURED ON TV. The long line outside the theater made up of friends, it was getting there, into the films, that was half the fun. We would stand there, or rush up and down saying hello, Garry Taylor, his arms full of the then-struggling eight-page *Free Press* wandering by, hey buy the *Free Press,* he would hawk it like a barrel of apples. The line itself was our fashion show, Vito and Sue, now reportedly either in Haiti or Sausalito, standing there in their tatted lace which was the forerunner of the now high-priced boutique fashions we can no longer afford to buy, the beginnings of Indian styles, boots everywhere, we were beginning to be recognizable.

Inside the lobby, those who were friends of the manager, a smiling and enthusiastic supporter of the real underground movie makers, named Mike Getz, would welcome the regular crowd of freeloaders. We would sip the free lemonade from paper cups and chat about the week's events. There was Jack Hirshman and his wife Ruth in her Garboesque hat and matching face, and Wally Berman who had made the marvelous poster for the midnight movies that some of us still have, and David Ossman talking about his new book of poems and John Thomas enormous and intimidating in blue denim with his old lady Rosie who always smiled and spoke softly. It was the time when Richard Register started No War Toys and had a display of his sculpture in the lobby, and there were other paintings too, on the walls and upstairs near the bathrooms; it was really a club house then, if you didn't know everyone, you felt that you had only to speak to them to find some common bond.

Finally inside, the regular Saturday night show patrons gone, we wandered down the aisles, more hellos, sliding into our seats, eating the imported chocolate bars Mike sold from a little pushcart in the lobby. Then Mike's disembodied voice over the microphone explaining things haltingly but with care, about the films, or places we should remember to go, like peace marches and poetry readings, and then, finally the films themselves, almost a second act to the drama. There was Batman to be yelled at, and long tedious Japanese films full of intellectual symbolism, Stan Brakhage and collages and little two-minute things about smoking pot or fucking. Sometimes the projector broke down and we would all clap and laugh and urge the show on; it was after all our show, it was something we were a part of. When it was over we would hang around some more, discussing what we had seen, planning to come again next week, seeing those friends we only saw on these occasions, but who were friends nevertheless.

It is all different now; Mike Getz is away in some woodsy retreat planning shows for a whole chain of theaters, the front of the Cinema has been remodeled, the funky advertisements replaced by slick sexual come-ons displayed behind glass. They were losing money, someone said, and now are doing what so many other theaters are doing, are charging too much and showing deviate films and sensationalistic art films and anything else that will make people come there from a wider and more affluent population than we were. I still go there sometimes, to see *Lonesome Cowboys,* a fine and raunchy and very funny film, or Dylan's *Don't Look Back* or whatever else they run that appeals to me on its merits, but I don't go there as my theater anymore, and I've only gone once at midnight. It was very strange, the people outside were silent and aloof, the manager strange and formal, the films just played there and we just sat there and perhaps it was only in my head that I heard the sounds of the talk and laughter that had made it a special place to go. But I understand, it is more businesslike, and more efficiently run, no more free lemonade, no more freeloaders, and surely more profitable, and will survive and flourish without us.

May 2, 1969

Who Was the Fool?

Comments on the cosmic scene reflected on the comic screen for your delectation and enjoyment. In the temporary guise of your Hollywood reporter a small glimpse into the variety of experience.

There we were, atop a hill overlooking the Strip, our car whisked away by a kid in a red vest, signing the guest book and through the door to Tommy Smothers' house. The printed invitation with stub for door prize had said, "You are somehow invited" and we were, to meet or mingle with Donovan at the Smothers' house at 6 P.M. Some preparty driving around Beverly Hills getting our heads stoked, besides we don't want to be the first ones there. Arrival and descent into the gracious spacious which is a Hollywood abode. Friends, faces of friends, greetings, and there we were, the long-haired money makers who hang around the music industry spreading joy among ourselves and occasionally among the people who pay us to put out the rap that sells.

Sitting down for a while and then up to case the food situation. A large table rimmed with imported cheeses, each with its own hand-lettered identification and in the middle a parking lot of fruit, melon, and strawberries the size of tomatoes. I swoop at the food and achieve a half pound of Camembert on a slice of pumpernickel plus a wedge of Grape which is a French cheese that looks as though small birds had shat on it. Back to sit on the sofa with a grandstand view of the arrivals, noting guises, fringes, feathers, foaming hairdos, smiles. It is somehow, in spite of being a P.R. party, very relaxed and friendly. From the big windows I can see over the Strip and down La Cienega and across Wilshire toward the wilderness.

Tommy Smothers! In person! In his own house! We all ignore him (out of shyness or cool?) as he wanders about lighting candles and incense. In comes Mama Cass! And Diahann Carroll! And two of the Monkees, the small one and the one whose face is like a rubber pancake that has been run over by a bus! I don't, and never have, cared from cool and gush into my cheese. Joannie Mitchell! Now there is someone I genuinely admire. I get up, tripping over a fur vest and fling myself at her side. May I, I ask, may I say thank you thank you thank you for all the hours of listening pleasure you have given me? She smiles back at me a bit bewildered and says, thank you. I turn and run, what else is there to say?

Downstairs at the bottom of the swirling iron-bound staircase is a patio, and I can see Robert comfortably ensconced in front of the shishkebab-laden table eating off an iron tong. I make my way down and join him standing there; we are next to the pool. The pool is irregularly shaped and at one end there is some sort of construction that looks like a cave overhanging the water. From the top of this thing water drips down into the pool which is lit in such a way that the drops seem to be sparks rising rather than water falling. We sit at one of the little tables round the pool and do more Star-gazing. Stills and Nash and Eric Burdon float into view, and Janis Joplin! Eyes full and up to there in broiled steak I go and explore the seafood which is in a game room off the patio. A table big as a king-sized bed heaped with lobster and clams and crab and shrimp. There is no one to count how much you eat so I stand there with Billy James and stuff my face. The grounds are aflood with waiters serving little puffy things filled with mushroom and pâté, and there are three bars, and even though I don't usually drink I seem to be consuming endless gin and tonics.

Full of goodies, Robert and I go off in search of a toilet and get swept into a parade into a small bedroom where we are squashed down onto the floor between a bundle of people all gathered to see the premiere show of The Music Scene. There is much ohing and ahing as friends appear on the screen and a man (obviously with some vested interest in the show) keeps saying, It makes it! It makes it!

The waiters come and go among the crowd on the floor dispensing gin and gin and whiskey and gin and ashtrays and a feeling of opulence. We smoke and drink and watch the show on the color TV on top of which is a framed picture of our host smiling at us.

TV over and we go back to the poolside; Donovan is going to sing for us! Murry Roman, script-writer and comedian on the murdered Smothers' show introduces the drawing for the door prize. Phil Ochs wins and wobbles up to accept. He starts off with a repetitive but essentially true statement about us living it up here and hearing lovely things like Donovan while all around us and at our hands people are dying. He is drunk and keeps repeating himself and saying how drunk he is and the people get restless and when he finishes there is a mixture of applause and catcalls. Then, as in slow motion, Phil leans over the pool and drops in his door prize, a basket heaped with cheese and fruit and wine. There is a sound of exhaled breath and a low moan and silence. Murry tries to rescue things a bit, and Tommy steps to the mike and says, Let's introduce a little class into this party —here's Donovan.

Donovan mounts the cave/diving board and squats in his white shirt and begins to sing of Winken, Blinken, and Nod while below him in the pool the basket floats over the watery grave where the cheeses and wine lie like corpses. Donovan introduces Paul Horne as

—The Krishna of Jazz—and Paul plays a soft flute accompaniment as Donovan continues his lullabying with Scottish ballads. He finishes and rises from the cave/diving board and silently plunges fully clothed into the pool.

What can possibly happen next? Phil has expiated our guilt to no particular end, we are like kids told to clean our plate because of the starving children in—where the hell are they starving this week—and yet Phil is right, and we are right too, for this life continues on and around just as that life struggles and what did Phil do that makes any difference in the end except to embarrass his host and get as drunk and well-fed as the rest of us.

We get up to leave, Tom Nolan is trying to throw John Carpenter into the pool where one solitary celebrant is diving for the wine bottles. Upstairs we retrieve our car from the red jackets and drive home in a drunken haze. Ah—Hollywood.

September 24, 1969

Snatch

Anyone who was fortunate enough to see a copy of Snatch Comics, a comic book by Robert Crumb and S. Clay Wilson, before it was removed from Moe's bookstore by Berkeley Police, would know that Pornography, along with God, is dead. (I think it wasn't sent through the mails so never got out of the Bay Area; the copy I saw was at a friend's house who'd brought it back from a recent visit north.) It is inconceivable to me that pornography could survive Snatch Comics. Since you most likely haven't seen a copy, let me describe it somewhat, though it is not easy to convey its visual raunchiness with words.

First of all it is grotesque, even in a world of grotesquery, it is utmost grotesque. It is Crude, Vulgar, Ugly, Offensive, Disgusting, Repulsive, Degrading, Filthy, Indecent, Violent, Shocking—all to the degree where these very qualities are negated by the exaggerated form of their presentation. It would be as though the Empire State Building emerged from the night-time dark one morning clothed in pinkish plastic covered with giant plastic fistulas and giant plastic pubic hairs reaching from the ground to the twentieth floor and giant plastic balls that sagged all over the streets blocking traffic from Twenty-third to Fifty-seventh, the whole edifice topped by an enormous head of glowing purplish plastic that pulsated and wiggled and spewed forth a thick plastic drool every twenty minutes or so which fell on all the neighboring skyscrapers clouding their window fronts, then oozed around the sagging pulsing testicles clogging the drains and the mayor made the following special announcement for the media: Pornographic.

On the other hand St. Louis might decide to turn its sexual symbol, the Saarinen Arch into a proper pussy and let it have lovely pink interior-lit plastic labia that could chime and swirl in the wind while golden silky plastic pubic hair could fall in soft clouds all the way to the ground, and little children could gaze upwards through this glowing vagina and see the whole sky as a womb with the stars as seeds and mankind as the sperm and maybe the earth would seem friendly and lovely and their mayor could say: Pornographic too only it would be like the name of a new art movement. Then all the books on the over twenty-one newsstand in lurid covers would seem what they are, cheap souvenirs of sex, and we could forget about fucking as being controversial and admit that it has historical precedent, even for ugly people.

John and Yoko gave us a big gift, their own selves utterly nonpornographic killing off the potential multi-million-dollar trade for teen mag pictures and stories about, "What does John say to Yoko after they shut the door" or "Does John really love Yoko" or "A visit to John and Yoko's living room (with a peek through the bedroom door)." There is nothing left to see, they are mortal meat and if she likes his penis (which one reader of *Rolling Stone* wrote to the editor to say she objected to, as though he should have a special one, I suppose, perhaps shaped like an electric guitar with amplified seminal vesicles and a Sergeant Pepper design in his pubic hair) and if John likes Yoko's flat flanks and Gauguinesque body and it turns out that Oriental women are not slanted, at least not in the visible part, and by this time the invisible part is all there is left to get worked up about, and who cares for views of the fallopian tubes besides gynecologists, it's OK with me because it frees me to face my own compilation of skin and fat and hair and bone with equanimity, all that keeps me from being one of "two virgins" is apparently the lack of talent.

If pornography is going to be saved, and I presume the law is very anxious to do just that, there must be an all-out attack on all specific sexual material, anything where the parts are clearly visible, where you see people (not fake plasticized air-brushed people) but real people fucking or sucking or shitting or licking or doing anything natural. It's all this license that is killing pornography, all this frankness and humor, this making fun of ourselves as human beings, seeing ourselves not as some item to be hidden away under cloth while we beg a well-financed god to forgive us, or a well-financed psychoanalyst. If the aim is to preserve pornography, which I am beginning to convince myself is a cornerstone of the Establishment, then they were right to grab Snatch out of Moe's and bust Open City for publishing an advertisement showing two men ignoring a totally exhibitionist girl, and force prostitutes and call girls and other sexsellers underground where they can continue to maintain their mystery and therefore their commercial value.

Pornography has traditionally been one of the best tools for political campaigners, and this is a local election year coming up, so grab a can of beer, relax in your chair, turn on the T(itillating) V(iewer) and watch them blow it up so they can suck it for everything it's worth.

1969

Stoned in the Aisle

Art experiences are everywhere. Last week was no exception. Anything is art, or art is anything. Why not? The new director of the Museum of Modern Art in New York said, in some interview I read, that art should be fun. Fun is also an art. Enough of this. (Side-remark: I had this experience yesterday which I think must be totally unique among experiences. I was riding home on the bus reading my column of last week about riding on the bus and sitting in front of me was the fat man that I wrote about as sitting in front of me and over my head was the recipe for creamy celery sauce soup gravy and pork chops that I also wrote about. I was tempted to hand the fat man the column and say look you are the fat man in this column but of course I couldn't do that.) Back to art.

Went to the Pasadena Museum because wanted to see it. Also I wanted to check up on what it looked like since I had so flippantly said in print that it looked like a public toilet based on what I had seen on the TV as a background to the Rose Parade. Well, I owe an apology to the Pasadena Museum because it is very handsome, and even more than that, it is life size, comfortable, pleasant to look at and be inside of and surrounded by and for viewing pictures. The current show is very contemporary art from New York 1950/60 and from California in the sixties. Among the California stuff is a glowing disc by Robert Irwin. This plastic disc glows and transfuses light and has an almost invisible rainbow hue pearled over the surface and casts a suave shadow and the whole thing iridesces and infuses the eye-ball and you float away on it and into a dreamland vision. Beautiful. I was of course stoned. That's something Robert taught me. I used to take museum going very seriously—now we are going to go to the museum and see great things of a cultural nature, etc., etc. Then Robert, my sweet guru, showed me that art was to be enjoyed, participated in, a source of fun for the eye and head.

After making it up and down the art-filled aisles for some spastic amount of time, gobbling up patterns and slashes, messes and contortions of color, we went out into the courtyard to get some fresh air, etc. There was a crowd out there, including Ruth Ashton whatchamacaller from Channel 2 news. They were all there to document a visual happening by Judy Gerowitz which consisted of a lot of colored smoke flares which were lit simultaneously. It said in the brochure that this was just part of a series of "atmospheres" created by Miss Gerowitz around California. It was rather pretty although the colored smoke turned into smog a bit quicker than I liked. On the way out of the museum we stopped and bought Edward Ruscha's book on the Sunset Strip which is a masterpiece of documentation second only to his book on the Royal Typewriter.

The second art happening of my week was the press conference given by the Fujiyama Odyssey. Seems the "World's Largest Festival" is to take place at the foot of Mt. Fujiyama sometime in August. It is being put on (that's the right word too!) by a mishmash of lawyers turned entrepreneurs dressed in (1.) purple velvet robe, (2.) approximately $300 Indian medicine man type fringe and bells outfits, (3.) suit. On the same platform was also a gentleman in a kimono who represented the Japan Beauty Congress, his translator (for a moment or two), Miss Japan and other notables. I would dub the general tone of the proceedings as Doublebubble think. There was talk of $3,000,000 investments, the ecology of portable toilets, the community of love, Manly P. Hall saying it was a good year to go to Japan, the 1971 Boy Scout Jamboree which would take place at the same spot, raising the consciousness of the world, Hog Farm people who would help the audience to "regulate themselves" and so on. There was supposed to be refreshments, but all there was were some sweetrolls cut in slices and some dried fruit. Hardly a $3,000,000 spread and I tend to evaluate performance with my stomach, well, partially! Why was it an art experience? Well, there was a creative attempt to boon swoggle people done with a certain amount of plastic flair. If it wasn't art it was bullshit and I prefer art! (There goes my free ticket to Japan!)

January 23, 1970

Phantom Cabaret Strikes Back

Now that Tiny Tim's wife is pregnant perhaps we can forget them. The horror of their exploitative wedding on live (?!!) TV was presumably based on the assumption that Tiny couldn't get it up, a slight reversal of the pornopleasure of watching the Newly Weds and imagining their plastic balling. Well, Tiny presumably got it up Miss Vicky and soon she will add to the population bomb. I suppose Miss Vicky will now want to be called Mrs. Vicky, which leads to the problem of who's Vicky? The whole thing is icky. Yecch.

I remember a time when Tiny Tim was at the Phantom Cabaret, a thing that took place at midnight in LA and featured the talents of Severn Darden, Tiny Tim, Hugh Romney and Del Close. Times change and Darden is a movie star, Close has cropped his hair and left for Texas to run a youth club, Tiny has become tremendous (financially) and Romney has become Wavy Gravy, a sort of peripatetic non-rent a cop for those horrendous things known as Rock Festivals (let he who casts the first Rock Festival, etc.!).

The night I went to the Phantom Cabaret the Merry Prankster bus was outside, and there was Kool-Aid which I hopefully sipped (I hadn't taken acid then). The Kool-Aid wasn't spiked, but the humor of the performance was. Romney was charming in a raggle sort of way, and Del Close made a magic light show. That was before light shows deteriorated into Christmas lights in plastic boxes for $25 at your local psychedelic exploiter.

Tiny Tim astounded me that night, he boopled onto the stage, feyed around, sang (or twittered), threw kisses, and was pure joy. I loved him, I adored him. Why do I now deplore him? Overexposure, wrong circumstances? I hope it isn't because he is a public fool now rather than a private delight: I suddenly suspect myself of snobbism. Hmmm . . .

March 27, 1970

Not What I Had in Mind

Everytime I try to get to the movies it seems such a big excursion: first I have to find the Sunday supplement or the *Free Press* or something that will tell me what is playing where, or rely on my own recall, like I think *Fanny and the Doctor* is playing at that place next to the Swiss restaurant. What place he says—next to what restaurant? You know, I say, don't you remember? We ate there once, the guy who owns it is fat and the food is terrible, we ate there with George and Jill. George and Jill who—he asks. Oh shit, all I wanted was to go to the movies, not play life history. Well, here is the paper, let's see, aside from the "adult" films, there are thirty-seven films on neurotic cowboys, fifteen about the life-style of hippies, two on World War Two (neat), seven with old comedians in search of new reputations, and five in French of which three are dubbed and two have subtitles, not what I had in mind.

What I had in mind was a sort of super *Mildred Pierce*. That old goodie had Joan Crawford extending her mulberry lips over a career of sordid detail, hinted at perversion, dressed in fancy clothes, placed in glamorous settings, and a "don't tell what Mildred Pierce did" ending where all the baddies died, especially her ungrateful daughter (an actress whose name escapes me but not the face unfortunately as she was one of my unfavorites). They don't make them like that anymore or rather I think it is me, I am not made like that anymore;

when I saw *Mildred Pierce* I was only sixteen and a virgin—things
have changed.

What we usually end up doing is watching TV. Where is the fucking guide—oh yeah, over there under the pile of papers and shirts
and stuff we emptied from the overnight bag when we got back from
our last weekend trip and put the bag away but never put the stuff
away. (Well, we could leave at a moment's notice by just stuffing
the stuff back into the bag, same old unanswered letters, same old
book I meant to read, same old comfortable shirt.) Found, *TV Guide*
found, let's see, lots of crap I say . . . maybe if we get stoned it
will look better.

Have some friends we just met, just met them but they are friends
is what I am trying to explain, and they sit there watching Channel
52 which has all those really explicitly dull films shot through boiling
oatmeal of some guy fishing in the Adirondacks. They watch those
films and get bombed, totally smashed, limp and out of it and the
films flicker comfortingly about nothing to care about and so they
control their environment. She says she never goes out because out
is so rotten, just staying in she can see everything nice, like views of
the Adirondacks and Canada and how to sew tepees or play croquet
and it's no threat. Myself, I don't have the iron constitution to get
that much into boredom as an aesthetic, though I can take it from
time to time, limpness must have some virtue (as the actress said to
the Bishop!).

Anyway, the TV is lousy and the movies hiding out there in the
traffic are far away, unknown and costly, and too much trouble to
figure out. It isn't like there was a Main Street and you drove by the
Roxy and the Bijou and the Palace and the Paramount on your way
to the butcher, there isn't even a butcher to go to, it's all a mess.

Mostly we end up doing nothing at all, drinking too much coffee
and arguing over the relative merits of *To Tell the Truth* and *Truth
or Consequences,* both of which actually have no merit at all. That's
the way time goes. I could go to meetings I suppose and propose
courses of action or volunteer to raise funds or learn to be more
sensitive or just hang out, but that's a drag too. (Don't write me letters about social responsibility. I've probably been to more meetings
and raised more money in my time than all of you put together—I'm
just pissed off with committees.) Finally it gets so bad around here
that I start reading, seemingly a last resort these days (and I used to
read so much) and then it gets better.

Reading, however old-fashioned, is still the best of the alternate worlds. And then of course there are always those personals at the back of the *Freep* (very good for reading while at stool!) and in desperation the various propositions on the ballot for the upcoming election. Yeah, get out and vote folks, the choices are nonexistent, the outcome foredoomed, and the whole process insulting. So what's at the movies?

1970

Superstar

Ting a ling . . .

Hello, who's this?

It's me, Viva! I've just written a book.

Oh, really! What's it about—making movies?

Some of it, just a minute—oh, ahhh, mmm, it's about my life; it's autobiographic only I disguised everybody.

What do you mean you disguised everybody?

Well, I call myself Gloria, see, and I gave everyone else other names, all my friends, like I call Andy *A*, see, mmm, wait a minute, I want to turn it to pulsate, there, that's better, mmmmmmmmm . . .

That sounds fascinating, so it's a novel? I mean what happens, you know . . .

Oh, it's about . . . mmm, ah ordinary things, the usual, you know, fucking with Coke bottles and sucking pricks and talking. . . .

Talking? You put it in written dialogue, I find dialogue so hard to do, to get it to sound natural; didn't you think that was the hardest part?

No, umm, it was easy, I always carry a tape recorder with me, EVERYWHERE, a little tape recorder and so all I had to do was transcribe the tapes, umm, I mean not all of them but the ones that I thought were important or explained stuff, ummm, oh it's too strong, wait a minute, there, that's better, it costs a dollar and fifty cents an hour to run it, but All Life Is Art, so it's making art and I wrote about the phone call when *A* got shot too, and what I did, umm, and what that bitch Infra Red did too and, ummm, I think I'm coming . . .

Coming to California?

No, I'm coming on Dolores' vibrator, she lent it to me for the weekend, here, say hello to my husband Angelo.

Hello Angelo.

Hello, how iz eet in California?

Fine, how are you?

I eez fine, here eez darling Gloria.

So you see my book is coming out in November and they are giving me a party at the Gotham Book Mart, and it's going to be fun I guess, have you tried a sweet potato?

Tried a sweet potato?

Yes, someone said it was better than a cucumber, but my clitoris is so small, can you find it?

Me? On the phone?

No, I was talking to darling Angelo, wait a minute till I move over a bit because Dolores is going to pop me, ummm, speed really makes it good. . . . It starts off with my childhood and my father, he used to lie on top of me and beat me, he was a Catholic doctor, you know . . .

Oh, do you think that explains it?

Explains what? I don't explain things, I just tell about them, about the filming, about the band-aids on my nipples.

I remember that, it was in *Lonesome Cowboys,* wasn't it? Yes, but I call it Creepy Cowboys, see if I have to change the names I can get a little editorializing in too, they can't sue me, and I tell about how I don't really fuck in the movies, and how Groovy and Hippie in Adele Vargas' movie, *Tigers Tremble* are fags, there are a lot of fags in my book. Stop it!

Stop what?

No, I'm talking to Dolores, she's sticking her rubber cock into my thigh, stop it. Dolores is funny, throwing all those photographs of pricks into the gutter. . . .

Listen Viva! Gloria! Wouldn't everybody know who you are writing about anyway?

Well, I guess so, and if they don't they wouldn't know who they are anyway and if they don't know who they are, then they don't know all about it anyway, and they will think it's all perverse I guess though I don't see what's so perverse about any of it, it's just the way we live, I mean, ummm, ummmm, I mean everybody that I know lives like hat it seems, ummm, ah, I'm coming again, that's sooo nice, ummm, you should try it, I never get bored with sex, do you?

No—Yes, well, did you use a lot of photographs?

No, I don't know why, we just didn't use any, but it has tapes and pages from my journals and poems and some of it is first person, you know, I say I did so and so, and other parts I take a more removed approach and write about myself as Gloria, like . . . Gloria fingered her clit, stuff like that, the book is called *Superstar,* do you think that's a good title?

Oh fine! perfect, yes I mean you are a super star, I have always thought of you as a superstar . . . I loved *Naked Restaurant* and *Lonesome Cowboys* and *Lion's Love,* they were great.

Well, thank you but I'm not going to make any more movies unless they pay me. You know they hardly paid me anything for those movies and I'm suing *A*.

What's that buzzing? Hello—Viva, what's that buzzing? Hello?

Ummm, that was, I was trying to stick the receiver in my cunt, I guess you heard the vibrator too, it's in there, hard to get it all up at one time, I keep trying, here, talk to Dolores for a minute. . . .

Hello? Hello. . . . Dolores?

Yes? How are you, Up, I'm up! oh it's so good, you should read the part about me in the book, I tell some farout stories and stuff, you haven't seen me in the movies because I have these stretchmarks I'm ashamed of. . . . I want to pop again, here, talk to Viva.

Viva?

Dolores has these funny inhibitions, but only about her stretchmarks, everything else comes right out, I've got it all in my book, ummm, you should see the cover.

What's on the cover?

It's this terribly beautiful photograph of me by Cecil Beaton, and it's wrapped around the book so that one of my eyes is right over the spine, and it says "Superstar" in gold lettering, and it's going to cost $6.95, but I think it's worth it really because it's so interesting, wait a minute while I suck your nipple, hold on there, ummmm, Angelo would you please put your finger up my ass, ahh, that's better, hello?

Hello? Yes, I'm still here, what are you doing?

Hello, ummm, hold on a minute, I think I'm coming. . . .

That's OK Viva, you go right ahead, I have to hang up now, I have a date with a Russian Wolfhound.

November, 1970

Down with Dirty Movies

When Narcissus looked into the pond the only pollution he saw was his own reflection which gave to him a sense of the skin of things but also, perhaps, was the birth of art, if art is the effort to improve and make manifest our conceptions of self and its extensions.

And when on Friday night last a dozen or so young ladies of astonishingly matching age and look paraded in front of the Paris Theater yelling "Down with Dirty Movies," they too were manifesting their art, for I'm sure I have seen, blurred though they were, their faces there, at the top of the photo, coyly peeking over their down front and center split beaver and bush all mine, yours, the world's, in packets of a dozen for ten dollars available now.

And when I sat with Paul Morrissey in a dark corner of the Black Rabbit Inn (where the atmosphere is more edible than the food because they serve too much food so that you are forced to leave it lying mutilated on your plate and mumble over it while you try to keep your cool with cigarettes and coffee) and he told me about Hollywood! the Stars! like Claudette Colbert! and Olivia de Havilland and Simone Simon! ah Simone Simon! didn't I see him settle back into the cushions and pass the pastor another cup of tea with a sigh the aspidistra in his eye giving him a tousled air, "the young people nowadays play with fire, ah me," and he crossed his ankles and rang for the maid.

It's all one world, Joe Dallesandro, star of *Trash,* sitting on the curb, for a moment, in the movie, stopped twixt futile encounters trying to get it up, the needle up the arm by way of the prick up the cunt, sitting on the curb watching nothing and behind him a meat market and carcasses floating in the window like so many naked Mussolinis hung by their feet or anatomical renditions of the musculature of chorus girls and the title to it all is *Trash,* of the soul, of the times watch out, Narcissus, for the pool is clotted over with spittle.

Michael Sklar looks thinner than he does in *Trash.* In the movie he plays a social worker who has this thing for shoes. "I think I'm going to faint" is Michael Sklar's favorite expression. Michael was worried that his mother would take it all seriously, he was afraid his mother would be upset, didn't tell her about the movie he was in, but she found out, momma knows, momma always knows and said, "It's not important what I think, it's important what Joe Dallesandro's mother thinks. I've only seen four naked men in my life, your father, you, your brother, and Joe Dallesandro." (Such is the broadening scope of art.) Of course momma was right except that Joe Dallesandro doesn't have a mother, he was scraped off the curbside, and although he moves naked through Warhol, Morrissey films, the most naked part of his body are the pimple scars on his buttocks; all the rest is decoration.

Look, this is a very serious article. I am writing about the movie *Trash,* about Paul Morrissey who directed—no, he says that's not the word—who produced it sort of although *Andy You Know Who* (which is not to deny his name but to phrase it in the lingerie lingo that simply simpers simplifies the information), and I am writing about Michael Sklar who plays a part in *Trash,* and I am writing about some very boring thing called *Adultery for Love and Profit* which had a gross premiere on Friday and I hope that's the largest of its gross, and I am trying to put all this together to tell you, and I might as well come right out and say it because it is getting all mixed up and contrapuntal or baroque, that *Trash* is a highly moral picture about an immoral world and that *Adultery for Love and Profit* is a highly immoral picture about a moral thing: love, flesh-lust, pleasure, desire, warm and wet.

When I heard I was going to NYC in November the first plan I made was to see *Trash,* because I thought it might not get here, as *Brand X* seems destined not to get here, and I wanted to see it real bad because ever since I'd seen *Naked Restaurant*—but I've written about what Warhol/Morrissey films are, I've told you that they are the penultimate narrative explanation of our consciousness now now now for as long as we tolerate New York City as a conception of a place for people to live and plot how to wipe out other people across the waters and admire that pretty building with its multinational hostesses who walk you around and say—here is where we keep the peace, piece, the uniformed cuntguides at the United Nations of industry on land donated by Rockefeller, and you know where his head is at for shit sake. NO NO NO, I'm not against the United Nations, just puked with the farce of it, letting South Africa keep its mandate over South West Africa. Now that sounds exotic to you, doesn't it? South West Africa? It's a piece of land on which people live and are crushed by the genocidal intentions of the South African government which has this little mandate from that beautiful lovely glass building on—that's all I meant by that.

What has all this to do with *Trash,* with dirty movies, is this narrative too nonlinear or too linear for you? Are you waiting for the commercials? OK. Go see *Trash* and save your skin. AND NOW A WORD ABOUT THE SPONSORS. I mean what the . . . what is going on? Effete, effete insight, decadence, decadent insight, takes one to know one? Is that what it comes down to, for know one, be one . . . He made the picture, and you think you are going to meet some kind of dope smoking Arnold Toynbee with a movieola and you meet a decadent effete fellow full of goodwill who makes the best damn movies of our decade and you have to say to yourself that something is rotten and it isn't necessarily in Denmark.

I sat in an office once over at Paramount talking to the publicist for a kiddies' TV show who when he referred to his boss, the producer, aways put his hand over his heart and said, "Syd cares." I couldn't figure out if it was show-and-tell about Syd's feelings or he was trying to hold his angina in, but I tell you "Morrissey Cares." Morrissey cares that the stars are gone, and by that I think he means the stars in our eyes, for stars were our enlarged reflections of our self-projection. Didn't all the Joan Crawford period women wear purple passion lipstick and the Jean Harlow generation float in chiffon and champagne, even though it was Canada Dry. So he misses the image, the image that was self-loving, he misses the times when beauty, whatever banal form it took, was the message. So he finds stars, he finds the most beautiful examples of our common culture, these driftwood transvestite cold and spaced automatons and tells us that this is what you must want to be, folks, because this is what you are creating in this world.

Michael Sklar was stopped outside Sardi's and asked for his autograph after *Trash* came out; it was the first time he was asked for his autograph, ever (I think I'm going to faint), and he was so excited by the request that he misspelled his name.

Michael Sklar can't get any credit cards. Well hardly. He has credit at Tiffany's and Rosenthal's and Hamerker Schlemecker and Georg Jensen, but he has been turned down by Korvette's and Ohrbach's. That's not funny. Tyfinny's and those folk know it's almost all over for them, but Ohrbach's and Korvette's know Andy and his gang are out to wipe out this system. Bombs, butane, and bounce. They are the Chiffon Panthers, the Westport Weathermen, the Chic Chicanos.

La Raza berry. The Young Laddies, aiming their cameras straight into that pool, that same pool where it all started; they just put some people near the pond and photograph their reflections only they don't do that: They turn the screen to water and let you look in. You? Is that you there looking in, is that you with the blank eye and the cold despair and the dope-ridden brain and the fallapart part? Getting uptight? So am I.

There is no sexploitation in *Trash,* but there is plenty in *Love for Adultery and Profit,* and exploitation renders the humanity out of man, and the humaneness is gone; it sucks, literally. *Trash* takes you, thrusts you, plonks you into a purity, forces you to seek purity. In much the same way that *Weekend* forced you to recognize the growing callousness of your watching self, *Trash* makes you decide for Christ. Billy Graham is an amateur.

I am a little bedeviled by guilt here. I spent two hours with Morrissey and two with Sklar and saw *Trash* twice and wish I had met Warhol even once, though years ago I got a postcard from John Wilcock and thought, because the signature was at that time unfamiliar to me, that it was from Warhol, and I went to the Paris Theater to see *Adultery for etc.* because I was also going to start writing a column called "Lick My Column," thinking it might be fun to get into porno films free and write about them from a woman's point of view and everyone thought it was a great idea and a ha ha and all I want to do now is cry and weep and shudder—and I hope everybody understands that it all means something, doesn't it?

February 5, 1971

Comicosmicapers

The wall that is the outside of the building is at the same time the inside of the street. The skin which is the outside of me is at the same time the nearest that the outer world can get. Aside from puncturing holes in my flesh and stuffing the world inside of me, the only other alternative seems to be to use the holes I already have to let it all pour out. Oh for the cosmic touch, the giant eternal fuck in the sky, the my bones are your bones, your earth is my soil, your trees are my limbs, those stars are my eyes, the waves my breath, clutch and hold, reach, touch and desire, lust for the livingness of everything, despair for the final union.

Now Now Now Now Now Now. Be yourself, a great friend and teacher said that to me. Be yourself. Who, who is my SELF? Plunge into words, make maps, charts, sign language, draw the code from the blood and translate in the daytime of the mind. The mind, a computer for my feelings, sending me memory signals and warnings, telling me what has happened and what may occur, a braking system, a guide, but not to be believed.

The best way is to stand on the edge and jump. My favorite poem is by W. H. Auden, and it is about Icarus. So what if my wings melt, how bright, how warm is the sun, how beautiful the view, how great the flight.

Chew Well, You're Eating My Days!

All places marked by food and love. Landmarked by passion, prints, imagistic visions forever superimposed upon the reality of geography-permanent superimposition. Tastes as guideposts. To return to Paris, as I did, packed into third-class carriage with French-labeled Coke bottles, doors with precipitous wooden steps to fall out of onto strange Gallic platforms, past upsprung pastel workers—apartments hung with Belgian linen, into the Gare Du Nord, assault on taxis (have the White Russians all withered away like the state? this driver spoke only French) and into remembered restaurant. Same menu, same sawdust, same taste, joy, love all the same.

Greenwich Village of the fortyfifties, down steps to the wooden tables of Drossies, to bowls of borscht, mounds of blackbread, and hours of talk. And now on Sunset, Drossies again, Mrs. Drossie all round with hospitality, same waiter, same soup, same bread, but tables different, yet the taste and smell of memories. Chopped liver on its platform of lettuce—chopped liver follows joy like a banner— black coffee is sad aftertimes taste. When there is something I want and I don't know what it is and it isn't love, is it smoked salmon?

German restaurant in Santa Monica—are they Nazis? Only dollarfifty for home-cooked meal. Father serves, mother cooks, daughter passes from gangly to maiden while we come and go. Near corner, Fourth and Main.

Strange smorgasborg on Pico near Fairfax, cooks Armenian and Jewish. Herring, a carrot salad with dill that tastes like cold mussels. Barragan's, a small Mexican café, now enlarging, on Sunset near Echo Park, Mommakitchen restaurant, four booths, some counter space, regular truckdriver daily mystery menu, salad with beautycolor things, red cabbage and carrots, crowded, hard to find, genuine food-place, cheap.

Italian, nonsoggy, spiced and delicious Milanos on Hillhurst. Red placemats, thickcustard pastry, food gorging, bread eating, resplendent warm comforting service, about twofifty, but oh pleasure and no hustle. Ugly plasticgrape semi-decor, but look into your plate and it glows back at you, pastaperfect and saucered.

Red does something to my stomach, makes it quiver and surge. Drossies has red walls, Milano red placemats and wallpaper, in London a red restaurant with tiffany lamps from the tiffiny times, in Cape Town the Café Royal all red leather and Moslem waiters in red fez—but don't go to sad South Africa.

Taix's manufactures a round, flat, hearth-baked sourdough bread. Cradle it on your chest, push it between your breasts, pull it apart and chew on its stretching crust, cheese, butter, taste it. A Mr. Felix makes German pumpernickel. Markets it in cellophane with his Victorian-perfect face on the label. Keep it in the fridge and eat it all week, full of grain, and dark sultry mountain-climbing taste, as though it were the last taste on earth.

I should like to sleep in a bed of Jewish doublewhipped cream cheese, squeeze it between my armpits, smear it on my belly, kiss it into mounds of fleshly love. I get lost in the sensuality of food, colors, smells, textures, all the world to copulate. Grass is to sing between fingers, shove in ears, wheat to plait through hair and caress the sensitive undersides of elbow and knee.

Rocks are the oldest ancient messenger of time, extolling survival in leaping heaps of hard responding iron, cragged and spilled across hours of traveling, strata singing to the light of its heaved borning sunwise, powerful with permanence. Air in sunlight pricks on the skin reminding of seasons, of light pouring in gushes for hours of opened-up time. Water tastes of fernmud paths down great heights, of reed pipes and lizardtrails, and spills into the unclenched throat open-mouthed at streams-end, while eyes swivel at the horizon of tree and flower and bird-swell tying with their calling the patchwork surroundings. Warm cowdung between toes, tiny prickles in the muscled calves, burrs, seeds, rotting bark, bending weeds flowering, too much a spring day, too much feel, movement, taste, touch in everything, cellular and running along a million secret juicy channels, in me, and through me and passing down furrowing into coolth of earth never lit, heaving with mineral and sweet growth.

Too much and all of very little and everything of nothing and all-thing together twined and bursting in pomegranate red succulent lovebuds, spilling and self-nourishing. This earth's religious fanatic wanders in praise.

March 11, 1966

The Strawberries Are Dead
and the Cream Is Curdled

When I was little and the Revolution was still going to come, like a nymphomaniac in analysis, there were strawberries and cream over the Life Cafeteria coffee cups and not all this deathdoom talk to curdle the cream and send the bright-eyed kids screaming into the streets and dance halls balling away the lastlust hours of this diminishing society.

I crawled between the legs of the last true men off to war in Spain, and held the hand of the shakeapart noname man we imported, a bit of waste from the camps of Europe who sat gluing leather into the shape of football purses, left us to be a janitor in the cement of the east Sixties, and coughed his way out in a cellar in the middle of a New York January.

Fine famous men these were, with slogan hearts and thin wives who shared their love with freedom in a sanctified adultery. A time of windy corners with mimeographed loveletters-to-the-wind sticking to woolly mittens, blowing down the gray curb, lying blacklimp in the guttering holes of the drains and swampbrown pools of citywater.

Vast glowing congregations in Madison Square Garden waving dollar bills for Nine Negro boys, for Tom Mooney, who later, out of his prison walls, stood in a crowded lot on Sixth Avenue, encased in a darkblue suit and monumental pallor, and shook hands and died so soon and marched on in my heaven populated with visionary soapbox orators, gaunt passers of information, the starving slum children for whom I shook rattling coincans on long afternoons.

Oh vanished rooms with pinned up notices of action, of art sales and lectures on the economic origins of poetry, of songs of antifascism, and all-night picketlines with you can't scare me. Oh great opened bright floweryellow sunred grassgreen future, so soon, oh love and song and tomorrow.

Heroes of another time I sing song for you through this new time of anxiety, of dehydrated hope and bangbang hours where the dead are over the seas and yellow and have unpronounceable names. Where we have too many causes and too small a world. Where the prisons of Europe and Asia, of Africa and America hold the golden throats of our heroes silenced in their screaming. Where war is our condition and peace as vague as God and times. Where even the borders of infinity become the territory of conquest and the space-ships bear cargoes of flags and slogans.

Yet stopped in the dream by horrorhistory, by the ovens of Europe, by barbed-wire horizons, by the generations of anonymous dead, I shall still be moved.

March 18, 1966

Statement

One:

There is an impossibility of communication./ That is why it never ends/ the painting and the poetry/ closing in/ toward that vanishing point. Closer now to the perimeter/ to the target's eye/ grab at it with the clenched skin/ the strangling muscle/ the orbiting ear.

HOLD IT!

Two:

Someone tells me that love is creating/ is love/ is nature. That is one item. A psychiatrist phoned me/ he said/ you must have a lot of courage to spill out your guts like this./ These are the only guts I know./ If I spill them like this/ maybe they will speak back to me/ let me into that pit/ the excavation of the universe/ to the hot liquid/ the before I began/ to when it started/ to what it is.

Three:

I ask you—who are you./ Approached in your costumed gaze/ words that you spill at me glaze my notion of you with brittle varnish/ as the treasures of the museums have maps of time whose veins corrode the painter's strokes so all you add to my preconception/ beautifies beyond the original/ intended or otherwise./ I have more confidence in your reality/ than in mine/ I can touch you and record the finger's deep sensation./ Touching myself I have a counterpoint of feelings/ the feeler and the felt.

Four:

I do not think the senses lie/ I believe that trees exist/ these are not the problems. I am talking to you about/ it is not their reality that worries me./ Let me say simply that we are always becoming what we do not know ourselves to be/ even this exploration alters the form/ so that what we are/ will/ by definition/ vanish at our approaching.

Five:

I appear to be concerned with identity/ my own/ others. I have become aware of the dichotomy of person./ the infinite recessions of the mind/ the plunge into quiet.

The thought of what lies at the base of personality creates in me the same nausea as/ the contemplation of the infinite. The analogy here; space/ time open endlessly out—the personality/ endlessly in.

To go within the superimposed frame/ the smeared visage/ the granulated body/ overcome my own perception/ to the dissolving flesh/ the boned structure before my knowledge/ their history/

I CAN'T EVER

Pain is singular./ I think Auden said it forever in his poem about Icarus/ but it comes to my mouth over and over. / Jesus alone between the bandits/ alone on the nails.

Face to face is agony/ is everything/ is nothing to say./ surrounded by bellowing transistorized authority/ I accept the presence of invisible others./ I know this—when you stir water/ the ripples spin outward forever.

April 5, 1966

Paranoiance

Everyone is bombing me with their eyes. They are zooming in on me for closeups of my soul—they have all their hands in my pocket and they are counting my seeds. They are making mosaics from my parts. My nipples are eyes—and my belly button, my God, my belly button is at the bottom of the page and I shall have to turn the paper over to find my ass.

Outside the trees are waiting. Every finger leaf is twitching to topple on me. The steps are being catapults to launch me off into the charred summer weeds.

The light hangs from the ceiling. It hangs from the ceiling in the middle of the room. It is a talking light. I CAN SEE YOU but I'm not there. The room is blanketed with peanut shells, and glasses of perfumed water drip onto the mat.

Why does that kid keep coming in the door—like an old Austrian weather vane? Dancing in my door to tell us about pigeons and waving flashlights at us and teetering there on his ugly little legs. He's lethal. He's going to rush down the hill pointing back at us with his chewed fingernail, the rim as black as an old car fender—I SAW THEM, he screams to the listening neighbors. THEY ARE IN THERE BEING HAPPY!

The kid's a refugee—we have to let him in. We open the door to his tapping and stand mutely listening while he tells us about his nothing go nowhere day. But he's counting us and gathering speed. He lunges slowly through the door to spread the news.

Sometimes I think I wouldn't go home at all. I think I'll hang on the curb outside the house, half hidden by the sword fronds of the cactus, the amber light making a nimbus around my head, and pass myself off as vegetation. A vegetable holograph.

There are too many things inside. Dishes with dried egg scumming the edges. Old towels with spots that smell, hanging on the bathroom rail, half collapsed with damp and rot. There's too much food. Cans and cans of food, lugged up the stairs from the car and shoved away in all the cupboards as if disaster must be faced on a full stomach. TO THE CELLARS—AND DON'T FORGET THE MUSHROOM SOUP. How many cans of tomatoes will I have to eat before the end, how many bowls of spaghetti to unwarp the desire to cram it down and fill out the hollow that does not come from hunger?

So the bomb goes off. Quiet and silent it goes off. Quiet as the ear bursts before the touch of sound.

It goes off every day, every hour, all the time. Ricocheting me around the room, splitting the now sense into the now and future sense,

I see my own shadow and its walking and my body is its mockery and I feel the sinking earth and I hear the closing of the eyelid.

July 22, 1966

Inner Graffiti

Will I be absolutely ancient before I can walk into a room of people and not visualize their private lusts? Will I one day talk face to face without seeing the groan of pleasure slip like a silent secret shade across the mouth, their hands become tender, their bodies twist with pleasure? No one escapes my sensual gaze.

The old lady behind the counter at the dry cleaner's hands me my clothes in their slippery skin of plastic. I see her returning at night to the old man, the television set, watching Doris Day in lace orgasm, Humphrey Bogart in steel kiss. She unbends from her pillowed chair, turns out the kitchen light, puts some water down for the cat, and attacks the old man with a forgiven fever. Thank you, I say, and leave the shop.

The bag boy at the market, his face flexible and unworked. His hands when not cramming fruit and cheese and noodles into bags, lying curled within themselves for fear of touching. His ears straight out in the astonishment of the sudden grown world, his feet with their boot toes pointed inward, he stands there naked and trembling and untried. I feel his little-girl dreams, his night confusion, his desperate calming of himself under the covers, his gigantic dream rapes, his endless beginnings of conversations planned to lead to that final mysterious act. Thank you, I say, and leave.

A couple at a party. How do you do, I say, examining his width of shoulder, the bulge of thigh muscle, the turn of wrist. HE with HER? These two remote people, she, all smoothed and set out, thin body, combed hair, blackened nylon eyelashes, gold chain bracelet, looking at me with status and grandeur. He, in a jacket of some strange twentieth-century material, now he glows, now he doesn't, choke collar, tie with pin, matching handkerchief. They look at me with polite curiosity. What was your name again? He asks, innocent, courteous, not knowing that I see them sweat-disheveled, clasped on a Queensize bed in a neon motel at the seaside, a quarter in the Magic-Finger box, the bed vibrating in counterpoint. Outside the chocolate bar melts in the glove compartment of the Buick Riviera and the crumpled Kleenex in the ashtray smells of gin.

The first time I actually saw people fuck, it was a revelation. It wasn't like all these endless musings superimposed upon my acquaintances, laid over the strangers in public places, coming between me and the instant to create a "now I know you" secret knowledge. It was a gloomy movie made many years ago, made around a pool and in a cardboard room. The gray participants, after listlessly projecting a story line, boy meets girl, playful tussle at pool edge, let's go into your room for a drink, or his room, or any room, proceed to impinge each other endlessly and soundlessly on a rumpled sheet. After a while, having like trained seals, taken all the postures they were told, and I could sense the director off camera saying, ENOUGH OF THAT—NOW YOU ON TOP, they ceased. The girl, or woman, or at least the body with the breasts, went to a telephone and summoned a friend. The friend arrived, there were hardly any greetings, the story line was forgotten. The two women then created a sort of togetherness with the man. It went on and on, they became cows, dogs, sheep, anything. We lay on the floor watching, no one giggled, no one squirmed. It was like an old newsreel of a war in which you didn't care which side won.

Still, I go on with my endless lustful private game. This make-believe adventure, this inner voyeurism, and it's lovely, and enjoyable, and I can't think of any reason to stop.

August 19, 1966

Hunger

Hunger, my eyes are hungry for all the delights of skin. Sunskimmed golden shells of flesh with faint hair bending toward the pore sprung warmth. I bite the flesh of my arm sun warmed and taste the skin fantasy of perfumed salt.

Hunger, the sound hunger of the empty ear, hollow for a chamber of music to catch the roundness of a note bouncing off the finger-held hole of a pipe, or the inflection of a voice upswept in a sigh of love and wanting.

Hunger, the taste of sweetness in the air early morning bathing the nostrils, as going down steps past growing bushes of flowers, the day hangs in whispers along the folding horizon.

Hunger of joy, with every moment's ecstatic embrace of the now living going outward clutch at feeling, and the agony of the memory of the orphans of days whose birth was denied in ignorant refusal of recognition.

Hunger for the touch of fingers, thighs and polished wood, bark and thistledown, for the cool of salamander skin caught in the mint ditches at the road's edge where the orange glow of their lizard bodies testified to the end of rain.

Hunger for childhood heedless rush pursuit of uphill daisy patches and overburdened cherry trees popping with juice, and the crack crunch of their splitting globes of fruit between still small and sharpened teeth.

Hunger of the evening of lapsing time, when outside the lights of other houses echo like applause, and inside I stare at all the possibilities of meeting and revival and make sodden journeys to the kitchen for the compensation of a cup of coffee with just a bit of sugar.

Hunger for the fullness that never oh never happens even at the moment of utmost engorgement, so that mouth full and running over with the honey of returned affection, the sallow taste of nothingness clots the tongue.

Hunger for nothingness in purity alone, the empty falling out of everything, the backwards countdown to the circle of zero like a halo over the heart endlessly illuminating the singular and isolated quality of self.

Hunger, hunger always stuffing the raging hole of needs and loves and half-found brilliances of color and of time. Stretched between the moment of conception and the birth of the new and fiery hunger always there.

October 21, 1966

Unto a Child from Us

There is a small unnamed boy of the Warsaw ghetto that haunts me. He is walking with his family into the camera and on to the concentration camp. I look away, but he comes into inner focus like the obverse of a bright color when the eye is closed. I once saw a series of films of the First World War, the deep mudded troops looked upwards through their clay masks. I remember the children of Guernica stacked in rows along the pavement, neat, timeless, and dead. I remember the child of China, alone and half clothed sitting beside a railroad track, midpath in destruction. I turn away from these images, they have happened, I have protested. I boycotted Japan and Germany as a child of the thirties, I asked for the embargo on Spain to be lifted, I sent a dollar in friendship to Russia, I collected tinfoil to fight the Fascists, I did what I could.

I have here before me, a section from the Christmas issue of *Ramparts* magazine, Merry Christmas to you. It is called, "The Children of Vietnam." Vietnam? They are the children of America. Vietnam does not grow napalm amongst its crops, we supply it. The faces of these children stare out at me from their burned bodies. None of the children are crying; crying is a luxury reserved for a society that knows compassion. They stare, that is all, they stand there in their prison of shriveled flesh and stare. I do not turn away this time, there is no place to turn to, they are my children.

What shall I send them this Christmas? A super spy kit, a rubber sword, a plastic rocket? The shops are full of Christmas carols and toys of destruction. It is hard to shop for children I have never met; perhaps the faces will give me some clue. The small boy without his arm, perhaps he would like some beads to string with his toes? What shall I send to the baby suckling the mother? They are both lying on the ground, her hand is bandaged and her spine severed and she is dead now anyway, though three days before she died that picture was taken, the baby suckling on the exposed breast. Perhaps the baby will settle for a nonbreakable plastic bottle, safer than glass, or mothers. Merry Peaceful Christmas, deck the halls with the names of the dead and dying, Angels we have heard on high and they sing escalate, the twelve days of Christmas are someone's anniversary of death.

Do I sound polemical, should I say this all in swinging syntax and poetic simile? What simile is there for the murder of children? What time of the year is this when all the houses are lit with multi-color lights and the stores are popping with the commerce of goodwill in the shape of guns and war machines? The lady from the Salvation Army stands on her piece of carpet on the sidewalk and rings her bell. Put a penny on the drum just to buy a turkey. While they are waiting to eat she can tell them about God as their stomachs clutch together and they remember the direct communication and love of a thousand bottles. They have pushed the bums off Pershing Square, they have watered them off the mayor's lawn, they have slammed the kids off the Sunset Strip, they have driven the flowering minds of a generation underground. Merry Christmas one and all.

Celebrate with me, carry flowers. Walk through the streets of this dispersed city with a flower in your hand, look happy. It is the best place on earth and we are spreading the joy to everyone. Sing hallelujah that we haven't dropped the bomb on your house, thank God for countries far away, for the silence of children who don't cry, for the international democratic bar-be-que. You have been invited. Don't think you haven't accepted the invitation.

December 25, 1966

Which Way to the Exit?

Having discovered late that all I have to sell is my time, I have bought back my rights and here I am—emancipated! I could make more money, but all I could buy with the money would be things, and I have enough things. At some point during the last year we discovered that we owned seven transistor radios; that's when the rot became apparent! So, I've dropped out . . . well, a little bit anyway, and from Wednesday afternoon to Monday morning, the time is all mine.

This first week has been overwhelming. I've spent hours looking out the window at the changes in the sky. From our hilltop it is another full world for my exploration, and when the cranberry sunset slinks down behind the cement ghosts of Santa Monica, it's pure kitsch delight! I've talked with friends, arriving unexpectedly, sprawling on their floor, rubbing my cheeks against their carpets, playing their records, eating their food, sharing their fantasies, and never wondered should I be somewhere else.

I don't know why I hung on so long, spending days like inflated coinage, waking still asleep, sleeping still awake with dreaming, driving off in the dark of morning, oozing home in the dark of evening, the sun and air of the day as remote as the weather reports for the Eastern and Seaboard states. What was it I wanted that I traded time so lightly, was it another car or another bit of clothing or the big numbers on the yellow stubs of checks? I must have lost myself somewhere in the marble isles of bargains, caught myself on the fine print of time payment, and I don't even know anyone named Jones. But, never again, no more, no more.

Being free is very full of obligation. Now there is time to do all the things I said time would not allow. Time to use to work and grow in work, to mold, to fit to shape the form of days, time to talk and listen on the same occasion. Time to see where I am, leaving the blinding goal unfixed, time to note each passing item, My God, even time to walk!

I've driven down the same streets day after day never seeing anything but the hindering traffic or the accursed pedestrians. But when I walk the same way I see such wonders, such marvels. Some windows tell you everything about their owner deep inside. The spotted half-drawn yellowed paper shades of old age, the washed pale curtains, the folded newspaper on the inside windowsill. Behind the army of off-white curtains in the Hollywood apartments are acres of off-white carpeting, whole casts of thousands sitting at formica tables eating Minute Rice, Spanish Style, off Party Paper Plates. They have bathrooms in color schemes and golden dolphins hold their face cream soap, and in their armpits they grow dollar signs instead of hair.

There are painted wooden houses where generations live in the blue light of television sets, and stagger off to beds full of stainless dreams and antihistamines. There are closed doors where no one goes, and stores where no one buys the old bread and balls of string, the man stands behind his counter on his platform of wood listening to the talk programs, cursing the commerce that did not make him king. There are light-poles all tacked with notices of sales, a new fridge and a fold-away bed, forced to sell, moving, cheap if you just call. How long have they been gone, the notice looks so old, perhaps they are in another town now, buying beds and ice and promising to pay.

The children run along the curb, one foot up and one foot skimming the road, their eyes are round, their clothing short, they shove aside the space, people, disaster, and a sense of time. I run behind until they see me, stop and laugh. They point and giggle and I jump up and down, wave my arms. "Crazy lady," they say and run away.

I often think that when I am very old I shall go about on roller skates. There I shall be, all hung with scarves and protest pins, flying down the street on wheels, doing figure eights at intersections and nobody will say anything, except maybe—crazy lady—and I'm used to that!

January 6, 1967

Dropping In

It's easy enough, once it becomes clear, as it is easy to say, That is the sun, that remote orange globe whose heat intimately coats my skin, who sucks life up through the tender tuber roots of plants, who bends the rigid tree to its radiance, who shuts off the day in slow red descent beyond horizons, leaving us with cool memory air and the pierce cloth sky, the slit eyes of stars, the solemn pale moon's quiet whisper—I am beauty still. The day comes as the moon passes and the hot sun rises and then the blood turns again through its secret channels.

It's easy enough when the heart marks the salt rhythm of the blood, when the self rises in the sea bowl of the belly and demands the shore, when the apparency of life becomes as the sun, regular in its insistence on attention, total in its power of sustenance. We mistake the lights of cities for the movement of the stars, the hypnotic winking of the neon signs, the rush of blindly glowing cars in flight down freeways bereft of grass, where no footsteps mark their transit, where the slick of oil lies on the road bed like matted hairs, all these we mistake as tracks of natural passage.

We wander prisoners in our own cement castles, looking from the tower windows along an aspect of used car lots. "I'm up here among the stars," we shout half spilled from the narrow windows, "up here among the diamond stars." Below, the silent mass of featureless faces turn for a moment in our direction and murmur, "huzzah."

It is easy enough, once you fly past yourself and see your body stranded there upon the face of the clock, pinned there, stretched between the nine and five, singing, "I shall still endure," the eyes rotating to their own silver shells of silence, the fingers messenger to another order, blabbering along the surface of strange objects.

You see yourself silent and alone among the pins and paperclips, among the clicking slot machines whose dehydrated mother's milk spills into Dixie cups, among the dancers' epileptic rhythms, alone in the cardboard house by the sea. The sea is muted into category, tamed by the blinded eye, extenuation of your landscape, a green sofa, one of blue, this cardboard house on this sandy cliff, this thick white rug of cloud, these hours at the table sipping coffee, reading magazines and jackets to the latest books—"His protest is not mine, though it speaks to me, I am here within my plastic kitchen by the sea."

It is easy enough, one moment you are split and splintered on your days, reaching out for shreds of self, gluing all together with a flaking glue, rushing down unnamed and unremarked streets to destinations which somehow never flower. And one day, one day—you stop.

You stop anywhere, but mostly in your body, and you know, you hear the song. You hear your creeping progress from the sea, you note your eyes' fixation on the land, whose pebble by pebble support has magnified to mountain size, whose rolling undulations escape your eyes, whose skin of sky is lost above your head, and you say in soft surprise—from sea to land is not the total movement of the mind. Then, pushing down with open hand, gritting sharp rock into your outspread palm, feeling the resilience of the earth between your drying fingertips, you rise upon your knees, throw back your head, back upon the bending neck, growing from the flowering rooted spine, and see the stars and sun and moon and breasts of cloud and the swirling lover to this turning mound of earth, the sky. You rise further still and join with your body's growth the three continents of your world, the water, the earth, the keeper of your time, the sky.

And then you walk, you pace this world with measured step, you dance and celebrate, you touch and sing, you plunge your fingers into air, you grip the ground with humming feet, and through your open singing mouth the first breath passes into space. Then tree and flower, rock and sea, and the turning passage of time, become part of your body's ecstasy.

It is easy then, because it . . . IS.

February 17, 1967

The Ladies' Home Journal

Victim. Really—occupied territory—maybe. Every month my womb spills out into neat traces on the convenient hygiene product, and with it, my mind and soul rise and fall. Oh deep depressions, listlessness and soul-shattering remorse, the sun, clouds, time, mock me. Frail creature, tossed, wood on the rushing stream, pliant and accursed by my woman's body.

Then—just before—LUST. Big groping lust, nipple rise at midday, rubbing thighs together at the dinner table, a mind filled with melons and cucumbers, dribble longings and skin itch, finger sucking, restless book reading, urges, urges.

Then—stomach heave and tense, muscles pull and recapitulate the pains of birth, the groin tightens, the breasts swell and ache, and it starts. Headache, listlessness, stomachache, boredom.

Then—it's over and the pills are set in their little container for twenty-five days of non-Papal bliss, and I forget, think myself my own continent, proud, self-determination, cool, in charge, the tingle and wing all self-controlled, desire sprung of love or lateness of night and the immediacy of flesh next to mine, warm and lazy in half sleep, containing the drama of possibility, the starting touch, the half images of the day, the finishing of an imagined sentence in a self-scripted drama, the word that answers, and fading into the other language that overtakes it, the words spelled by fingers and tongue, the eyes that are flesh and the ears of moisture and the transposition of self into wholeness and—

So a woman turns around herself, viewing the buttocks that support in sitting and in love. Coils the hair spilt along the shoulders up onto her head, lazy and in morning confusion, makes a cup of coffee.

A man, back within his isolation and strength, flutters his lips in sleep, the breath lies heavy over the sheets and blankets and hazes the room with the warm smell of his sleeping.

I try to explain one theory: Man's ambition is motivated by sexual desire. To get ahead and be somebody—that really means, to have a wider choice in bed. To fight a war is to rape a village. To climb a mountain is to seduce stone. Argument—what about Schweitzer, what about the Pope? Maybe they both fuck God?

It's seasonal rutting then, like the pigeons and the prelate we went to see. Thought we were going to see a new religion—"Home of the Prelate of Tibrun"—sign on the freeway. Wow—wonder what that could be. Much driving along divided freeway surrounded by shining stars of beercans until the cut-off and the turn-around, then much driving back through same reflective path to the sign again.

We went up the dirt road, next to us a small stream with two ducks, wooden? no—they moved off with their ground-paralleling waddle. Further up the road, dirt and poplar trees, divided, "To The Office"—the sign said, we went. The office did not look religious, squat and whitewashed with steel-framed windows and a Mustang, with a racing stripe bisecting its enamel, parked in front. We turned around—there behind a wire fence was an enormous bull, black and shiny with his low body almost touching the ground and his big valuable balls swaying between his legs. That no doubt was the prelate.

On another day we went to the old ghost town and looked in the windows of the souvenir shops at plastic snakes made in Japan and imitation cut-glass cigarette lighters and rusty objects with typed cards describing their antiquity and use. Oil lamp, used in mines. Spoon for measuring gold, one lump or two? Off, down a side road, a yoga academy, the woman out back hanging up the wash looked at our license plate—"You from California? Everyone here seems to be." Inside—where the sign said "Monastery"—people typing and sorting cards. Shoe boxes with photographs stapled on the outside. Later we saw in the brochure that they offer correspondence school in yoga, communicate and know you by your photograph, very personal. A young man takes us into a big room with mattresses on the floor, covered with Indian bedspreads. He squats on his legs, his face is hairless and his hair is shaved on the top of his head but hangs long to his shoulders at the side. He shows us a picture of his swami. I wonder why he hasn't any hair on his face and who gets to lie on the mattresses. We leave—I should have asked him why he shaved only the top, I said. You said I wonder if he gets laid.

It seems to be a preoccupation, but I can blame it on my belly seasons, on the urges of my muscles and the lining of my uterus. Men, I guess, have to have some greater plan.

May 26, 1967

Mouth Love

I set my mouth to your mouth, with words.
With lips, with tongue, I explode.
It's mouth love when I meet you—
Hello
Hello
You look well
So do you
Doing your hair a new way?
Um
It suits you
Younger, makes me look younger, does it?
Yes, I like it, do you like my dress?
I was noticing it as you came in, nice color, suits you
Thank you, heard from Charlie, phoned or anything lately?
No, but Mirabelle says she saw him Saturday at the March . . .
That's mouth love, I die for it, banal it sounds but the words are just the saliva, it's the nonthought, nonverbal mouth love I crave.

Mouth love. I rub my lips along the baby's skin and suck warmth and the faint ammonia scent, the thin skin against my lips, eyes shut, the body held close to my face, my cheeks, my head becomes a mouth, skin sensitive to touch, I kiss the baby for all babies, for your babies or all the babies I might have produced, for the innocence and the dependence and absence of malice, I need it, mouth love.

Mouth love. You kiss me geographically from north to south, from lips to lips. I swell with singing pleasure. My body is a mouth to answer your exploration with skin words, with warmth sounds and moisture music.

Time solves its mystery and dissolves itself, space is declared void, gravity becomes the arms that hold me for you, mouth and arms join, gs, belly seas and loin plateaus, toes curl in sentences, knees paraphrase my hope of joining my entirety to your entirety, mouth love.

Mouth love. The Twinkie on the grocer's shelf in its cellophaned virginity. I shall rape it, squeeze it, lick its white delight, coat my mouth with its sweet soft satiation. Twinkie lust at midnight, spun out an evening, pasting colored paper on cardboard, searching the refrigerator and met by the hostility of leftover boiled potatoes, salad dressing, wilted lettuce. Twinkie lust propels me into fantasy, my lips form kisses in space, my tongue curls over my teeth, my eyes widen and my hands flutter, mouth love at midnight and the stores are closed.

Words, flesh, food. All feed the mouth, the mouth that first delineated the world, when blind and uncoordinated in my crib I lifted my hand in random motion, sucked and found—finger. Mouth love when I laid a caterpillar on my tongue to taste its fuzzy softness, mouth love when I greet my friend, mouth love when I explore the warmth of your body, when I sing, even when I cry with the exquisiteness of tasted sorrow. Mouth love.

July 14, 1967

cene One, Take?

Get me out of this skin-tight chamber of horrors where the cues are whispered by some interior maker of disaster whose script is full of the clichés of past years. Unhappy childhood speaks, rejection overcomes me, unhappy childhood dances over the meat tissue stage, the petal lids curl closed, and this older withering slowing crusting body crumples to child tears, to under the blanket ten at night fright visions and the sound of the stopping of my own heart.

The prompter grows fat; he is amused at ghosts who never forget their lines while the live people out there shaking my hand wonder why the fingers grip them back in hope at once, slacken and let go, busy themselves with typing out these written words of the scenario that never reaches its ending but continues like some fantastic plot to keep me alive so as not to miss next week's installment.

Some person once told me that the Jewish holidays are very cleverly worked out, one being happy and the next sad and so on going from manic to depressive and back in orderly procession, fully documented and promoted. Good. Good for the holy Jew who can swallow his laughter in time to cry. But what of me whose days go up and down, who feels the utter anguish of everything and the ultimate ecstasy? It makes for changes, God only knows that makes for changes, flexibility, even acceptance, and a sort of crummy optimism, or suicidal barrier because you never know how beautiful the next day will be, it always gets beautiful, it always gets tragic.

How much of anything can justifiably be said to be under control, how much of the apparent vibratory environment is the prime mover, how much comes from that repertory company of disaster and remembered fear that plays in the off-Broadway of the heart? How much of anything, I can as easily look at it either way denying my instinct to repudiate and discern. But I want to discern with cleared eye and fresh brain and kissing mouth all things flowering righteous and singing. I on the other hand may not be able, due to miscasting, judgmental screw-ups, missing pages, revisions and translations from the former speech, clearly to perceive anything. The analogy is a crutch and a cuteness, but the drama is real and the cast sifts onward through my head.

Out, out, it's a little experimental stuff that's needed here, some way of making thought as non-meaningful as the words of Dada Poetry. I could do everything backwards, like trying to change my handwriting or draw a face not the way I always draw faces but the way someone else draws faces. I am unable to sustain it for long though, it's slow and awkward, it doesn't fit.

Disaster, I shall have to admit to disaster. Me, disaster. It gets more complicated, I am more adept at fooling myself, I know that it's not going smoothly, the trying is getting out of control, the actors are stumbling and the monster inside is throwing out cues at random. A cup of coffee, some candy, suck my thumb, maybe if I step outside for a moment they will go on to the second act without me, must it have a happy ending to be a success?

October 20, 1967

Oh! Say Can You See?

They are all gone. Gone into the historical woods and wine deep sea, the explorers with pith helmets and wooden craft, lashed to the wheel, sails furled, looking for the edge of the world, or camping under the tigermouthed African moon their hearts ablaze with territory, carving their message on a tree, forty-seven days since we departed the coast and have not found the river yet. Gone. Gone these explorers, gone over the edge of the world, down the river forever. Are there any mountains to be climbed that no foot has touched, any rivers to be followed from their tearful source to their hysterical copulation with the sea? Any seas to be sailed toward unknown destinations? Only in the mind, or up into space, and no one I know can make their own spacecraft and man it with volunteers, we are tied to the earth with our guts to examine, our brains to explore.

Hail Beatles, hail Burroughs, hail Andy Warhol. Hail the retired and the forgotten and the too-soon absorbed. Hail Antonioni and Leary, hail the Queen of England pioneer of the Absurd Theatre. There are new explorers' clubs in every city, many of whose members are busted for illegal navigation, but the maps continue to explode all over the dining room floor and we all get to see new worlds every day.

Hail Salinger up on his farm, mutely leaning on a fence for *Time* magazine minding his own business, having given us a continent he leaves us to populate it, and we do. Hail Mouse who made us read not from left to right or right to left but not at all, or with our eyes blinking like inbuilt strobes, the message only a visual dance for eyeballs.

Your name is your flag and your game is your map and the only restrictions come from inside where it's all flexible or all tight, thwarted, and dead.

Second Stanza

Overpopulation also means too many people on the same trip, too many people hanging onto the mind's threads, too many people painting by numbers following a score making the same picture in dilutation. Overpopulation also means too many people selling what is supposed to be given free, like love, which a few years ago was never to be mentioned aloud. Some terrestrial explorer rediscovered love, extended its boundaries to include everyman and we all said love outloud with the same bravado as the little kids in the bathroom who shout over the flushing of the toilet, fuck mummy, fuck daddy. Love, Love, *L-O-V-E,* but what does it mean now, nothing, it's been oversaid, oversung, oversold. Love, there wasn't enough brain food, and the United Nations had no jurisdiction, the World Health Organization said it was contagious but not deadly, the War on Poverty disclaimed responsibility in favor of budgets, the civic authorities worried about toilets, the county never heard of it, so they called in the press and the TV and the cops and they overwrote it, oversaw it, and overclumped it on the head, rid the streets of it, and the green grass reverted to desert, and the birds fled, and the flowers died, and only Madison Avenue remembers the word, love.

Maybe the time is not ripe for large public explorations, rather to sneak off somewhere leaving behind only false maps with impossible directions . . . soak twice and swallow, take a warm bath, run out of money, turn left, bribe a mother, fell a tree, watch yourself in the hubcaps going by for a new view of speed you didn't count on, then count it, divide by 200,000,000 and sell to the nearest dealer (try the White House first), use the profit to support yourself in infancy which is just around the corner every day and it's a breech-birth so call the doctor and tell him to bring some bombs because the baby's stuck in the canal and the canal is an international zone and where the hell are the police with their butterfly nets?

If you discover a bright and true and valid and soothing and loud and harmonious inner upstanding banner-waving self-explanatory place, cover it with camouflage, here's the recipe: Ten tons of smog and paper foil, soot silt and oil, all the yesterday's newspapers rolled up and covered with sauce, syph, clap and applause, tickets to the theater for the first lobe second convolution to the left, and pistular sores cured only by hand.

Or: curl up in your bed at night with your head unscrewed and tucked under your arm, your legs neatly folded on the chair, your heart at the dry cleaner's, and pray for rain, any rain, drip, drop, drip, drip, dropop, driip, droooopop, pop, op.

November 3, 1967

Channel Novocaine

Nothing is painful. Immortalized, the fang-toothed blood suck flicks across my screen, and I, though half asleep, do not believe the scene; the clothes are ancient and the fear has turned to dust. The chains split with the alloy silence of their painted rust, the clubs of balsa wood hit with a softened thud (black and white does little for the red of blood) and I am old and wise beyond my fears. Crenelated castle walls whose plaster backs mock their disguise, lean sodden in the storage yard, and all of Spain has turned to mold and crust and sags against the studio debris, the door to paradise swings open in the smoggy breeze, and plastic snow is all of freeze there is, and there is nothing painful in the world of pain.

Nothing is painful. His plastic scars do not mar his famous face, his deafened ear is tuned to verbal cues; they tumble in the bed, their bodies hidden by the sheets, and tears of glycerine obscure their view. He is stabbed, stabbed now, he is dead and crumbles to the floor, he writhes, and catsup spills, she, turning, smiles once at the barricaded door and pops the poison pills, and the flashback sight of their approach, warned by telegraph or phone, or chariot rushing over plastic cobblestone, reassure me of her rescue soon. On celluloid we never die alone.

Nothing is painful. I saw Oswald die, then walk the corridor and die again, and just before I went to bed I saw him die once more. He had more deaths than I shall ever know, he had a whiteness in his face, the hand with the gun was half obscured, it was some trick of Nouvelle Vague I'm sure, and I shall see it done again, there was no pain, just a moment of surprise. His image falls before my eyes, falls, and falls again.

There is action though there is no pain, the cliff edge fight when distance is a painted place, and though the trampled body hurtles through the unreal space, there is no pain that is not comforted by popcorn joy. She takes time off from her technicolor rapes to tell us things in interviews—I am sometimes bored, but it is just the job I do —then—see my sofa (recently acquired) it was owned once, my decorator swears, by a queen of France, who was taken from some country château dance to be decapitated, but I have had it mended and redyed. She plumps the cushions with an owner's pride and fiddles with her silvered hair. I sit immobilized, and stare.

Nothing is painful, the pictures merge, the blood of Asia is a foreign dirge and grass knolls are beautiful to see. The dead are phantoms of the flicker-screen, the pain is plastic and the fire is naphthalene, and justice to be done is justice seen. The police report the killer killed. The deceased leaped from the window and then he died, became deceased. I saw him leap out through the glass and fall, he moved his head up from the lawn grass just once, and saw his own death's head reflected from the camera's eye, he did not make a sound, he was deceased and acted out his part, with no respect for art, he simply died. Not one announcer cried, they switched to cigarettes and jokes, and told me what brand name to buy.

But I saw it, with my eyes and brain, and it was not painful, was not pain, I was watching channel novocaine. With clean hands, with clean clothes, I watch their programmed death, with cleansed hands, with cleansed mind, with cleansed breath.

March 22, 1968

What's New

I was going to write a long, as a matter of fact I did write a long, piece on Terror in the Street and how it was the Police who were creating that terror for a segment of society that was in no wise constitutionally criminal. Then I thought Oh Crap, the paper is full of grimness, the streets are full of grimness, the election postmortem will keep Huntlybrinkcronk grim for weeks, who knows but what we will all get emphysema and croak from smog anyway before anything else, and, if I have this public voice why not use it for joy. So here is a big har har for you all.

HAR HAR.

I found Elliot Mintz very poignant in last week's *Free Press,* and understand and sort of agree with much he said, although I think his alternative is not clearly stated and his projected future more strawberry than rosy. I am glad he said what he said because I harbor fears that being "older" may have quenched the revolutionary fire within me, for God's sake I was at Peekskill, wasn't I, and tried to free the Scottsboro Boys (no kiddies, not a rock band), and toddled up the gangplanks of German ships with bags of groceries for the dockworkers who refused to load them long before our government even thought Mr. Hitler uncouth. So, I worry, maybe I am becoming, you know, re-act-ionary, because I just can't bide militarism in any guise, or racism, and have always thought black if not beautiful, no worse than white which never struck me as beautiful to begin with (actually I think that yellowish olive skin that Syrian and Lebanese people have is the most beautiful).

It has become a problem to try and differentiate activism from rampage, protest from mindless steamletting; I can understand that the black man has a lot of steamletting to do, but often when the mouths are opened, all that comes out is hot air. As in most countries where repression is on the rise, the judiciary is usually the last part to corrupt. Not that it doesn't, but if one can get into the courtroom without being completely broken in bone and spirit by the policeman into whose custody the law has entrusted us, and if those same police do not lie, or more realistically, if those policemen do not lie convincingly, or even more realistically, if one's lawyer is able to demonstrate that they have lied, there is a decent chance that the spirit of law will be enacted. Remember, folks, as of yet they don't actually put you inside for twenty or gas you without first allowing you to make your way up the appeal court route. What I am meandering on about is that it is still the minions of the law who are doing the violence to us, not so much the law itself.

Example: the Metro Squad's activities as reported in last week's *Free Press,* entirely illegal. Witness all our friends who are stopped, presumably for some traffic violation like no-good taillights, only to have their person and their vehicles searched, quite illegally. Witness all the people we know who are physically attacked by police in the street and then arrested for resisting or whatever, only to have the charges dropped and that ends the matter, doesn't it, no police heads ever fall (perhaps that's one of the problems, no police heads!).

I think it is important to realize that these stormtrooper-like tactics of the police must be known to their superiors, and to the superiors' superiors, and all the way up to persons on highest, who in turn are supported by campaign contributions from even higher (moneywise) persons and so on. So while it is the police who visibly perform the garbage duty of our system, it is someone up there who doesn't love us that is issuing the orders. It is to that someone, or someones, that Elliot, myself, the Yippies, Black Power, voter might, enraged youth, student radicals, etc., ought to turn their attention. After all it is really not relevant to tell a garbage man he has dirty hands; it is only relevant to make sure he doesn't wipe them all over us.

November 15, 1968

No Shortage of Issues

I get up medium early, and because Robert has already gone to work, I turn on the television for company. This week I watched Jacqueline Susann try to estimate the amount of fish that would fit into a pelican's beak—it seemed most appropriate. (What I want to know is—how many fish can Jacqueline Susann get in her mouth?) Before that little gamey show goes on I watch the *Today* show, catching glimpses of things while brushing my teeth or making the bed. A few days ago there was a remarkable lady on the show. She was one hundred and three years old. There she sat, scroonched up, shriveled, peeking over the table top, sitting next to the glamorous and imperturbable lady hostess who kept asking her imperturbably bland questions. It seems this old lady had in her time been a suffragette and a racing car driver.

"Tell me, Mrs. Wilson"—I can't remember her name so I will call her Mrs. Wilson—"at what age were you a suffragrette?" "Well," said the halting-voiced Mrs. Wilson, "the most important thing is to enjoy life." "Oh," said the hostess. "Well, tell me Mrs. Wilson, you used to drive racing cars, see we have this picture of you here, when was that taken?" "I think," said Mrs. Wilson, "that life is wonderful, a wonderful thing." "Yes, yes," said the hostess, "but tell me, what do you think of today's youth?" "Life," said Mrs. W., "is a wonderful thing, living is wonderful."

I was beginning to get nudgy; I couldn't quite decide if Mrs. Wilson was going to live till the end of the broadcast, and if she was, was she senile or something? I mean all she said was that life was wonder-

l. The hostess gave one more try, "Tell me what you would tell the
oung people today, what message have you?" Said Mrs. Wilson, "Life
 wonderful, life is to be enjoyed, life is a wonderful thing." They
witched to the commercial, and I went on brushing my teeth.

Then it struck me, here was this old, old lady, I mean one hundred
nd three years old, that's more old than I can hope for, that's more
ld than anyone I've ever spoken to, or even seen on TV (although I
member some photos in *Life* magazine of peasants from some re-
ote part of Russia who were even older). But here on the TV was
is ancient woman, and she was answering questions with difficulty,
nd using what energy she had, and what time, trying to say what to
er was the only important thing. She was saying something which
ad ramifications no matter how trite it sounded, for if life is wonder-
l, then killing is a disaster, if life is a wonderful thing, then the most
nportant thing is to be supportive to life, if life is to enjoy then one
ould fight all the elements that prohibit joy. She was simply sum-
ing it up in short sentences, and very succinctly, and I was too used
 polemics to grasp it at first.

A few days later I had to go out to Pitzer College (for women) in
laremont to give a reading. I read some of my columns to the som-
er stare of the students, who although quiet, were definitely not
apped by what was going on. "But what about your political com-
itments?" they asked. I had been reading columns about feeling,
bout finding one's own way of seeing things, about relating to other
eople with intensity and spontaneity, about what seem to me to be
asic things that have to be self-achieved before you can do much
bout convincing other people. I don't mean that there is no necessity
 be a political activist, but everyone can find a way to not only
 and up and be counted in marches and demonstrations, but to also
ffect changes in their face-to-face encounters. Anyway they had me
ummoxed. They seemed to want me to write "up against the wall"
 stead of anything lyrical in celebration of humanity and its capaci-
es.

"What do you do?" I asked in return. They had a problem, it
eems. Everything was too good, they complained. If they wanted to
hange something at Pitzer, they had only to go to the administration
nd the administration changed it. The classes were small (perhaps
ecause the tuition was—I was told—$5,000 a year!) and the teach-
rs great and the surroundings new (and to my mind sterile and de-
umanizing, but they didn't seem to notice). What they wanted was

something to fight, all the other campuses were in turmoil, protesting fighting, trying to make changes, and there at Pitzer it didn't take fight or boycott, it was all negotiable. Well, tough shit, too bloody bad, there they were in an optimum situation, able to get the kind of education they wanted and they were frustrated by not having fashionable enemy, by not being able to "do their thing" which wasn't their thing at all but just what they seemed to feel was the new life-style.

After the reading was over I was invited to go over to the ROTC building at the men's college where about thirty or so people were sitting-in. I went over and found the office occupied by some kids sitting around singing and playing the guitar and pasting (very neatly very carefully) Moratorium notices over the pictures on the wall. "What's happening here?" I asked the middle-aged ROTC brass who was there watching. "Well, you can see," he said, "nothing much They are occupying this office." "What are they doing?" I asked. " don't know," he said, "although they have covered up all the photos of our handsome boys," and he smiled. They were very tidy—one girl opened a desk drawer full of files and hesitated, then she delicately placed a leaflet over the files and slowly closed the drawer. There were ashtrays and everybody was using them. "What's happening," asked someone from the occupying side. "We are occupying the building," he said. "It's because of the Moratorium, we wanted to do something." "What will this do?" I asked. "I don't know," he said "Maybe it will stop the ROTC. You're from the *Free Press*," he said "Sort of," I said. "Do you have a press release I can give them?" A press release, no, they didn't have one. I left, everyone was smiling the ROTC brass and the occupying army, all relaxed and doing their thing.

So how do we effect change, and what is it we want to change and isn't it important to change what needs changing and to be constructive and creative with what opportunities we have? And if they really thought for themselves, wouldn't they be happy to have a college where they could form their own curriculum to some extent and use their energies for other issues? There is no shortage of issues, all they have to do is sit down and think a little. As I was leaving, the student who was walking with me to the car said, "You know, I think the faculty here is more hip then the students."

November 21, 196

Bummers

I'm tired of bummers. That's all. I don't want to have to turn a Christmas season into a session of doom-calling. I want to celebrate peace at the season of the Prince of Peace. It's a rain-dance, it's totem-time, I want to sing "Joy to the World."

Our police chief was interviewed on television. He commended the people of Watts for their sobriety in the face of the slaughter of the Panthers. "They acted well," he said, contained. "They were not provoked. Why," he added, "they acted just like you or I would." Hello, paleface.

I sat down to read the Atkins girl's description of the Tate murder in the Sunday *Times*. (Why Tate? There were four other people, but I guess this is Hollywood and she gets top billing.) I tried to read it but I became nauseated. I used to read gory murder stuff with an obscene relish. Not this time. There has been too much murder. It's beginning to seem real—really happening.

Scientists have invented something called polywater. If it is released on the earth freely, some say it will gobble up all our natural water. You can't drink polywater. The makings of phosgene gas are lying in rotting containers half exposed on a dump just outside Palm Springs. There is a curve on Decker Canyon road that seven cars have plunged over in the last year, taking their occupants to death and disfiguration. The highway commission is still trying to decide whether to budget for "curve" signs at that spot.

But—I don't want to do this, I want to be merry. I want to think of the generations of men who have celebrated this season, Chanukah, Ramadan, Christmas, Winter, whatever it is called. It is a time of asking nature to be bountiful to us in the coming year.

Nature. Whatever that was. Outside Mount Storm, West Virginia, a man who grows Christmas trees has had his crop blighted by pollutants from the adjoining power plant. He used to grow 10,000 trees; this year he will be happy to harvest 1,000. They are going to erect a third plant near there next year. Power plant, not green growing plant.

Los Angeles County is infested with rodents. It is estimated that there is one rat for every person. Share the wealth.

Food prices have risen. There are too many people on the earth. The mayor of Newark is indicted for extortion. In South Africa apartheid flourishes. South Africa is part of the American subsidy program for sugar. That means we buy their sugar at inflated and above market prices. Political prisoners are rotting in the jails of Greece, Spain, the Soviets, Africa, America. Merry Christmas, Huey Newton.

God damn it, I want to be jolly. I want to have joy. I want to be able to celebrate. Enough. My wish for you is that you will investigate your creativity, find the courage to believe in the innate goodness of man, the energy to implement your beliefs, the opportunity to survive.

December 26, 1969

Click Click

I was over at the laundromat comparing the whiteness of my wash, oh, the razzle-dazzle of it all, the chocolate stains, the fruit pies in the night, the dismal yellow put to flight, the sparkle set to right.

That lady's hair holds a curl; I am limp. Dangle straggle and no bleach, her husband pursues her down the supermarket aisle, theater of passions between the beans and oven cleaner. Now that Dow doesn't make napalm, can I buy?

At the carwash the customers crowd around me examining my extras. Concealed tearducts, super tread toes, and an automatic hiccup. I am moving up to the fender generation, and memories of running boards dance in my head. Once it was good enough to make it to the next town at 35 miles an hour. Where has the bliss gone? Less chrome, more power and automatic indigestion.

He left me because he didn't like my coffee, and the rain smeared my windows beyond repair. I sat there on my massage chair, the rollers reminiscent of a night of love, and watched the glow of the shampooed carpet diffuse the room, throwing its nylon reflection on the washable walls. Next door I could hear the foreign lady boiling water; an endless parade of people passed through her rooms. Oh, Mrs.

Olson, how do you do it? I hear she gets it straight from Michoacán —mountain grown.

It behooves me to prepare for my future; I bank my money and enroll in a course in abalone diving. Abalone sells for five dollars a rubbery pound, and they say I can make millions piercing the oil slick and heading for the harbor bed. There among the secret silver, inside Oriental chambers, I shall make my fortune ten months of the year. Above me the clouds darken and the sea life dies. There on the ocean bed I shall thrive—plastic pearls for eyes above me.

They came to remove my furniture. There were six Vietnamese orphans sleeping on the convertible sofa, but they took them, too. And my eye-level oven with its poppin-fresh dough just about to brown. And my 5,000 free Blue Chip Stamps. You should have bought home-owners' protection, a continuous roof of safety—the man said flashing his ultra-white, sex-laden smile at me. Well, I've come a long way, baby blue, to get where I'm coming to on the bathroom floor, my nostrils clogged with the masculine scent of lime. Above me his armpits radiate perfume while he gestures at the Necessary Negro through the wall-less back of the medicine cabinet.

Click click and it's all over; the silence crowds the room. Beside me the unread books turn to dust. One swipe with my magic duster and I can see my reflection, eyes covered with the now color of Maybelline green, in the mar-proof, stain-resistant surface of the French provincial bedroom suite.

Next door, the Swedish lady is still cooking with gas. Would you have it any other way?

March 20, 1970

Woman's Life

Just as the moon pulls the astronaut to its mottled harbor so its waxing and waning pull the blood and lining from my womb. Man can fly, and woman can wax and wane. The touch down on the moon was man's first step into a world that has ruled me since puberty.

See-saw Marjorie Daw now I'm up and then I'm down again. Both sides present themselves in an interior verbal advocacy that convinces

me, the courtroom of my own crimes, that both are correct. I understand everything clearly and thusly not at all for all things contain
their opposite and are, therefore, singular. Everything is one thing
within which I swing and lunge a solid empty form. I am joined to my
madness; I am my madness.

If I could stop and separate so that I could view myself from outside, I could judge myself. (Judge not lest ye be judged.) Yet they call
two selves schizoid. If my one self of two selves is one, then it cannot
be madness. They must all be mad. "A common conclusion of the
insane." That's what they would say (but that might be their madness
speaking). (Or—is it my madness?) Which is an example of the
whole.

The point is that in any argument of emotions there are always
two, if not more good sides that can be taken. There is the motive,
and the motive that ascribes motive, and the motive that ascribes as-
cribing motive. (On the other hand—which in itself is a common
saying denoting just this very problem—the sun rises and makes day;
the sun sets and makes night; both are realities and keep repeating.)
Perhaps it's just that I am going to have my period soon that makes
me want to cry all day. I should accept grief as another set of activities, sadness and gloom, silence, grayness, just an angle of vision.

Today I was wishing for a finalization of some kind; what will the
end be, I asked Robert. Death, he said, which is a correct answer but
not the one I wanted. I remember that when I arrived at college for
the first time I projected a welcoming committee with music, something to signify the start of my adult nonfamily life. It was mostly silence that met me, and confusion, and general dispassionate curiosity
—where was I from and what was my name? I wanted them to tell
me those answers. Today I wanted something to happen, something
that would say—it has all been for this, leading to this, this is it,
THIS IS WHAT IT IS ALL ABOUT.

Outside the smog glides by and the day passes from light to shade
and the TV news is sodden and Sunday-minded and my stomach
hurts in anticipation of my scheduled discharge and the electricity
continues to work because we have paid the bill, paid all our bills, but
there must be something else.

It's not God, or not the gods I'm offered. Last week the Almo's little band of hostile God salesmen grabbed me on Hollywood Boulevard and shoved their Jesus down my throat. But you people are so

hostile, I said, why wouldn't you listen to what I have to say? They didn't listen though; they looked past and through me and kept on shucking Jesus as though he were the soul's vacuum cleaner, new model, low-down payment, just sign up and follow. I suppose it has helped them in some way; it seems to have freed them to attack strangers walking down the street, but I'm not ready for that kind of taking over.

I've thought about chanting, exercise, diets, moons and planets, ankhs and stars, Freud and after-Freud, Indian mystics, Lower Eastside fanatics, vegetarians, rice-eaters, Zionism, Krishna, they are all there offering the answer, but I can't hear it inside my head. I keep laughing; I laugh too much. Once I was being initiated into something, and while the man was chanting over me and making offerings of rice and flowers to the little over-brightly tinted picture, I looked behind me at the box from which the rice had been taken. It was a box of Minute Rice.

This is the way I am today, and I know even while being in the midst of this despair over existence that tomorrow I will be otherwise (again a clue, other-wise). Meanwhile (a very mean while), I am going to get up and go into the other room and turn on the color TV and watch the world go by. Whose world? It must be mine, for I am watching it.

July 17, 1970

Lovers and Enemies

Nighttime raga in the form of an anatomical landscape for a self-absented lover:

I have never known this, so late to come, and now I am freaked out by it, situation. Don't know what of the what is real, don't know from the time of beginning at writing these thoughts till approaching the ending, for it never seems to end, but rimples onwardly outwardly on, if I am still of the mind I was at the beginning. When.

Loins ache but it is a secret down between my fuzzy dreamscape ripple tides—no warning to the outside folk who temperate and sweet bend forward but not to peek twixt. I hurt with sizzle needs of lubricating timelapse loose lapse lips sip flutter lips bruising of the tight now gone loose opening cave of want it. Never tell.

Night glooms near. Bluescape shadows flicker on the TV set transvestized into silent slide and roll color patterns with mouths, more mouths all clean fresh and white as the laundry and nothing is happening toward me and I will sleep it off, off being the only thing that is possible.

I present it unsorted as it comes through with its confusions and disillusion or illusion or perfume or sensory private details and then you will see it, perhaps only while crumpling it endlessly into paper logs for the never-lit fire, and answer?

Oh you will not answer me ever, nor even once, by look or gesture, but enigmatic always, like the limerick sphinx or—perhaps—spare me one austere signal, some dream lady prince and gentleman raising a hand to beckon. I remain torn and tied to you for my history and can only plan revolution when certain of your government. The roads are closed! The wires are down! Danger!

Everything above is ample declaration of what can be said. (It's ended, the thought ate itself and the thinker tinkered on with the sound of the keys dug deep into her arm shooting up words in the night, feeling the rush and speed of it, the blast and cool of it, the ice between the eyes and the pulse between the thighs and the highest of the high is someone else than Meher Baba.)

Daytime returns in all its lucidity and produces these lines:

I didn't tell after all, nothing. Secrets tucked into flesh pockets. I pull apart the curtains, the light shafts in on the empty brandy bottle, the glass, the roach in the ashtray, the piles of records (nude black lovers waiting for their cardboard jackets). My head aches, my stomach rumbles, I don't know who that is in the mirror.

Last night I listened to the words for fantasy (as all of us do when we lead subterranean dream lives). This morning the sheets are twisted and the pillows lie on the floor. Perhaps I shall get up and drive over the mountains to find myself sitting in a field of clover with my dark and demon lover. I get up and tidy the room, wiping the smear reminders of my existence, my landscape of souvenirs. No matter, no one will notice anything else unless they glue my clues together, and even then, they may know already.

The ultimate joke is when the joker falls, flails, and crawls to doom from laughter, and after, watching his own disease, charts his fever for his own attendance, finds a cure and plays with death. Again, no matter, the world turns and we turn with it though we may be going in opposite directions. It keeps on happening, and so, I salute you from my cells.

January 15, 1971

The Carrot or the Plastic Spoon

LONGINGS for the green, for the eye suck and stretch of green-ness. I have a recurring fantasy life, me Earth Mother, me baker of bread, me weaver of cloth, me Tarzan's Jane. I tried it for about eight months, up against a mountain and surrounded by blossoms, but all I got was nudgy. It seems that the country smooths me out, and being smooth is no condition for work. Why work? Because I am the result of an upbringing which fixed me in the principle of reward for effort. Not just money, but that great sigh of released tension comparable to an orgasm which wells up and spills out after I have done something from the inside, outside. In the country everything seems so attuned, so naturally flowing, the necessity to make change, alteration, lay my being over the ongoing reality, seems an absurdity. But what about the great sigh? I have to return to my natural habitat, the cement and spittle environment of cities where the disorganization and tension, the human electricity, and the pressure of time force me to go through the work/release syndrome.

Yet there are many people who I love who look on me with pity, think of me as caught in a giant machine. I look on them with love too, and tenderness and great compassion for their trade. Their trade seems to me to be hours devoted to anxiety about where they will get the $20 they need to fix their Volkswagen brakes or pay land tax or buy flour and wine. Between that labor they take time to write to me about the beauty of bucolic laid-back existence and how they feel for me. It's nice, all of us busy feeling for each other.

I seem to have wandered from the subject of the greenness, but the precarious existence of life on welfare or scrounged vegetables is also a part of the new bucolia. That's the other reason I never was able to stay down on the farm.

Nevertheless, I still harbor, like an old addict with a new habit, romantic ideas of getting away to the woods, running naked through the tall grass, eating food I myself have grown (though I hate to weed as much, or more, than I hate to make beds!) and sitting on my porch, watching my sun go down, writing letters to my poor friends still trapped in the city. Conflict, conflict, the cream or the celery, the sweater or the raincoat, the pill or the baby, the trick or the treat, the carrot or the plastic spoon.

Santa Barbarians

Magnificent ecstatics dance on the grass, flower fed, the heads twirl toward the sun. The hills rise their green flesh away to the intensity of blue, the oranges burst upon the trees.

We did the town, lolling into shops and touching. We touched the ribbons and the hard plastic curtain rings, made imaginary necklaces of the golden-coated rings, thought the ribbons into bindings for our hair.

Outside, a boy asked us where he could buy Tarot cards, asked us and we answered him, and an old lady kissed another old lady's dog.

In Montecito there are great silent Spanish houses behind gates. Service entrances punctuate the drives which spring away from the road with hard disdain. A pink wall curves along the tree-straddled roadway. Its gates are wrought iron and end in the pattern of a peacock's tail. Beyond the gates, swung to and bound by chain, the bending phallic flowers grow, dripping their pollen-heavy stems in waxy white. Along the path, silver blue, the cactus rise like fans, pointed and hard and planned.

When I was lying on the beach asleep you gathered flowers and a piece of wood and built a window so that I, opening slowly one sun-clogged eye, looked through an arch of green and gold down to the white-topped sea. You danced along the sand writing my name with a stick and the five old people with a transistor radio walked carefully around my identity.

Isla Vista is small and tends the campus—four bookstores, a taco stand with flaming pits, two laundromats, some clothing shops. The students flow along the streets making sounds. One evening we followed a boy playing a harmonica down to the sea. "Which way to the beach"—we called, when he, distressed by our following bodies, turned his singing head in our direction. He pointed and we went, down the tarred incline till, stopped by the inevitable immensity of water, we stood, then sat, at the foot of the pavement, our feet balanced lightly on the sand.

The ocean at night illuminates itself with foam. The breakers shoot suddenly white, pause at their crest, then slide gush to gush along the line of their tumbling advance. I heard once that every seventh wave was large, that the waters in the sea do not move toward the shore, but heave over the tide's pull as the skin heaves over the straining muscle.

The stars seemed to move, each bright star dancing forward and falling back. "I will find you a moving star," you said, "or a satellite or rocket." Once in college I had wandered across the Oregon grass listening to a thin boy name the constellations. "There's Yerxa and the Toads and sweet Penelope with almond eyes, and there," he raised his hand and pointed west, "there is the great constellation of Aristotle." I went the next day to the library to get a chart of the sky, so that I might also have, within my head, a Baedeker of names for what had always been light remote and silent against the black pain of infinity.

I could not find his stars, his clusters and his constellations, though the chart was rich in allegorical formations, Diana with her bow, the major and the minor bear. I did not keep the book long, and have remembered the chart he gave me all these years.

"We are living like gangsters," I say to you, twining leaves around your body. "We are a two-man mafia," I tell you, leaning against your arm in a roomful of dancing people. The party is on a hill and the members of the band are aged somewhere between thirteen and sixteen. They swagger and stamp out sexual energy with their still-unexpanded limbs. We went with Harvey to collect them from the old adobe house on the sea cliff. The house was stranded between the apartment buildings, the landlady would soon, perhaps soon, maybe not for a while yet, we all hoped not for a while yet, tear it down and build a set of matching cages. The six boys tumbled around the white-washed room. "I'm sorry about the mess," the woman said, "but they are old enough to clean it up—if they want to live that way, it's up to them." Her thin hand circled the space in gesture. "I'm sorry," she said again, "it really looks terrible." In the bathroom the raw wooden beams were painted black and on the sink were tooth-brushes and squashed tubes of paste. Four of the brushes were chil-dren's size. Taco, the leader of the band, was crammed into a stylish suit. "Hey man," he said to the boys sitting on the amplifiers in the back of Harvey's Volkswagen bus, "leave my hair alone." Then turn-ing to me, putting his chubby hand on my knee which was pressed close to his in the confined space, "I dig your slacks," he said.

A man from the Agricultural Department is coming to the farm to tell the foreman how to grow lemons. The old man has been here forty-seven years and gets up early and drives his tractor through the orchard cursing the department, and the times which have made the lemons grow better for men in suits.

We sit with our morning coffee, on the porch, and hear the birds. We see through the dispersing morning haze the rim of the sea and the black steel-masted boat, but really oil rig, which last night glowed with lights and seemed to be some passing sailing ship alive with pi-rates.

March 3, 1967

Keep America Beautiful

Stood early morning on Michael's balcony and saw the Glendale hills roll away to the smogged horizon. I could, with effort, defoliate the hills of their pale houses which sank sullenly along the line of the rise and fall. I could imagine the bare expanse of California, the hot days and the desert-cool nights, the silence of a hundred years ago. Except for the Builder, whose Disneyland of Death lay greenly before me, all was chewed and destructed. The Golden State Freeway, like a rubberband, stretched through the cleft below, minuscule cars silently fled along its taut pathway. They appeared so small, it was like look-ing at a gigantic display in a toy department of little self-animated tin cars. But those freeway cars were real and inside each was a driver bent on committing some daily obscenity in a no-dust office, com-pounding the annotations of civilization. I think automation is already upon us; we are the machines.

"Some view," Michael said, spreading his body in the smog-filtered sun. I thought of the mountains, and orange trees in our canyoned retreat. "Yes," I said, "it's some view."

Well, it is some view, any view is some view. *Objets trouvés*, kitchen-sink, Pop art, the glorification of the ultimate ugliness. John Thomas says ugliness comforts him; it never fades as beauty does. Perhaps—perhaps that's an answer to the desperate condition.

Ladybird sits on her husband's head feeling his napalm vibrations between her thighs. "Lyndon dear, let's beautify America . . ." Why not. Flowers for a dead society, wreaths for the industrial revulsion.

Sleep upon the riverbank, the foam detergent is summer snow, soft the banana peels and beer cans flow, down to the sea. Sit upon the grass, there on the roadside, while the belch of exhaust blasts your dreaming eyes.

Music in a hall, loud and pulsating. A thousand amplifiers invade the silence creating a silence of their own. The brain dances within the skull—but our bodies do not touch—we save that for hand to hand combat.

Ladybird has little eyes, Lyndon has a scar, and Lucy is pregnant. The Dutch princess married a German, some say he was a Nazi. Madame Ky had her eyes opened and elongates them with mascara.

The search continues. I know a boy who sits and meditates in a basement. He is the pimp of San Francisco, and, therefore, a saint. I know a woman whose belly is bursting with child. "Will the acid affect my child's mind?" she asks me.

Ladybird wears strict clothes; her suits are of tight wool and her underwear is laminated silk. Lyndon spends a lot of time in the bathroom; what is he doing in there?

There are a lot of kids hitching rides on the roadways. "Where are you going?" "That way," they say, pointing in the direction we were going. "OK, hop in," we say. Later on, they get out, and I look back and see them standing where we dropped them, staring vaguely at the traffic.

I saw a garden somewhere inside the fenced-off development that begins three miles from our house, down at the beginning of our green road which passes unimproved through orchards of walnut and orange. It was a square house with wiggly bits around the windows and a postbox supported by a welded serpentine chain. The garden was full of plastic flowers.

Every morning I look from my bed, over Robert's shoulder, out the wide windows to the lemon grove. Soon the trees will be surfaced with blossoms and the perfume will confuse me with its indolent perfection. I'm going to write to Ladybird and tell her how I breathe deeply, doing my bit to beautify America.

March, 1967

Bang Bang, You're Dead

Daybreak and the streets are deserted. The sun rises in the east, I know I know, and my east is a curving road with buildings and smog on the horizon. And the clouds, whoosh are raining gumdrops, what the hell and my mailbox is full of tears and the destitution pleas and soon the dawning will give way to twilight for a brief five minutes before the neon time takes over. Days away, days adrift, days upon days of doing whatever, whatever did you do today my love? Oh I knotted the shawl of twenty colors to bind my love to you, I plucked the songbird's feather and bound my feet in leather, and if all my dreams are true, the sailing ships shall sail forever and find an island new.

Those were the days, the Indians coming over the horizon all painted up for genocide, buckskin and taffy pulls, wheatlands almost, sage and scrabble, wide sky and no markers to say where the road turns. Come, let us pray. I heard on the radio today, driving in my car, a fireman telling Mr. Jackson that LSD makes you insane. Another lie on the airwaves, another inch to the gap, they are vanishing thataway and we are vanishing thisaway and we all pay tithes to the same government.

Bang bang you're dead and don't get up till the next commercial. I gotta get out these stains, do you have something that removes the brown of sorrow and the black of regret? Can I soak it in your message until clean, and is clean white? Hare Krishna Hari Krishna, they sold me some incense on the street, it is called Limes, now my house is heavy with the perfume, it is beautiful, what is beautiful is what pleases me, pleases me by soothing some capacity of mine, my skin to his touch, my tongue to its taste, my eyes to its design, my ears to its sound. Beautiful beautiful beautiful.

I compose messages in my head, Dear supermarket owner, if I have to stand in your goddamn line another hour just to buy these tasteless items I gludge down every evening because I am too tired to cook I shall . . . what shall I do? Dear radio station, do you think we are all idiots, LSD does not make you insane, I am perfectly respectable lady, I am perfectly respectable lady? I don't wear stockings. I don't wear lipstick. I do vote though that too makes me crazy. How can I go on year after year voting for those people? I don't want to vote for them, I want my vote returned to me, my real vote, I want to be represented somewhere, I've been on the losing side all my life and I want to win a little.

I really felt nauseous looking at those drawings on TV of Bobby Seale bound and gagged. It was me, the me they were binding and gagging, only they are more subtle usually, and I can write for the *Free Press* and say what I mean so I am a little ungagged, but not enough. I want more parks. Spent last Sunday in that small grass thing called a park next to the County Museum. That's a park, I suppose, because it has grass, and it has the La Brea tar pits, carefully enclosed in wire mesh so we can't become fossils, and cement statues of saber-mouth tigers and their babies, and a place guarded by police dogs where what look to be students sift through mud looking for more fossils. The museum is having a Van Gogh exhibition. The waiting line to get in stretches about two blocks long. I asked the guard if that was usual, such a long line. "He had a very tragic life, you know," the guard said, "he painted all those pictures in so few years" (I forget the figures the guard quoted) "and so everybody wants to see the pictures." I guess that's a reason to go to an art exhibit, or a proper reason for Hollywood anyway. Back in the park the old people sat on benches in neat rows. Why weren't they provided with awnings and tables to play chess and checkers on and little beds of flowers? Perhaps I should write another letter—Dear Park Department, why don't you use more imagination and make parks comfortable? And while you're at it, why don't you tear down the buildings and make more parks?

Days, more days, what did I do on Monday, or Tuesday? I can't remember the time and that makes me nervous, all that time losing itself in nothingness. The anti-cigarette commercials say you lose a minute of life for every minute you smoke. I lose minutes of life all the time. I remember when I have done something unusual the time stretched to the pleasure. Afterward that segment of time continues to illuminate. But all these hours like little bits of spinach in a cream sauce, sliding down the mouth of time. Wow!

The body continues to function, sort of, the mind continues to go its divergent ways, part of it matching the yes-sir smile, part of it dancing along a lunacy route which cannot be made into sentences. The days continue to continue, and so do I.

November 14, 1969

I See Myself as a Belly Farm on Legs

A million birds sing. Early morning I rise to the intermittent hum of the battery clock, the hum that continues from the inside of suitcases, or liberated on a table reminds, time is passing. The birds continue. They have nestled in the Japanese lantern over the porch, a redfaced redbreasted bird and his mild brown mate. They have occupied the semi-cellar that we hope to fix, into Turkish seraglio? Indian meditation corner? paint it red? beige? hang drapes over the exposed light cables? cover up the bird's nest? There are birds in every tree, the avocado is a virtual slum of birds and large testicular avocados, their bottoms pecked away. The fruit hangs up high and unreachable, a paradise for giants.

Sometimes I imagine great rubberized creatures mounting the hills and lolling down toward us, through the blond and dried grain that silvers in the wind, past the prickly trees and up and over our fragile wooden house. They have electric eyes and hum occasionally, like the clock. Apart from them, I cannot imagine disaster here, in this bowl of green, unless all the birds should choose to sit, at the same time, on our faded shingle roof.

Baby birds fall out of their nests like dead flowers. Their tender bones and limp feathers melt into the weeds. Linda's cat crawls through the mass, its eyes carnivorous, its movements hereditary. At night the deer's eyes are reflected in the lights of our car. They stop and we stop, then watch them go, in a smooth grace of disappearance, down the long brown isles of earth between the walnut trees. Those same walnuts had been bare, brown wooden candelabra in a meadow of yellow crowned weed when we first came. Now they stand on the plowed acreage with great spread of leaf. Looking up between their rows in the daytime, it is like some formally shadowed garden of a European palace.

Bob has planted a garden and yesterday Linda showed me the first zucchini, small and shiny it lay in the palm of her hand. We grew it ourselves, she said. She looked like a piece of the sun, her bright orange rebozo blouse stretched over her ripening belly.

Everything here is growing, the birds are coupling in flight, the fine giant wings of the hawks cast slim shadows over the meadows and on the apple tree small nubs of fruit are sprouting. I feel like a vehicle of procreation, I see myself as a belly farm on legs, and can imagine how in the plan of things all intent is on my survival till I bear. The spring is definitely a time for getting pregnant, the whole world is like an illustrated children's book on procreation. The swollen flower buds burst to oranges and to apples, even the hard bark of the fig shoots out its sweet fruit.

I suppose we will leave the nest in the basement room until the birds have gone, and in the lantern too. We will only move the rats' nest made of red and green paper from our scrapbook. They have left their gypsy home, full of feathers and bones, and moved on. There is nothing to do but wait for the birds to fly and the apples to grow red and juicy and my belly to swell in echo.

June 23, 1967

Excellent Opportunity for Development

I have seen houses whose amputated walls reveal the flowered paper and brilliant paint of their former inside state. The toothless fireplaces hang in midair, and the broken water pipes stick out like cut trachea sucking at the void. Until I saw such a house I had not realized that my room and all its decoration was merely an attempt to disguise the box, on top of another box in which I lived.

The countryside is then, simply, where they have not yet built. This wonderment of growing grain, the thistle, twig and waxy rock, the slide and sludge and spike and sudden green, are all, as the realtor says, merely "undeveloped."

But I know that that is the real world, the world of grass and drying waterbed, of bird rest branch and lizard lair, of snake and bee swarm, gnat, fly, and moth, of frantic morning chirping from the trees or midnight croaking of the frogs who bang out their songs of lust on rubberband guitars.

I know this world of rising with the light and sleeping in the dark, of watching growing things and touching warm things that get their warmth directly from the sun, of drinking water as it rises from the ground, or eating berries off the prickly bush, I know it is real, is the way things are, and yet . . .

The bird who lives in our cellar has built her nest on one of the rough wooden beams near the ceiling. We want to cover the beams with cloth, to make a seraglio or something somehow exotic out of what is really just enclosed foundation, but we must wait. We cannot hang up cloth until the nestlings fly away, away through that same hole in the screen that lets in the bird, and the flies and gnats and moths and things that hum in the night and have large green eyes. The bird "owns" this house as we own this house, through necessity of shelter and delight in trees. Neither of us could live on concrete.

There is no happy ending though, for if the bomb doesn't get us, the housing developments will.

The bird that lives in our basement has shit on the stairs. Oh well, no one owns anything anymore, we are owned by our times. We are turned to despair by the bland announcement of wars over the radio, or made radiant by the sun's bright warmth on our faces in the morning, then discouraged by the neon signs and square houses that creep inexorably toward us along the wide ribbon road. Up and down the state the markets bloom, the laundromats and automatic cleaners, carwashes and bowling alleys, churches and hamburger stands, the discount monsters with their rich displays for the poor in spirit, sold with come-on prices and no personalized service. The land is squeezed and churned and leveled, and the woods curl up and retreat.

The cities swell with people and with dirt. The streets crack and the grass slides up between the pavement and is trampled flat by feet objecting to this sign of earth. I grew up in the city and never knew, until I saw an excavating machine chewing up that too solid flesh of cement, that underneath was dirt, earth, real fertile land, stone, seed. A billion seeds must lie dormant under the metropolitan slick waiting for the final great destruction.

June 30, 1967

California Lullaby Daze

Visiting LA is sure a Strange Trip!
The rhythm of city things sets blood gonging through templed veins. Along Laurel Canyon trees suffered with dust, thin veils on leaf color, leaves twinge in circular car move air, make rosaries of atmosphere, of gray dream skies, of our pass hours between destinations. Desire for green curls at the roadside. At the bottom of the road a bunch of flower children are stranded, are clogged with fumes, are melted into the rubbish outside Pandora's Box, from the brown paper landscape and the boom boom sign boards comes no echo of their song, only the sound of the newsboys crying Oracle.

Driving down Fairfax, avenue of the miraculous appearance of the psychedelic Elijah, I note an announcement, there will be free lectures on Tantra Yoga Monday nights at the newspaper office where the ink bleeds off the pages and the printing disappears. Out on the streets it is wandering Jews, all of them, renewing the ghetto avenue with ankhs for mezuzah and for scrolls, licorice paper. "It's getting better, better all the t-i-m-e." I pick up the message woven in Indian tones, the nodding heads, the moving bodies, up and down the coast from San Francisco to Los Angeles, "It's getting better all the time."

Visiting in a large, cool, joyful room above the Sunset Strip, harvesting gossip, chewing over intimacies, how is, and what has happened to, and where have they gone . . . I'm told that Vito named his daughter Groovy. My head takes off for some private touring, though the body is still being polite. Groovy? Will she be obsolete in twenty years along with Flower Power and trip posters? Or will the God's eye passions, the old lace bibs, the uncut hair and the bells circle her with the new-time religion. "In a hundred years—all new people." Zap—it clears the head! A world of bell ringers! Of bead stringers! Flower makers! Weavers! Song singers! Trailers of the long California lullabye daze! Stompers and whistlers! Meditators! Makers of small things to dangle and large things to lean on! Watchers of the afternoons catching the air on open eyes, tongueing the colors of sound, and at night, the light from the candle radiant in the silence, the beads! The twigs! The posters on the wall! A new geography of joy!

In the evening we went to see the Dylan movie at the Cinema. Saw him moving through England, saw him in one shot with the face of an old bubba stranded on a bench at Venice beach. Saw the small mouth open, heard the nasal remorse of his voice let out the cry of his people. Back in the car—turn on the radio, I want all the news right away, even in the middle of the song! The teletype voice of the announcer says in monotone—"Rioting broke out again tonight in New Jersey—but first this important announcement." There goes my head again. I want to know of all the bone crush and the slam cut, the crack and thundering fall, of the people who can't stand it anymore and fill bottles with fire, who take boxes of shoes from the glass orifices they have opened between themselves and their material desires.

(Inside head accompaniment to the news . . . Don't they get sick of destroying their own cages? Aren't they going to move out, one day, one NIGHT, out into the white plastic scape of the neat down payment suburbs, do a little burning there? Will the cozy cottages burn and the black chicks dance in mink on the lakeside lawns? And then what will the fashions be, the tie-dyed throwaways of the creative society or the captured car and the new rich of the blacks? Up the ladder we go, up up and over the top. Flower children pollinating the air, blacks wanting "in" on the "great society," substituting the money manacle for the old iron kind, wanting to win the travesty game. But—"It's getting better, better all the time" say the boys. The garbage is richer, the time is slicker, the sounds more confusing.) I'm getting sick all over myself and head for the hills.

The houses creep up on me on dollar bills, but the sun blinds me for the moment to their shadow and I'm busy moving my hands. My hands are always moving, making totem ornaments and fleshy bread, cleaning and planting. Planting small seeds, almost invisible, spraying water onto the drying cracked lip soil, hoping for another day, for a little growth, for some heat, food, the reassurance of skin, the touch of body, no dreams in the quiet night, the brilliance on closed eyes in the morning, the absence of television, an hour of silence, a moment of stillness to watch the deer before they leap into the bushes and disappear, an image of beauty, a word, a sound of voices, a hope, perhaps, that it is getting better, better all the time.

July 28, 1967

Grok

Love, it is announced, is at the Earl Warren Showgrounds, perhaps playing at this very moment within the round cement building with the windows like slanted eyes peeking through a veil. Love is everywhere. Oh rock and groove, roll and grok, rule and grook!

Rule and grook in Isla Vista, free coffee at the Unicorn but no milk, nice sunshine through a big tree outside the Thunderbird Jewelers. Our first day on the beach we saw a live pig and a ball ten feet round, motorbikes doing close monograms on the sand, and, louder than the waves, the PCIF band playing at the end of a rubber umbilicus tethered to the house above, where hung, visible through a window, a poster photograph of Allen Ginsberg in top hat, pointing west.

Rule and grook in Isla Vista slithering into the campus for a free Wednesday noon concert, trying all the toilets, adjusting faces to the other faces in the scholastic mirrors, whose reflections are fittingly serious and hopeful. Case the Student Center, a megalopolis of slot machines, gum, chocolate, coffee in its permutations of—with cream, without cream, with sugar—and oh bliss, whipped chocolate to drip down the chin and scald the throat. Stood by a glass exit door listening to the University Wind Ensemble whose rhythm paralleled the walking people by the lagoon, the surge of birds on the horizon, the silence of a dark-as-eggplant-colored flock whose bodies knobbed the treetops, scraped against the blue sky. Saw history and passion in the anonymous movements isolated by the watching eye, saw the water reflect the buildings, the buildings: Eyes of glass shout back the water's shine.

Rule and grook in the grocery store. Judge the contents of the student stomachs: eight dozen Twinkies, thirty boxes of macaroni mix, packages of fat bacon, eggs, polysaturated everythings, and all eaten under hair lathered by antidandruff shampoo, with underarms mum clean and nails melon pink. The minds of a nation are fed on artificial flavor, di-cresyl-toluene, and edible vegetable colorings. We were carrying incense. "What's that?" the lady behind the counter heaped with Fritos and bubble gum asked. "Here, smell it," the Love Hero answered, doing his courtly presentation dance before the altar of commerce, handing the smiling lady some sticks. The next time we were there she told us she had taken it home; it had smelled lovely. A customer in the line of customers giggled; we bowed in delight.

Rule and grook across the prairie lot between the Kisch and the Donut Shop, putting feet into holes darkened by the deep and non-reflection night, feel the grass wrap your passage with the pull of earth, a million centipedes take refuge in this piece of land harassed from their burrows by the multi-dwellings, dormitories whose design is middle-aged Los Angeles Versailles. See the students walking home with books on botany and thirteenth-century music, through the glass doors of Fontainebleau and Flamingo, under the plastic chandeliers, across the intersexual lounges, and up to their virginal bedrooms in the chicken seraglio.

Rule and grook on Colegio Road, our car out of gas, the night big and bright above us, the windows of the dorm sullenly curtained, the lot of bicycles, whose spokes in sunlight contrapuntally shine, thrusts glint silver in our eyes, refractions of the headlights of our rescuers. "Can you take us to get some gas?" we ask. "Well"—he looks at us— "OK." We begin our circuit cruise of Isla Vista after ten. All closed, the empty stations mock our need. "What's it like here?" we ask, smoking furiously in the back seat of the Volkswagen, our knees wedged under our chins. We are new and eager for information—any riots? any protests? are there urgent factions in small organizations, mythic personalities in the chemistry building, isolated geniuses on certain floors of the dorms, who silent behind closed doors plan the future inheritance? Yes and no, there is incense burning on the fifth floor and rows of shut windows and no boys in Francisco Torres after hours. There is going to be a big *Fuck-In* soon, but we can't come as we are not registered students. No outside agitators at the *Fuck-In,* only official thighs and registered breasts will meet on every floor and groan the rules into oblivion. "If we can help in any way," we offer, and they laugh.

From where we live, plotting vast enterprises, at the end of the canyon road, up against the green reality, it is twelve minutes to Isla Vista and the Magic Lantern. We drive off to go to a movie, often, but we never get there. There's the visit to the Unicorn to drink coffee, getting hung up in a book of Afrikaans' poetry in translation, borrowing a pencil, then some paper to copy out a poem by Robert Creeley about a lover pissing in a sink, the poem really understanding, the process of copying word, punctuation, format of another mind, enlightening. We resolve to copy all the poems we like, make large immutable plan to include all of everything, maybe even the New Testament, or even the *I Ching* in original Chinese, oh rule and grook.

The poolhall has an excellent selection of ten-cent belly busters, imitation cheese-flavored plastic corn bubbles, salted pretzel sticks, diminuendo Milky Ways, free mountain spring water and book matches, clean rest rooms, and pinball machines. The Love Hero explains that the pelvis rules the world, shoving his elasticized bones with sexual delicacy against the wooden nymph-box whose Protestant threat of "tilt" keeps it a perpetual seduction. Bang, the catapulted hammer sends the ball up the channel, oh, it lights the labial stanchions one by one, bounces and bells, lights and gongs, the titillation trembles toward the extra charge, the small perversions of the bonus points, the vacillating targets' precoital judder, the big come of a free game. I watch his promiscuity and chew the salt offerings from a plastic bag, it's a man's game after all, rule and grook.

July, 1967

Help!!!

We got the letter three days ago—quite formal, it said, we have to leave our cottage in thirty days. It didn't mention the deer, our vegetable garden just ripening, the quiet, the peace, the sun, the trees, the birds, but we have to leave them too. My stomach turned in on itself; I became paranoid! Three weeks ago the Estate Management came with a shame-faced man whom they introduced as Mr. X, the "Termite Inspector." (Who were the termites?) He went through our cottage, looking at my batiks in the windows, the ones that said "Peace," that said "Flower Power," he looked at our God's Eye, the three-dimensional one Robert made glowing from its string tied to the ceiling beam. I think the termites made this dust over here, I said, pointing to the door frame, but Mr. X was examining the Modigliani postcards of apricot nudes that were pinned over our bed, the bed with the ten exotic pillows in hand-dyed batik design. I was making bread, my hands covered with the clinging skin of dough, excuse me, I said, for not shaking hands, I'm making bread. They stared at me silently, was it, I wondered, an obscene activity—"Couple, makes bread, desirous of meeting others for fun and loaves."

The weaving I had traded for at the Renaissance Faire two years ago didn't have termites in it, I'm sure it didn't, but it was examined, as it turned slowly on its rope in front of a window, delicate strips of weaving, beads, a sort of three-dimensional string and flax poem. They were so uncommunicative, or really, their silence shouted. But I got the message, and now, three days ago I got it in words, thirty days please.

They say they need the cottage to house farmhands, until, that is, Santa Barbara City Cottage takes over in a few years and turns this paradise into—what? What will the farmhands think of the windows I painstakingly overlaid with delicate patterns of tissue paper, windows that now glow and transfuse the light, where once dark curtains had hung? I spent hours making those windows, finishing this nest, where I hoped to be able to, within the arms of beauty and silence, finish a novel.

We had turned a mousedung, rat-habitated wooden shack into a pleasure garden. I had swept mouse dung into sacks, hauled the rotting carcasses of rats from the semi-basement, scrubbed, disinfected, scrubbed, deodorized, and, at last, with a clean box around me, begun to make a container suitable to my joy. We hung old Indian bedspreads over the raw and electric-cabled ceiling, we haunted the Salvation Army "As Is" Yard and returned triumphant with dollar carpets and old-fashioned kitchen utensils. Robert cleared a fire break around the house, working for ten hot wet days, chopping the dried thistle and weed. We painted walls, and in the kitchen I scrubbed the soiled linoleum tile to reflective splendor. We built a sun shade on our deck, the deck which swung out from the door into the belly of the orange trees, so that I could lie on my back waiting for the oranges to fall onto my head giving me a golden concussion. We smiled and shared our delight with friends, and believed Paradise was ours, that at last, after the work and the scrambling around, the nailing and the scrubbing, the painting and the decorating, we had finished our nest and could live in it.

We are in despair now. What will happen to our vegetable garden, the flowers we transplanted and nurtured, the novel I am trying to write, the days of equilibrium, the hope for peace and a little time to

ve away from the plastic holocaust? All yesterday, and the day be-
ore, we drove through the hills of Santa Barbara looking for a home.
Ve drove through Carpenteria, through Montecito, everywhere. The
tory, the same story, nothing, nowhere, can't help. Friends sent us to
ee friends who wished us well . . . and if they could . . . and as
he day ended, so did my hopes and I felt myself shrivel up and dry.

Why not, Robert asked, write a column and ask people to help, ask
f anyone has a house, a cottage, a barn, shack, temple, stable, castle,
abin, cave, anything, anywhere, where it is quiet and things grow,
vhere we can be quiet and let ourselves grow, matching our flowering
o that of nature. Why not, he said, someone must care, must under-
tand, must be able to help, why not . . . and so I have.

August 4, 1967

Down the Drain

I begin to understand vibrations. Or is it ESP that makes me
hread my nerve endings with yours even while we do nothing but
tand there making mouth love, hello, how are you, fine, how are
ou. People say and do, show and tell, but the story isn't the one you
ee, hear, but another more vibrating thing that tangles you up. Tan-
les you in their thing which may be good, or bad, but sets your own
iming askew.

If there are vibrations from people, then the vibrations are com-
ounded by cities, and cities add strange goals and unnatural timing.
ities flower in the dark, glow with color at night, in the daytime the
rumble shows, the chewing gum melts on the pavement, it's the La
rea tar pits coming back to claim their own. Crowds then, are
trangely overpowering. Good crowds more so. At the first Love-Ins,
ots of clear light flowing like sugar and wine and spinning in the re-
eptive mind, and opening the body to pleasures, sound pleasures,
exture pleasures, to colors as reality, not as disguise for rot, for infe-
ior construction, rouge on a corpse, tint over gray hair, substitute for
ppearance, disguise.

Mostly it's spectator sports. You are placed somewhere and the
cene moves for you. You go out in the car and the streets move for

you, the car stays the same inside so it doesn't move in the mind but the streets move past, playlet, episode, accidents for melodrama, red lights for intermission, destination for climax. Inside the house the TV moves the world for you, disasters are dehydrated for instant use, famous people sit in your living room and smile at you and adjust their skirt lengths.

In Disneyland you move, or are moved, but the moving is only incidental, passing things that do things for you. They blow steam or heave their plastic bodies up out of the water at you (safely) and the guide shoots at them with blanks and tells you you missed your chance to throw your mother-in-law (safe All-American one step removed anti-Momism) overboard (where she would get eaten by plastic crocodiles? or would they only eat her pink curlers and luminescent earrings?).

There are two kinds of people. People who make speeches at you and people who talk to you. I find an inverse ratio of intelligence there, the more they make speeches the less words they have to say. I have spent much of the last week having people make speeches at me. I suppose it is my own fault because I keep nodding my head. Can they see my eyes unfocused? I see only the chance for quiet when I can escape to the toilet in the pause that will surely come.

Toilets are the last place to be left alone in the city, but they don't have good views.

After scattering around the city, visiting people at popcorn speed, in the door how are you, refuge in the toilet, must come out, flush, look at self in the mirror, is that a pimple, if I squeeze it will they notice, will they know that I have been in there malingering? Out the door, may I use your telephone? what for, to make more appointments to use more bathrooms, look out of more windows, explain what we are doing in town, looking for a home, just a place to stop all this circling around and sit, not having to hide in the toilet.

But this time I am bringing vibrations with me, surrounded by them, loaded down with them, sloughing them off on other people, making them uptight. I'm confused, harried, pursued, anxious, homesick (for where? for tree/space). Hello, good-bye, hello, good-bye, come and see us, we don't know where we are going to be, but come and see us anyway. Tidbits of history are shoved at me, who kissed who. Someone who used to live with his wife and child now lives with two women because he has found real love, we should visit him. We wouldn't, too complicated, maybe next time he will be back with his wife and child and that's easier.

It is five days later, and I'm bloated with hamburgers, eighteen-cent hamburgers and nineteen-cent hamburgers and cardboard cupfuls of ice with a trickle of flavored syrup and flaccid French fries with watered catsup and tacos that crumble on their greasy yellow paper beds. I am constipated and have diarrhea and we are still going places in the city and hearing speeches and the toilets are getting noisier and if I don't get out of here I will never make it back. But where is back? only two more weeks in the cottage and then? Lock your bathroom doors! I'm coming to visit you and you may as well help me to face reality standing up.

August 25, 1967

And Silently Steal Away

Stained glass objects hanging in the window, hanging in light space, color, turning the room to cathedral. Dried flowers in a bowl, once in colors, blues, pale and deep, yellows and beiges, now subtly somber with a new color no less ecstatic than when fresh in bloom. Weavings and posters, small collages, tacked against the wall, spaces of design, chairs too, whose spindle backs sift the light in rays across the carpet, like the rain in ribbons seen across a total space, the kind of space where the curvature of the earth is made visible. I can see the room, as it was, even now while sitting here, in someone else's house, with all our treasures packed in small square cardboard boxes.

Coffins, it is like coffins, when the house is stacked, packed, and crammed into boxes. The walls denuded hold pale patches where objects hung, the floor has scratches where the chairs were moved, dragged to the table or turned to face the open door so that sitting there I could see the fields fold away toward sky.

We make homes as though we never will depart, each thing becomes proprietor of its space. The salt cellars always go just there, month after month, just there, next to the jar where the pineapple top grows, its silent energetic tendrils of root curling in the water, its top sprouting green fronds which turn back softly in smooth design. Each thing takes its place, and becomes part of its environment; it is as it has always been and will ever be, or so we think, wandering around in its familiarity feeling home, next, safe comfort.

How then it hurts, like an operation without anesthesia, like incision into the flesh, to take these things and pile them into square cardboard boxes. The sorting out, the enforced rejection of small bits of paper with so much potential, beads, string, old magazines, scraps of cloth, unwearable clothes, once casually dispersed within our room, hidden away because if of no immediate use who knows when they would become essential, now reexamined with dispassionate eyes, their magic denied, their existence violated.

It's all over now, the sunlight filters through barren windows, an army of nails occupies the kitchen wall, slaughtered in boxes, the mugs and spoons, the red enamel frying pans (the eggbeaters which never worked but looked so like sculpture stuffed into the bottom of the garbage bag). We are gone from there with all our goods, we are evacuated from our handmade womb, refugees from our secret nation, our flags are down and wrapped around the dishes and hidden in boxes.

It will start again, when we find another home, the sorting and the planning, the windows hung with color, the posters unrolled and thumbtacked onto walls, the pots stacked for use, the newly acquired pineapple top set in water to grow; each thing will find its forever place and we will forget how these monuments to our flowering eye could ever have been anywhere else, could ever have been packed in cardboard boxes.

September 22, 1967

Natural Resources

How to keep hold of the white light in the neon night, in the silver paper day, how to hold the inner infinity in a delineating society when we are measured in the mirrors of commerce and named in statistics, we tremble on forgetfulness and fall into inner oblivion.

What will return me to the insight which came so strongly: Nothngness, nothingness being everythingness and all things being a continuum. The me being eternal and transitory, these relative measurements noting nothing. I am, each day I am, because I say I am and that suffices. As Maharishi said, I smell the rose—who am I? I am the one who smells the rose.

I thought for a while that to go among trees, unmotivated trees, trees that are because they are and stay as long as they are, and stop when they stop, would be to walk among signposts. For a while it was. The feeling of the unity of nature, the seasonal aspect of natural life, clarifying the seasonableness of inner life, the birth of thought, its flowering, its withering, and yet in its death it becomes the enrichment for the next thought, much as the dying leaves melt into the ground to nourish the shoots of next year's plants. I thought that this visible process would align me to my own rhythm. It did, for a while it did, but it was, I think, really a retracing of my own steps, through a retraining of gait, a relearning of motion, a clarity of progress.

In the end, the lesson absorbed, it became a matter of seduction, for we are not trees, we do not flower in passivity as does the bush, we are not rooted in the ground or indifferent to a multiplicity of stimuli. From that green and pleasant land we could only take the information that we are not tied to the earth with roots, but are meant to grow from an inner soil as we move, and do, across a varied landscape.

So, I am back in the city, which is a totally man-made landscape, where the forest is people and the weeds are people and some bear fruit and some bear only copies of fruit, dry and dusty, though their appearance is deceptive, much as next to each fruitful plant you will find a weed, growing in imitation, similar in leaf and habit, but unfruited and sucking nourishment for no creative purpose.

Then I must always examine, to separate the fruitful from the weed, the fecund from its imitator, and it is more difficult in cities where society mixes up the vocabulary, denies the values, superimposes the look for the honey. I must search for a deeper more solid ground, my own earth, soil, from which to view everything, as though I were to take my own plot of ground with me to nourish me and the world of flowering. Weeds grow everywhere unaided; it takes a lot of weeding and watering to cultivate a flower.

September 29, 1967

Sea Shell Sounds

At the salt water's edge. Crackle shell under foot, still wet, slime
skinned water leaf, grains of glistening sand, glow of slug in half shell
leaving trails of silver marking its slow perambulation. Roots of se
plants, amber tubule split, anemones, their brush petals all to on
side, limp and fading. The sand rises thickly between my toes, spurt
up shallow water, sinks again in silence. Bubbles rise from tunnelin
shell bearing small no-eye creatures. Gray stones shoot brillianc
from their mica decorations, wood wastes in layers and melts into th
sand.

The place where the tide has been. Here the heave reached it
peak, this mark the measure of its expansion, here it faltered an
fled back, halted and slid away, lay for a moment thinly wet and as
piring to reclaim the world, then followed the moon back to it
oceanic bowl. The sea bowl of tipping weed and luminous fish wa
below the eyes' reach, mountain ranges never seen, floor of jewels
mermaids, horrible many-tentacled creatures that rave, swirl, an
suck open the shells of giant clams.

The sea bowl that holds swallowed centuries of iron and silver
trunks of treasures, bolts of silk, ladies in their prime, and gallan
men who fell, still pointing at the stars. The sea slid back to its hord
of treasures from the land at this tide line, leaving the white salt lich
of its desire like dried sperm on a long pale thigh. It left mussel shell
with tiny sparks of coral, white and articulated, ghost bones of cal
cium, hollow tubule homes of spineless creatures evaporated from
their architecture by the dry hot air. Jellyfish, grim thin and melting
flat with no glistening pearl-like depths and shake-a-body movements
A Portuguese man o' war, its blue stinging tentacles empty of poi
son, limp beside its melting body, defeated and impotent, falle
away from his floating glory, for it rode too high and was left, still fo
a moment complicated, armed and lit by an inner luminescence, o
this last shore of the sea. It is lying next to a Dixie cup lid and a piec
of pinkish plastic which does not melt or fade or shine with any ligh
or sag, although it's split in half, multiplying, so that there are tw
pieces now. The sea, if it comes back to take these things away, wil

pit up the pinkish plastic on another beach. This plastic reject of the earth will wander forever among the chalky homes of beasts and waxy seaweed turning oaken brown and rotting Dixie cups and splintered wooden spoons.

Above the tide's edge. The dry crust of sand splinters beneath my feet. Walking lightly I try to skim the burning heat-retentive sand, pushing small fragments of shell into the rented surface, stubbing against stone from the cliffs above, staining my skin with smears of oil and tar from pitch-stained wood. Wood that comes from the sea, bleached and swirled with grain, or wood from the land still barked, trunks of trees, slats of boxes. There is a piece of tire half-sunken in the sand, graying, its curved interior a repository of wind-blown pebbles and bits of plastic bags.

The cliffs at the beach's edge. Chunky, with clumps of wild grasses bent all one way, scruff juniper with roots exposed, rocks held by impacted sand, chalk remains of shell, gray patches with rust designs, lichen in yellow bloom, succulents with water-swollen leaves and stems, bright blossoms that close at night. High up, a piece of string tied to the remains of a paper kite, flaps and tangles on the rock and foot.

On top of the cliffs. An open space of dirt and sand and grass grown brown. Plastic bags balloon in the wind. Paper swirls and struggles against sticks of wood, skits the ground where some shells lie, totally white and strange. Broken glass reflects the light, tin cans catch the blowing dirt and barricade themselves and disappear, or roll in piles against the rock and weed, a sneaker laps its canvas top. There are cores of apples with faint teeth marks, drying orange peels, broken sunglasses and bottles of lotion with sand sticking to their oily labels, bottle tops shining like quarters hint at treasure. Dog shit, drying in the sun, makes targets for peacock-colored flies with berry-balling eyes who dart from pile to pile.

At the curbside bus stop. People waiting, carrying beach balls in plastic string bags, their bathing suits bear the patterns of their sitting in sand designs. Arms with towels, arms with red bites and thin golden hair sand sprinkled, hugging thermos bottles, Sunday papers, hair full of curlers, hair wet and sagging, hair hidden under straw hats with fancy straw designs. Sunglasses reflecting the houses across the street.

Across the street. Houses with faded wooden window frames, with gardens of cactus and white stone. A burger stand, whose counter is striped with mustard stains and lumps of dried catsup, a box of nonabsorbent papers to wipe your hands tilts against the smeared window glass. There are plastic sticks to stir your coffee, or to carry away, back to the beach below, with the plastic bag of burgers, where you can sit in the sun and eat, letting the wind take the bag and using the stick to make your mark upon the sand. When you are gone, the tide comes in to deposit its salty grief of dead upon the sand and takes away its souvenir of earth, the Dixie cup, the plastic stick.

April 26, 1968

Gray Power

TV comedian joke: A man goes to New York City, but doesn't like it; he comes back to Los Angeles because he felt nervous in a place where he couldn't see the air. Barf.

Move to New York and die of the soot, it's a little more granular than smog and soils the clothes and destroys nylons, but it doesn't make your eyes water.

Stay in Los Angeles where the boogers in the nose turn gray, will they still taste like asparagus? I'm too old and inhibited to find out. For every problem there is a solution.

Throw a lot of jello into the sky, from great machines, squirt the sky with jello, strawberry in the summer, grapefruit in the winter. At night when it congeals from the cold, send up helicopters with sterling silver blades to cut it into chunks, package and export as Los Angeles Smog Salad.

Blow cement into the sky, and water, it will mix with the smog and fall down in lovely gray chunks which can be used for cheap housing. To protect the heads of citizens, erect a strong steel net to catch the falling chunks.

Have everyone step outside at 11 A.M. each smoggy day and blow in the direction of Vietnam. The smog will float over the sea and settle on our "enemy" and choke him. Cheap warfare.

Burn pot, lots of it, tons of it, fields and streets of it, till the smoke fills the sky, everyone will be glad, happy even, to breathe in that smog. Then, because it's so nice it will be declared illegal and perhaps someone will finally do something about air pollution, that is, if anyone is able to concentrate. This plan will have to wait a while as there is at present a mysterious lack of pot around.

Or you could plug up car exhaust pipes with marshmallows, they would filter the smog and toast at the same time. Every evening they could be removed and donated to the Boy Scouts whose good deed of the day would be to eat them.

Wear a gas mask, this would protect you from the smog and the cops.

Launch Mayor Yorty into space, his hot air would blow the smog away.

Smog is caused by Communists; they have evil thoughts and these thoughts are transformed into carbon particles which are threatening the very basis of our constitution. The constitution of the United States is suffering from emphysema. Safeguard our constitution before we all become forefathers.

Everytime you buy a car send a bale of smog to Detroit. This will solve the problems of Detroit's black people for everyone will be black, and since all people are the same there is no way to tell a real black person from a smog-black one, there will be instantaneous enlightenment in Detroit which will compensate them for their early death.

Make smog attractive, have commercials for smog, with little catchy tunes, sung by hip groups:

> Jiggity jog
> I love the smog
> So does my dog
> It looks like fog
> I like to play
> In sweet LA
> On a smog-filled day
> Jiggity jog
> I love the smog

Or a top-forty tune with lyrics like this:

> The kaleidoscopic smog makes crystal rainbows
> In my unicorn brain while shreds of memories
> Take mind-trips in the acid rain
> And one-eyed charlatans grow feet of fire
> To stamp out dreams of gray desire

While young girls dressed in yellowed curtain-shrouds
Do oblivion service to the choked up crowds
And a peacock of the royal court
Fans choking throats with a glittering feather
And no one calls the pollution board
To ask about the weather.

July 18, 1968

Exit from Paradise

Naomi had big sad eyes and a slight limp that made her turn one foot in as she walked. I love her, Stanley said. She's married I said, she's only sixteen, she's married, and besides she's really dumb. She's charming and I love her, he said, and her husband is an idiot. She loves him, I said, or she wouldn't have married him would she, huh, would she? We were getting ready for bed which was a very involved procedure of skirting each other with our eyes averted, maneuvering within the confines of the small room we shared in Paradise Alley. He's like a brother, I told my friend Carol, really, that's all, I know it sounds strange but that's the way it is, and just because we share the room it doesn't mean we are more than friends, no one believes us but it's true. And it was.

Martin, whom I decided I loved because he had played a record of Schelomo while we made love, and gave me hot mulled red wine, and most of all, I suppose, because he had said he loved me, had left the room to both of us, presumably so we could watch over each other, me seeing that Stanley didn't forget him, and Stanley making sure I was faithful. Martin went to Israel to help win the war of independence, he sailed off in a Russian freighter from Brooklyn to Italy and from Italy to Israel and wrote cryptic messages to us about the Pal Mach. Stanley and I were both studying at NYU and wondering if we would survive the bomb; air-raid shelter signs were going up all over New York, those yellow signs which are now battered and dusty and part of the cancerous scenery of the city. Naomi lived upstairs above her mother who had been the mistress of someone famous, I can't remember who, and had borne Naomi, who was therefore the daughter of that same famous unknown person, a painter or writer I think, or perhaps just someone loud on the bohemian scene when I was about two or three. At night we could hear her mother fighting with her lover, or lovers; many people walked up the stairs past our room or knocked on our door looking for Sally, insistent and belligerent and never apologetic for disturbing us. That's why she got married, Stanley said, wouldn't you, to get away from that?

I don't think that's why she got married. I was brushing my teeth over the sink which was both bathroom sink and kitchen sink and sometimes a place to pee into when it was dark and cold and the trip down the hall to the shared toilet seemed too much to undertake. I think she loves him. Love, said Stanley, is an imposed frame of mind used to disguise lust or need for a relationship, and she might as well love me as that idiot, I'd at least teach her something. She could use that, I said. You're a frustrated bitch, Stanley said, why don't you find a place of your own? Why don't you? I answered. But we liked sharing that room; he was tall and skinny and, I know now with the wisdom of retrospective analysis, shy and awkward and uncertain. I was plump and noisy and nervous; we comforted each other.

Have some more soup, said Naomi, leaning over Stanley so that her large breasts brushed against his shoulder. We were having dinner upstairs in their apartment; we lived like a sandwich in Paradise Alley, Stanley and me on the bottom floor, Sally and her lovers on the middle, and huddled in the low ceilinged room which must have been an attic at one time, Naomi and Bernie, the husband. What do you think of Sartre, Bernie asked the space in the middle of the table, or apparently that is what he was speaking to for his small solemn eyes never looked directly at anyone. Perhaps he was tired having worked all day in an office where he was an accountant, and then coming home on the bus with all the bodies pinching him into his tiny space on the seat and waiting for the crosstown connection and coming up the stairs and finding us sitting in his room arguing about politics, or rather Stanley making his *reductio ad absurdum* speech about democracy and leaning over Naomi all the time while he was talking so he could stare straight at her breasts. What do you think of Sartre, Stanley answered, the mimicry heavy in his voice, his eyes, swimming with Murine brightness fastened on Naomi. Well, said Bernie, trying, I could feel him trying, to make some definitive brilliant remark which would pull his wife back to him from this threatening poetic seducer, I haven't read a lot actually, just *No Exit* which we saw last summer,

I mean I saw the play, so I guess I haven't read him at all but I thought you might have some ideas about him. Naomi tells me you are very interested in existentialism and so I thought . . . but whatever he thought he never finished saying because he started to cough and wheeze and Naomi said asthma, as though to explain it, and Bernie, and even perhaps, why she was married to him, asthma.

Asthma, said Stanley, later when we were back in our peeling crowded room, asthma is purely psychological. You see he used it as a tactic to overcome me, he knew I was a threat to him, to his marriage, so he used it to pull her to him, to outplay me, he has enough sense to see what is going on, instinctively. What is going on, I asked. Don't you know, said Stanley, she needs me, she told me so today, she loves me, she's just afraid of hurting him, that's why she stays, he's only laid her once in the four months they've been married. Oh, for Christ's sake, I said, is that what she told you, do you really believe that? You're so smart, Stanley said, so fucking smart, you make me sick, don't you have any sense of loveliness, or love? Love, I said, if I must remind you, is just a cover story for lust, you said so yourself, didn't you? But Stanley was looking out the small window at the garbage cans across the alley, at the sootmarks on the walls that were almost shapes, and I could tell from the way he stood there, silently, that this time together, in this small room, the two of us poised on the edge of the disasters of grown-up relationships, was almost over. And it was, because a week later Stanley and Naomi ran away together to Reno, and shortly after that, after days of avoiding Bernie and confusing discussions with Sally whose main concern was an ill-concealed fear that Naomi might come back to stay with her, I moved out and back to the apartment with my father, where he had been living alone ever since my mother had run away.

February 16, 1968

"Outtakes"

Little colored feathers whirling, but not feathers, bits of nylon on a hat, the old lady sits at a bus stop on Hollywood Boulevard and waits for the bus. The loneliest place in Los Angeles, the bus stop, who are these people who do not have cars in a city where everyone agrees "must have a car in Los Angeles." Who are the everyone I quote, just the everyone I know, the middle-class dropouts with middle-class orientations, we children of this mechanical world, we have hi-fi's (must have) and lp's (must have) and radios (must have) and cars (must have). I don't live in Los Angeles; I live in my sectioned Los Angeles, the one where my friends live, where we all have our homes and things we do. There are miles of other people, only that, miles, they are the area we drive by when we go from here to there, there being you, or a store or a place we are going to. It is said that 5,000 people come here every month, maybe the figure is wrong. Where do they settle? Some in the poverty of Watts and the poverty of other places I don't know, some in Beverly Hills, some in Hollywood; they all find their milieu.

(My) everyone is talking about, thinking of, leaving town. Barry says the oxygen is being destroyed by cement, Los Angeles is borrowing oxygen now, and if they cut down the Amazon the whole world's supply of oxygen might disappear! He is going north. The little girl selling ceramic-buttons at the Sunday art fair on La Cienega has already gone north, bought a small house by a stream. Some people are going to Colorado, to grow vegetables. The city is moving to the country, the country is moving to the city.

Here we are in twentieth-century whatever, trying to get back to the dirt, the same dirt that our ancestors fought so hard to get away from, giving up turnips for turntables. It's a pendulum, I think it is. I don't want to live in the country; I just want the values of knowing where I live and how and being related. I don't want to be forced to relate to cabbages; I like people and what people contribute to each other—imagination, energy, love, humor. I don't want to have to be alone with the trees; I like trees, I like green, I like silence, but I want neighbors.

Who are we, what are we doing? We are like wolf packs, snarling from behind our cage bars, escaping and biting the kids on the road. We are lost in our world; we feel strangers to our times. The universal electric brain is devouring us. But I don't want to have to live in a cave to be safe, I don't want to get off this whirling world, I want to find a reality in its midst. There are too many people? Too many for whom? Ask any one of the people if they, themselves, are expendable; do they, themselves feel that they are extraneous? Too many for whom, for me? And am I not one too many for someone else? Cities, awful. Everyone (my everyone) says cities are death. But they are real, they are the result of what we are doing, and if everyone of the "too many people" were to run away to the country to be alone, would there be any alone to be in?

We (my we) are sick of what we have too much of; other people are wanting what we no longer want. A higher standard of living—does that mean plastic wrap and picture windows and cars and processed everything? Sure it does, it's all a way of sharing the loot, distribution, leveling out. We complain, like desperate aristocrats staring at the peasants at the gates, they are trampling our rose garden trying to get into our castle. We are reactionaries, those of us who say "too many people"; we are no different from those who spoke of the Master Race. We are not preindustrial revolution peasants, we drag our electric mixers into the desert with us, we buy our stone-milled flour from health food stores conveniently located near the more affluent neighborhoods. We sit in comfortable chairs in well-lighted rooms listening to multi-plex stereo recordings while we learn to make our own moccasins—Indians? The Indians want to go to college, want fair opportunities to have plumbing, except for those Indians who want to return to traditional forms of life, but where, on their delineated ranges, caught between the complexes of paved roads and big industrial cities? What traditional life? Is that what their kids want? Or are they fed up with being second class, attempting to find pride in their traditions, looking to the past for the future? Is that valid? Was it ever valid? More important, is it even feasible now?

For me, the answer is to take what is, what is discernibly real, and try to live with it, try to change it so that everyone can live with it; I don't accept the idea of "too many people," "too many cars," after all, I keep my car, and I want to keep my life too.

March 14, 1969

Freeman's Harvest

The dandelion has a small bright yellow flower; it grows in vacant lots between the rubble and cement. We go out with a spade to dig it up, to harvest its roots; they are as thick as my middle finger. The roots are twisted through the drying soil, have little tendrils which clutch the ground; we shake them and twist off the tops, put them in Mark's sack, and dig some more. The flowers are so golden yellow, the roots so pale beneath their crust of dirt.

Here, Mark says, is this enough? We spill our harvest upon the wooden table, a boat hatch washed up upon the Venice beaches by the storm, now propped on bricks, a table that we lean upon. Marcie takes the roots and strips them of their fine hair like shoots, cuts them, puts them in the oven to roast; we are going to have dandelion coffee!

You see, says Mark, says Marcie, all the earth is contaminated; everything is full of chemicals and DDT. The air is foul, the soil is foul, the plants are sprayed, the fruit is sprayed. They are going to live off things grown organically, things growing wild, dandelion coffee and clover tea. Their house is calm, a rug to sit upon, that table rescued from the sea, some drawings on the wall, silence, and this last-ditch stand upon an earth that is being slowly destroyed by man.

Marcie makes flutes of bamboo; she cuts the hole to match our scale, plays windy tunes and little trills. Outside their small room her garden grows, vegetables in empty ice cream bins, each covered with its own greenhouse made of a bottle bottom cut away, their leaves protected from the graying wind. I think of forests, and farms, and all things growing wild, she says.

Stranded in the city at the edge of the sea, they walk their dogs along the sand, their dogs race the waves. I am writing songs, Mark says, and sings a sliding lamentation, part of the now time and part of his childhood memories of wailings in the synagogue.

We go back to the room and sit upon our legs, no chairs, the radio plays a Dylan song, "Love Is a Four Letter Word," we nod our heads. They have found a way while I am caught still in the cities' dilemma. The conversation turns to earthquakes. Earthquakes! The whole of this state falling into the sea, the buildings sinking, the neon signs adrift, the coupons for ten cents off soggy and unredeemable upon the sand. Yesterday the man who wrote the book about the last days of the great state of California retracts all on an early morning TV show. It was, he said, a parable for our national anxiety, our fears about Vietnam, our troubles over poverty. Ha Ha, no earthquake, just reality, and on to commercials for imitation cream. The husband moos like a cow, the wife looks smug, I feel the earth tremble; what we have is imitation earth no doubt, along with imitation death.

We have already dealt with death, dealt with it in waxes and plastic lace, have dealt with milk through imitation cream; we deal with ourselves through tranquilizers and pills that make us "up," wherever that may be, for even "up" has been abolished by men in rocketships who know the earth as down below.

Mark and Marcie try to turn from all confusion, digging dandelions for their coffee and foraging the urban beaches for their furniture, but still they talk of death and the splintering soil.

Is it some monstrous disaster that engulfs us now, made of bombs and DDT, of madness and illusion, of imitations of a reality we remember, the higher-priced spread that tastes so good but kills us with calories and cholesterol.

What has happened to the natural span of man, the childhood and the youth and age? The children rushing to be youth, the youth thrown into wars, the old men not allowed to die, but propped against a window, stiff and cold, for one last wave, for one last smile.

The dandelions grow in vacant lots, though not for long. Soon buildings twenty stories high will rise, all windows and cement, crushing the yellow blossoms, crushing the earth, cold containers perched at the edge of the sea where soon, they say, the land will crack and slide, and fall into the water. We tremble at the edge of our disintegrating times and look for answers.

April, 1969

Getting Your Share

I think if I have to drive down another traffic-laden street I'll go mad! And yet we seem to have to live in this conjunction to communicate and interact with each other and be productive. We are like a bunch of ants traveling a narrow passage. I remember seeing in parts of Africa, vast open spaces, spaces of nothingness, though not exactly nothing for there were flowers and stones and bushes and rocks and some strange crawling things, and then suddenly, in this relative emptiness would rise great cones of sand, perhaps four or five feet tall and in these edifices lived millions of ants, all of them hauling eggs and debris and shoving their way past each other in and out of their little tunnels. It looked strange, but it also looked exactly like our own city situation.

So we long for countryside, lots of empty spaces and eye room and breath room and room just for quietness and aloneness and yet we cluster, all over the world, people cluster. It must be our nature, or it must be the result of some vast self-perpetuating mistake, that we live in clusters which start off as villages and become towns and then cities and then gigantic extensive reiterations of town city complexes. Even when they are divided into districts with their own waterholes of supermarkets and shops they still remain tight and claustrophobic.

So I sit in my car and dodge other cars, each occupied with an equally harassed driver, rooting my way along the tar, avoiding holes and watching stoplights and keeping an eye out for police cars which, like dangerous wildlife, lurk behind corners ready to devour me if I don't play the game right. Even public transport, not that there is any that is reasonably supportive in this town, is hideous. Squeeze and shove and very expensive and jolt and sit staring into other faces as distressed or remote as one's own, all moving together encapsulated down the road.

I crossed the country by Greyhound a few years ago and that was somewhat different. You sit and stare out your foggy window as the states roll by and the voices around you change, the twangs give way to drawls and the drunks keep up a noise even though the cast changes. Everyone on those buses seemed to be heading for the city, some city, some place, though it is impossible that people only got on and never got off, so I suppose a few dribbled out into little places whose names I never knew but whose aspects remain in memory as a blur of one shop front and a gas station.

Even trying to get out of the congestion, out to the mountains or the sea plunges you into further conflict. Long rows of weekend escapees, like the remembered films of all those French people fleeing south as the Germans took Paris, roads clogged, all of us trying to get away from each other, stuck there on the highway side by side. I stare into other car windows, well, there's a face I'll never see again, this hopefully, and two miles on there we are, still ignorant of each other but side by side on the roadway facing the same direction as strangers.

I don't think coastlines should be owned. I could never understand how someone could own a piece of shore, a stretch of beach; in some countries all beaches are public. There is only so much shore, so much, but so much less than there is of land. Why can't I go down to any beach I wish, walk along and watch the sea? How can someone own this unique piece of the earth? Of course to the people who do own a beach it seems only right, otherwise how could they have privacy and quiet and not be inundated by transistor radios and thousands of fellow sea lovers.

I have this same conflict when I see the houses go up in the countryside, or the high rises along the shore where before was wilderness and perhaps a few cottages at most, spoiled, it's all spoiled now I say, and then, but this means that so many more people can enjoy a part of what before belonged to only a few, although usually the only people who get to enjoy it are the wealthy ones. Only it's not the same when there are many people, and yet, which are the people who should have and which who should not? A basic socialist training in my youth has proven very confusing.

There are always things that seem spoiled by too many people, or too much exposure, and there is always the concomitant thought that this is the result of the equalization of things, of letting everyone have his share. It is this same desire to have one's own home that has ruined the countryside, chopping away at nature until there doesn't seem to be any left. Yet if they were to build only multicomplexes of housing, how miserable I would find it to live in one. I want my own house, I want my own garden, my own view, space, solitude, and it is this common desire that has made Los Angeles so expansive and hideous.

I don't seem to be able to figure this out, all I can do is complain, to complain of the traffic and of the crowding and of the standing in line and of the gigantic sameness of everything mass produced which is the very method that has made produce available to the masses. The only room left seems to be the room within, the space inside where the creative and dreaming world continues while the surrounding reality slowly chokes me. It's either that or the moon, the barren pockmarked dry and desolate moon, and the sky, and the stars, and the spaces not yet controlled by man.

May 23, 1969

The Carrot or the Plastic Spoon

Trapped in the great divide, one foot on a carrot and the other on a plastic spoon. Letters from escapees—"well, we have planted enough to feed ourselves and Marcia is canning peaches and pears and plums and we have a basket of apples and some rice so come and see us—" but I can't. I am in the nine to five landscape, though not involuntarily.

Oh my heart grows green enough, and my brain loved the space and silence, and my feet dance through thoughts of mud between the toes, but something, some virus of city life infests me and I have to be where the action is, however tawdry.

It is ugly here. There is nothing to look at that doesn't mock ambition, cement and iron and glass. Views down the boulevard on the way to work of smog in the distance so that it is like driving into the dragon's mouth. But drive I do down the gullet and with a kinky joy.

Executive luncheons from twelve to two and traffic jams at eight thirty and five thirty, lying on the bed at home watching the news on TV, eating celery. Somewhere out in an undesignated space my friend Turtle is watching the stars. He sent me a message of greetings last week and an invitation to "come and see us"—the us being a commune in the hillsides, full of sweet smiles and good vibes. But I can't because tomorrow comes and I come with it fully charged with the pursuit of career and achievement and excitement that is doing something in the city.

I haven't seen Turtle for some years. I first met him five years ago; he used to visit me at my office when I was working at KPFK. He heralded his arrival with the sound of bells which he wore suspended from almost every protruding part of himself. He would float in the door and settle on the edge of my desk and unload a series of treasures from his pockets. He was like A. A. Milne's Jonathon Jo "with a mouth like an O and a wheelbarrow full of surprises, whatever you wanted he never said no and he had it in all shapes and sizes." (Well, my memory may be inaccurate but that is how I recall that poem.) Turtle would have a supply of little pieces of prismatically cut colored glass which he would hold up to your eye for you to peer through (while you were typing!) or he would hand you a roach clip intricately fashioned of some glowing metal, that he had made. All this was before these baubles became the commercial items of hipdom. Turtle was a Troubadour and a messenger of good times and so it was a joy to suddenly find him again, on the cover of *Life* magazine! (that issue with the elegiac photographs of the commune). I looked at those beautiful pictures of those radiant people and longed to be able to join them, or at least a part of me longed to do so. But the realer part of me, and it must be the more real part for it is the part that prevails, went on with its city dance.

It is a conundrum. How do you earn enough to survive: You live/ work in the city. How do you survive: You get the hell out of the city and live in the country. I know the real values are the ones that sustain Turtle and his brothers and sisters there on the land, so why can't I join them, why do I get frightened at the idea of giving all this up? All this what? All this excitement of being where it is happening, whatever it is, of talking to people, different people all the time and seeing the latest movies, and reading the latest newspapers, and eating the too rich food and driving down the crowded streets. Why am I happy with a life that I know is shallow and false and transient? Will I be content to have two weeks of the fifty in greenness, is that the answer?

Perhaps that is why I never admit to myself that I really live here, that this is where I am. I always think that this is just for now, just until I have had enough, and then, and then I will take to the woods. But it has been a long time, a long time that I have been standing here with one foot on the carrot and one on the plastic spoon.

October 17, 1969

Unnatural Resources

California rainy day psalm: the slither of sky, tears, the echoes of dying bird steps. Think—the sea a flotilla of oil! the sea birds waterlogged and sleek with death. The black oil pulses up, broken free of its plastic vein, runs over water where no oil was meant to flow. The rain comes down, drags soil turned mud over mountain roads, oil unfurls over the sea. The oil pulses upward and the rain comes down.

Wild birds trail dark streaks along the beaches, drag black pearly ooze from feathers too clogged, too coated, to float or fly. Bird beaks are slimed with tar, ruby eyes turned coal, with no view of sky or sea, but all of this vista of slick death, this unnatural caul of black-gold death, spreading over the seaside waters. The oil pulses upward and the rain comes down.

The beaches are choked with tar, rubbery roots of subsea plants wilt in sullen heaps and bulges, lie over dimmed quartz and shale, the sea air smells of dark petroleum, iodine, and death. The garland strings of bulbs, the flexing fronds, the little pinkish caves of shell, the brittle and the feathery objects of the oceanscape are storm displaced, lie tarred and fading on our shores. The oil bubbles up and the rain drips down.

Three hundred birds or so were counted, captured, cleansed, and returned to death. Webbed feet unused to cages, air voices weak and thin, untuned and lost in terror, their bird fears a mass of sludgy grease and tar. Three hundred of how many, of how many dying on our shrinking shores where the oil washes up and the land washes down.

How many care, the birds' thin bone statistics fly away as they no longer can, vie with our metal disasters and our plastic deaths. It all flies by, the moon is more or less the same on every side, so what, and next the sun, and Mars, a fine new kind of war. We can ignore the shoreside deaths by switching off the set, something more not quite right but best ignored, like pain or China. The television weeks go by while our good earth vanishes, mixing oil and water, for the oil pulses upward and the rains come down.

The rain falls and takes a mountain with it, smothers two old aunts in backroom beds, their grave is made of lath and plaster, their beaches made of bones and tar, their time was eaten by mud and water, and the oil pulses upward.

Go argue in capitols about gains and taxes, about profits and the resources of our land, sit in paneled rooms a forest fell to build, burn the oil for which whole nations die, and which now, set free upon our water, marks the suicidal slash marks of our insane greed. The rain falls down, somehow still purely water, clears the petrol smog and lets us see our mountains, carved and cleft with roads and subdivisions, bereft of roots, awash with rain, spilling top soil upon the white stone

lawns, and sending chips of roadway tar down to the dead bird
beaches where the oil pulses upward while the rains fall down.

February 21, 1969

Letter to Marcia

This is a letter to Marcia.

Your eggs plop out, your chickens karkle, your eyes sparkle, your
sky fills with sunshine. You share your trip with me and hand me a
sea of love and poetry written by pen in the drifting greenward hours
of your leafy silences. You cause me joy by your existence and cast
veils of flower hours around my smog love city. I am garlanded in absurdities and wealthy with a sense of decay. I thrive on the corpses of
sensibility and fly like the vulture after plastic prey born dead and
swollen pink with praise—to each his road—we can share love and
water.

Your time is measured in teaspoons of sea salt; the drying leaves of
strawberry and thyme, the round white eye of berry, the thistle stalk,
all decorate your teapot or lie swollen in the golden water. Your day
begins with the galactic rising and your evening follows melting shadows over the horizon. I see neon teeth on every corner and hungry
blizzard ladies, refugees from eastern snow-flecked tenements, walk
the avenues on golden spikes, their blue burst vein legs gilded with
nylon. I stuff the grease-slimed twigs of starch between my blackened
fingers and lick the blood-red sauce they carry.

Your water pulses between the fronds and buds and leaves, slow
pulsations; and across the moss, the glistening transparencies of liquid
fall into your jar. Above, three birds, in search of no author, sing the
latest from the sky parade, deposit eggs colored to reflect the sky, in
goblets of twig and down. Your hands hold water and let it fall back
upon the earth, your brown fingers curl upon a flower and leave it on
its stem, its stem tied to earth, its roots sucking the soil.

I tie the dried dyed thistles to an upright decision and pull the curtains. The curtains have a trace of butterflies and contain the day's
dirt and dust. The moats of light tickle the floor, fly over last night's

coffee cups and drown in crumpled black/white piles of yesterday's disasters. The TV world flicks its spectrum face, pulls eyes into electronic buzz, they dance, they sing, they introduce—Miss Sparkle Plenty to the author of a book on overkill. You don't need lessons, says the author, while along the avenue the buses fart exhaust, the vision mumbles.

Your trees make shade and bark and branch without plan, loose limbs for firewood, regrow, the new leaves tipped chartreuse, the dead upon the earth sink nourishment beneath the rot and roll of last year's bloom. You count the dapple on your arm, make songs of sunshine and love to the feathers in your yard. You kiss and twine the silver nighttime along your shut eyelids, let lapsing light slide silence across your throat.

I slit my wrist with a small gold watch, my palm knows the hours and my fingers charge. My neck supports my head, my head supports my body. I suck fumes for peace, inhale the gas of laughter until my lips go rubber and my brain goes mush. I circle myself with refuse and search for diamonds.

I am the meat treat lady in search of input and you are the queen of green.

February 19, 1970

Dope Strikes Back:
Hippie Scenes, Blossoms to Dust

THE WHOLE POINT of the thing is that it started somewhere. I pick it up around 1948 and the pre-hippie beatniks, take it through 1951, then leap to the middle sixties, because in between 1951 and 1964 I was living in Cape Town, South Africa, and London in a state more political than psychedelic. I was a Greenwich Village baby beatnik, and now I am a middle-aged Los Angeles Hippie turned mutant, looking for a place to lay my head. Head, I am a head. What a nice term, to be a head. If all the rest of you were dismembered, except the plumbing and the head, you would still be you. Since I have no lust to concentrate on the plumbing, I am satisfied to categorize myself as a head. Got that?

There were some fortunate aspects to being out of America for eleven years, fortunate for it allowed me to return with untrained eyes. It was all new, from styrofoam cup to "Make Love Not War." It was, for me, a foreign culture. I wandered and partook, as when in Rome, and I observed and changed. Changed because ultimately there are no observers, only participants. These pieces reflect both the external change and my own internal reorientation whose boundaries are marked pre-1967 and post-1967. Nineteen-sixty-six was the year I started smoking dope, that was my psychedelic adolescence; 1967 was the year I took acid and my head turned twenty-one. Donovan sang "Sunshine Superman," Owsley dropped from the sky onto the grass of Golden Gate Park where the Human Be-In was busy happening, and the "Downtown Swami" Hare Krishna'd his way to the West Coast.

As with most climactic events, we who participated were unaware of just how significant that event was, though I think for most of us at the Be-In it marked the point at which we became true believers in a mass culture and media freaks.

The year that followed saw the upspringing of all our gardens, we went to wandering in this state and throughout California. Incense, flowers, love, flying saucers, freakouts, handouts, moans, chants, overdoses, giggles, gaggles, welfare, squatters, parks, babies, posters, black lights, necklaces, Nehru, sitars, Indians (both kinds!) paisley, collages, bedspreads on walls, walls of canvas, beds of grass, communes, brown rice, victory through vegetables, love, noise, busts, bummers, oh those "groovy" pre-ecology days!

These patchwork memories amaze and amuse me now, my own naïveté, how blissful! To think I thought "we" were winning! On second thought perhaps we are, what with all the boys (who aren't killed) coming home from the war dopers and even Nixon saying this may be the last one. (Reminds me of the alcoholic's plea for just one more for the road, because we are still over there dropping incendiary and slime, grinding up babies into soured meat, taking the pride of a people at half-price, making the world safe for the fat bastards like myself with a house full of media input machines so that I can tabulate just how many deaths bought my last transistorized prize.)

But trips are always worth it, even if you get lost and don't speak the language and the bed isn't as comfortable as home and no one makes a decent hamburger. Trips and journeys, new faces and modes, swinging along with the eternal pendulum that breaks the wind of change and tolls a mysterious hour. Watch out for witches and control addicts, otherwise, after looking both ways, run do not walk to your nearest dealer.

Herewith a small history with two titles, a brief sociological investigation into the state of being set in the language of our times. Chronicles not of Martians, but of space travelers confined to California. Their journeys, my journey, faces, happenings, people, events, the elastic then stretched to its borders by euphoria. The Thesaurus is the imagination, the map is historical, the trip continues.

Flotsam and Jet Set

OK so you are wearing beads, and your hair is long and from the back you might be anyone, and from the front your face isn't too different either, your expression, is it an expression, is non-attendance, and your style is all I ever know of you. Style, it's all style and not much content, unless style is content, but what is the definition of decadence? Is it the substitution of style for content? Is that why so many love children smile a lot and score off you for everything they can get, cigarettes, hey man, lay a cigarette on me, or another ploy, anybody got a match? OK, now who's got a cigarette to go with it? Or you walk into an underground paper office where there is a big sign on the wall that says "Don't make magic, Be magic" and "Love" and you ask about something and receive cold indifference; they are too busy manufacturing love to give away any samples.

Hippiebums, dirty long-haired hippiebums with nowhere to go and nothing to do and they spend a lot of time using your daylight and your floor doing their nothing so that if you have something to do it is impossible. Who's that bunch of hippies out there in our garage-way mending their shoes and dancing and inviting the man to come and bust us, while we stand at the window and worry, from inside our ten-uous safety, where we just got through with a lot of cleaning up after a departed hippie community, washing, wall painting, and removing piles of animal shit from under the refrigerator?

Split, that's what it's come to, a big rift, hippies and hippiebums. Upstairs the acid freaks are screaming and shouting and beating each other up and chasing each other around in lace dresses and the child who lives there sits at our table asking for food and wondering where her mother is, only not too hopefully.

Hippiebums give you presents, like dirty feathers or one bead or the clap. Hippiebums tell you about mystical experiences while they finger your breadbox. Hippiebums start off on your floor and make it to the couch and then eye your bed. When it gets tight for them they split, but they let you keep the feather or bead or the clap as a souvenir. You're materialistic they mumble at you as they drag themselves out your door, their pockets stuffed with peanut butter sandwiches.

Hippiebums write bad poetry and draw ugly pictures and make you look at them. They sing dull songs to one chord change and tell you how it is, letting you in on the secrets of life. Hippiebums hitch rides with you and roll joints in the back seat leaving seeds on the carpet. Hippiebums are just leaving for San Francisco or have just come back. Hippiebums use your telephone to call Chicago and Great Falls and three friends in New York; they pass the time on your phone.

Hippiebums are always there at mealtimes but can't wipe dishes; hippiebums bring their friends over but never tell you their names.

Hippiebums come from middle-class homes and want you to be their parents, want you to pay their rent, want to make your world their high school. Hippiebums believe in the abundance of the Great Society, and want you to supply it. Hippiebums are predatory but wear a disguise of love. Hippiebums serenade you with their bells and dance for you, stepping on your feet.

I used to smile at everyone with a button or a bell or a flower. I used to think how beautiful it was all becoming, how rich it was, how sweet and good. But it's fantasy time, that's what it is, fantasy time in the twentieth century and style is where it's at, and only a few maintain content, and content, in the end, is really what creates a good world, and love, and being together with people and doing and making peace and feeling love and sustaining energy. So don't feel bad if you can't love every long-haired flower bell child in the road; things aren't always what they seem.

October 13, 1967

Diatribe

We sat on the floor drinking wine and listening to the Indian records reserved for such occasions, making little comments knowingly about the beat, the philosophical content, counting off with fat fingers against palm the groups of nine, eleven, or seven. It reminded me of the time I had worked as the curator of a gallery above a furniture store. As a tie-in we had held an exhibition of Japanese prints while they sold shoji screens and Hong Kong chairs. During the exhibition we played the same five Japanese records all day. At first it had been agony for me, the unusual harmonies, the seemingly distorted sequence of sound. Then it became familiar and pleasant, and a few days later it became Muzak, so that it does not surprise me to live with Ravi Shankar now, and like it.

However, I suspect my preoccupation with Indian music, with God's eyes, with the paraphernalia of quasi-mysticism, is really as trite to my world as the paintings of Keane are to suburbia. I expect to encounter the unexpected, and the unexpected takes parallel form all about me. In Los Angeles much of it seems to be an admixture of Orient and Homosexual, so that if the trend continues I should not be surprised to be overrun by a mass of Camp Zen Buddhists waving Tiffany lamps and chanting, "We shall over om."

But then, perhaps at this very moment, they may be sitting outside the Taj Mahal playing Wanda Landowska on portable transistorized Japanese record players. While all about me are taking flight with acid and pot, the Delhi government may be legislating against the use of Methedrine and Miltown. Our hair grows longer, but in China, are there any pigtails left? Confusion of cultures? It's one big shook-up world.

I suppose what I'm saying is that there are no new experiences. We are just moving around the international Monopoly board trying to pass Go. The cards change from Community Chest to Chance and we land on a lot of pretty far-out no parking spots, but it's that same marked-off square we are circling all the time.

Perhaps all new experiences have to come from inside, and we are in the end limited by our physical components and historical span. If I love you, there are statistically a hundred I could also love, maybe tens of hundreds, but let me kiss you, because you are here.

I don't say reject the new wild experiences, but are they new, are they wild? Only to those of us who have not experienced them before. It is disturbing to me to see the army of the enlightened preaching, because I've heard that song before, somewhere else. Go ahead, share the vision, but don't lay it on us with too much force, because some of us know it anyway. And the experience of experience, it isn't that new. Only the ability to feel, for those people who have shunted their powers onto the mass culture sidetrack, who have become blotting paper for the stinking pool of commercialized emotion, perhaps only for these people is the chemical experience such an eye-opener.

You may be expanding, but examine from what you are expanding, and toward what. You can only enrich that which exists; it is a process, not a quality. Feelings may in the end be all that we have, but let's feel for something.

Turn the record over and relax, if you like it, it's OK. But if you just think you should like it . . .

May, 1966

Saturday Morning Conjugation

Driving Somewhere. The detour is in the mind, is in the body. Items flash by, curbsides recede and flex inward. Painstaking attention must be paid to green lights, red lights, the ambiguity of yellow. Blocks circled, paint, shingle, brick, cement, crumble and fence off direction. I am discreet in my attention to the law.

Walking Somewhere. Obstacles straddle the pathway. Small stones leap to life and panic my feet. Moss, grass, tangled root of bush, fallen twig, grapple at my liquid pacing movement. Trees bend in green swirl, sky recedes in flow silently, a film running backwards. I am sucked into minute space and stranded.

Sitting Somewhere. Everyjoy, merryjolly tickle, laughter curls along the inside of my lips. My eyes withdraw from the tennisball sun stopped in its passage by my observation. Whooosh, splendor, sweet perfumed eyes of time lay velvet glances along my swirling spine, send kisses through my veins. My toenails turn sensual with pleasure. My body is a nipple and I sing of milk.

Lying Somewhere. Each hair turns sentinel to skin, the pores open and suck in measures of touch. The belly bursts its pod and seeds of lilac-colored corn sprout feathers and grow between my legs. Tickle turn and sprinkle, hair and wet longing flow, the grass lies down in quilting.

Listening Somewhere. What deep sound is that? Humming of the wooden boards creaking as the house sags. Bird nest burdens sway the roof, cat prints clot the yard, owl beads fall on the bushes, dog hairs surface the plastic-covered pad and crackle with electricity. The Japanese cooker is covered with gray ash and small birds seeking disaster mince across the pebble lawn under the eyes of an army of cats.

Looking Somewhere. Miraculous spider shells catch the light in mock silken traps. The fluorescent bug lies shattered in the web, the spider sleeps. A million ants make journey across the sill and spiral out around the dishes and the door. Their feet thump against the floor, there is no silence anymore but it is composed of growth and motion, rural ants with urban occupations.

Living Somewhere. Tomorrow's days are marked, last week fades upon the calendar. The black crosses signify the celebrations and disasters, when face to face the memory of the name was missing. Extended time lengthens the passage of hours. The shutting door repeats its motion, flicks against the eye, and cuts the light with sound. Against the window the colored glasses imprison the globular shine of early day. When you come home, I will be sitting here, doing nothing on a Saturday morning.

September 16, 1966

Softly the Empty Sound

I exposed the underside of the stone; it had lain buried for all its ages in the soft sandstone and I plucked it like a berry from the bush of the rock. The view undulated before us, the bracken and dried grass, the falling away of sand and rubble down toward the still spread sea. I turned and twisted that nodule of rock in its socket until it fell into my hand, liberated and heavy. From underneath, a centipede, translucent and yellowy-green, holding within its glow the quality of all subterranean creatures who bereft of sunlight cast their own illumination, emerged from the exposed socket and slid toward whatever nearest crack would furnish it oblivion. You said, "Capture it," but made no move, and I turned away from any disaster we might create, having only disemboweled that rock from the habit of touching and turning and pushing to which my fingers had grown addicted.

We got back in the car and drove upwards. Above us the spherical radar mounds were white and huddled against the outline of the mountains. We drove toward them and you told me about the couple in the flying saucer and showed me the tarmac cover to the ground, beneath which, you said, the Nike missiles lay, pointing toward the harbor and the always advancing enemy. It was quiet up there, those white obtrusions and the missile pads and the empty cars parked outside the wire fence.

We drove on, exploring the contour and the change of the heaving rock, seeing the upflung strata caught in flow and hardened in its transport of formation. The road circled the form of the mountain, twisted downward, and you played talk games of make believe. "I am Dr. Brines and you are exposing me to danger, I should be safe in my operating theater . . ." You talked on, but it was your game, and I listened to the voice and the sounds of the wind-rustled trees and felt the sun and the aloneness. We decided to buy some food and eat it up there where we had come from, in some wooded place where I hoped we might find a stream though you explained that there was no water in this season.

The woman behind the counter at the little roadside store was very nice; she smiled at me from behind her tray of doughnuts, and behind her a framed autographed photograph of Ronald Reagan smiled at me too. The men outside had not smiled, but they perhaps had seen my "Make Love Not War" bumper sticker. We went back up the road looking for shelter and chose a spot, a ravine running upward where the leafy trees bent inward and there was a path and a place to park. We left the car, and carrying the paper sack of food, climbed over small stones and bent branches until suddenly we heard over the sound of birds and snapping twigs, the sound of water against rock. Looking down through the tangle of bush we saw a pool and the small stream which poured over the mossy rocks and made that noise which always to me means cool and sanctuary. We slip slid down the bowllike sides of the ravine and sat on the rocks in the stream, dangling our feet in the water and eating the food from the bag.

It was almost like slipping back into my childhood in Upper New York State where we had carried straw baskets to the pond and spread our sandwiches out upon the rock and the farmer's daughter, whose name was Josie, said, "Don't mind if I do," instead of yes when offered her share. She carried a bottle of water in which there was a hair from the tail of a horse, and was patient in her expectations of its turning into a snake. I sat there thinking of that time, and you sat there making faces because the bread was artificial and the salami was plastic and in the end you ate only the tomatoes and drank the beer. We collected the bits of paper, and taking our cans of beer, climbed up the other side to a flat rock where we could sitting up see another pool further on but inaccessible, or lying on our backs stare up into the receding layers of leaves which overlapped and permutated their color and the light with kaleidoscopic effect.

I heard a rustling sound and looked and saw a man. "Someone else is here," I said to you, pointing to the figure almost obscured by the protruding rock and bush. "He's coming to attack us, maybe," I said,

being suddenly full of headline catastrophes and television sadism im-
aginings. He climbed away from us and I watched him with relief.
Then he appeared again below us and looking at him I said I thought
he was a Forest Ranger, but you said "No," and pointed out his
badge, "he is a sheriff." "Hello," I called, "what's this place called?"
He looked up, smiling, "I call it Poison Oak Gulch," he said, and
climbed up to where we were sitting, still smiling. He stood over us
and within a non-space of time his face shut and the thinned lips
opened and he said to you, "Show me your I.D." You stood up, as-
sembling your lanky young body from the worn suede boots to long
cluttered sun-streaked hair and stubble-covered rosy cheeks, you rose
up off the rock and held out your I.D. He looked at it, and still holding it turned to me. "Your I.D.," he said. I did not get up but answered softly, "It's in the car." "Whose car is that?" he asked. "It's
my car," I said. "Who is it registered to?" "My husband," I said. "Oh
—and where is he?" He looked at me and at the can of beer and at
you and his expression implied all of the dirt and filth and ugliness
that is so profitably sold in books way back, miles away, in the heart
of Los Angeles. He leaned over and went through the pockets of your
jacket on which we had been sitting. "You shouldn't do that," I said
softly, testing my voice for blandness. He looked up at me. "I can do
anything I want," he said.

There were trees and rocks and water all around, and I could feel
myself being catapulted over the edge by the gentlest flick of his arm,
to be hauled up and off for resisting arrest with no witness to summon
but the still voice of the mountainside. "Mind if I search you?" he
said to you. "Go ahead," you answered, looking past him to the tumbling trickling water and the variegated pattern of the sunlight on the
ground. He thumped at you and looked in your pockets. You had car
keys and some money. "Where's the marijuana?" he asked. We
looked at him, neither startled, nor afraid, nor with any real emotion.
"You've smoked a lot I bet," he said to me, "how many times have
you smoked marijuana, come on, got high a lot, haven't you!" I did
not stop examining the surface of the rock to reply, there was such an
abyss between his movement and direction and the tranquil reflective
morning that had brought us up this path like children in a garden to
eat lunch and listen to the still sounds of the vegetable silence.

He left us then, saying, "Enjoy yourself." We silently gathered up
our things and went back to the car. He was waiting there looking in
the window, perhaps trying to read the copy of the *Free Press* that lay

on the floor behind the seat. "OK," he said to me, "OK, show me your I.D. now." I opened the trunk of the car to get it from my purse; he reached in and poked at the accumulation of paper and bits of camping equipment that was scattered inside. I showed him my temporary driver's license; I had gone for my renewal the week before and was still using the slip until the regular license came. "Your license has expired," he said to me. "I presume so," I said, "that's why I got a renewal." "Your license is expired," he said again, but neither he nor I could develop that reasoning beyond its implied threat. He gave me back my slip of paper and I shut the trunk. He walked to his black and white car. "Everything all right?" you called out to him. He turned around, he was smiling again, but a different thinner smile, a smile that stretched across his young even teeth. "This time," he said, "but next time?" . . .

October 14, 1966

Is Wampum Obsolete?

The serious conversation went on around me, tribes, caring, loving, being for each other. Leary, it was said, estimated forty as the maximum number. I was asked if I have a longing to belong. It confused me, caught between the realization that I have always thought of myself as belonging, and this specific question. Where would they all be, waiting to use the same toilet, as John suggests with more than wry humor, or in the kitchen, as my fantasy has it, all chopping each other's vegetables knee-deep in peels?

I tried once to form a craftsmen's cooperative after the last Renaissance Faire. I was sick of selling to the unloving public and coveted all sorts of hand-woven and love-assembled objects for which I did not have the money. I sent out notices and spread the word by mouth and fifty or so people came. We talked about sharing our abilities, eliminating the middle man, not putting comparative values on our products but freely exchanging them as the flowers of our hands and vision. We sat in a circle and told what we could do, or teach. There were potters and painters and welders and glass workers and weavers. There was also a sandal maker. Our enthusiasm continued until it turned out that everyone wanted sandals, but the sandalmaker could only use so many paintings in his life, and besides leather was expensive. It was a good party, though, with lots of addresses exchanged; the disillusionment was drowned in Red Mountain burgundy.

In London I once lived in a house with twelve other people, most of whom fought with each other in pairs behind locked doors. We shared one kitchen whose multitude of cupboards were allocated and locked so we couldn't steal each other's cornflakes. It worked in a way, though not a very pleasant one. Recently I shared a house with five other people. One girl made a large poster in big red and black lettering outlining everyone's domestic responsibilities; I moved out.

Still I believe in communal living, but I prefer it like seduction, where the goal is never too distinctly explained. I mean if you move in for a day, and stay a year because you like it there, and help each other out because you like each other, and when love goes you go too, it's OK. Restrictive, conceptualized, homogeneous, purposeful togetherness has never worked out well for me.

To me we are already a tribe of sorts—all of us with flowers in our hair or eyes, who read the same books and hate the same war, who buy the same records and dance to the same pounding tunes. But it's not just on Haight or Fairfax or East Seventh. It's in London and Amsterdam and Paris and Piraeus and anywhere; its tribal bond is common values, not geography.

There is something about the word "tribe" that worries me. For all the implications of love and togetherness, didn't the tribes war each with each? Were there not tribal rituals which constricted movement and spontaneity, and are not rituals just little fancy civil laws dressed out in poetry? Does not "tribe" also mean, "exclude"? Haven't I all my life sought to break out of the exclude hocus-pocus of my world, the economic tribe of neighborhood, the religious tribe of birth, the mental tribe of a too-structured political belief?

Some months ago I lent a dollar to a friend. Give it back, I said, when you can afford it. No, he said, but I'll pass it on to the next person who needs it. That's pretty much the way I feel and I don't care whether he's an Indian or not, but then, maybe we're all Indians anyway.

April 14, 1967

Say It with Flowers

We were in the midst of that kind of nondirectional movement which has its own momentum, which moves small tangles of people through cities consisting of apartments and hangouts. First we dropped one friend at a coffee house to make his connection, then the other friend at his office to pick up his check which, if it were there, would provide us all with a meal. We waited in a parking lot in front of a topless bar, where later, high up a pole, in a glass cage, a seemingly inexhaustible leggy girl in a silver bikini would dance in the brilliance of a searchlight to gyrate customers over the top of Broadway's hill and into the bar. We watched the remains of North Beach sift along the street, mad gay queens in tight pants following fancy dogs on leashes, a few older classic bohemians, and the sailors, who paused at every display of topless dancers and stared fixedly at the photographs. It was 5 P.M., too early for commercial sex, too late to save the day.

How young the sailors look. I remember looking at sailors on another Broadway, 3,000 miles away, during the war to "make the world safe for democracy." I would walk along with my father in the evening, watching the crowd pass, hungry for adulthood and the glamor of love with a uniform. My father was headed for the oyster bar on Forty-second Street, and I was headed nowhere, or so it seemed to me, thirteen years old, never been kissed, red raspberry Joan Crawford mouth, my absent mother's ocelot jacket, and an undefined wet longing. "Buy me a sailor, Daddy." I would say it as a joke, not being brave enough to say it as it was, the furtive looks at the small behinds in blue, the white hat whose trophy value was incalculable. All that summer girls on the beach wore sailors' hats with the brims turned down and names scrawled on the dirty white surface—Joey loves Agnes, I love Bill—they bobbed along with their badges of conquest. Now, so much later, the sailors are still on the streets, the world is not yet safe for anything, and the glamor is gone.

The street depressed me; I got impatient sitting in the car, waiting. Behind us was the generator truck used for the searchlight which would illuminate the almost plastic goddess who would dance in that square of glass above our head, and turning to look at the truck, I saw a man was painting it bright colors, but without much enthusiasm. "Go ask him if you can help," said Robert, who instigates most of the comedy of my life, and so I did. "Sure, man," he said, "but I've got to go now, here's the paint, the brushes are under the truck, just put them back when you've finished." We started painting. First I made a sort of Indian design and Robert made flowers, then I made flowers and Robert made dollar signs. I made lines, he made spots, then we wrote Peace, Love, and Flowers. How hopeful we are, writing Peace, writing Love, writing Flowers.

How hopeful we were two days later marching to Kezar Stadium to protest the war. How hopeful I have always been, how many marches. Marches against the Korean War, against the Taft Hartley law, against white supremacy, against, against, against. How we walk along, smiling at each other, repeating magic incantations, Lift the Embargo on Spain, Free the Scottsboro Boys, We Shall Overcome, Peace, now now now. The speeches sound the same, talking to ourselves over microphones, we will stand together, we will demand, we shall achieve.

After the march and the speeches, the cheer for God (cheer for God?), after the Cantata for Human Rights, a multivoiced orchestrated objectionable self-serious piece of old-fashioned music reminiscent of the Norman Corwin epics of that other war (other war?), after an hour of boredom on hard seats listening to rousing speeches directed at the already converted, after all that hodgepodge of a traditional liberal revival, we fled to the streets and saw with great relief the new world really happening, or somewhat happening. They do it with flowers and bells, with dancing in the street and free bananas, with smiles and Salvation Army velvet dresses. The shop windows were full of peace posters, and flowers, and signs in psychedelic obscure penmanship for dances, and triumph of triumphs, where there had been a window full of the junk of the great society, old toasters that no longer popped, goldplated tin magazine racks, pictures of dogs and sunsets, were cards of buttons saying, "LSD for LBJ" and "If It Moves Fondle It." True the toasters and bottles and pictures were still there, pushed to the back of the shop, but they were, in a way, one step nearer to oblivion.

I wonder if I will continue to march, to listen to speeches, to be neat and tidy in my protest and have my numbers diminished by a press who should know better, or will I take to dancing in the street and try to say it with flowers?

April 21, 1967

Smoke from a Plastic Teepee

So we drop out, split, take off, go in. Some, like the kid on the road, to join the Indians. "Which Indians?" I ask. "The Jewish Indians," he answers, saying, "you see man, I'm Jewish and I want to be an Indian, so I'm going to Boulder, Colorado, to join the Jewish Indians." And the Indians, sitting in front of their television sets, what do they think of these anxious and bearded strangers who rush across their dusty village squares calling—Brother, I am come.

There they are, the Indians in stretch Levis and nylon shirts computing cattle sales and hoping for something better, and a long-haired pale-faced boy from Brooklyn rushes up. "I too am dispossessed," he says. "Yeah," says the Indian, wondering if this is some new VISTA tactic to make him part of the middle class. "Yeah, but can you tango?" or he might as well say that for all they have in common. "But you're an Indian, man," the kid says, "you're a tribe, you know where it's at." "Well, it sure ain't here," the Indian says, pointing to the rusty Ford in his yard, the broken fridge on the porch. "Why don't you go back where you come from?"

I mean, to the Indian today, today's Indian, it must seem as absurd as the white jazz player seemed to the Negro. You can't jump someone else's culture, shoot a little ethnic juice into your tired veins, because this is the twentieth century and you have to deal with it like it is. Tribes? OK, where, and whose land are you going to live off anyway?

It's a kind of cultural suicide, though not profitless. The chain shoe stores are selling Teepee Creepers, those little doeskin (dough skin $ skin) moccasins that the kids wore on the Strip last year. You can buy various "revolutionary" buttons, if not made in Japan, then in Hoboken, New Jersey, and at about the same places that used to sell the ones that said, "Kiss Me Quick?" Join the Underground . . . oh yeah!

An underground is underground, is opposed, is active, is rethinking, is searching, is doing against the sucking emasculature of the prevalent society. It isn't dripping with blue ink on the cover of *Life* magazine, charging three dollars to dance at the end of the garbage of Venice. What is more "in" than psychedelic? The Reno Atmospherium (run by a really drab university with lots of "Keep Off the Grass" signs on the only bit of lawn for miles around) is putting on a show called Psychedelia. It is no more connected to the psychedelic experience than the earrings sold at Woolworth's as Mind Blowers. What is it? It is commercial instant super profitable "sub-culture," that's what it is, and if it sells?

We've been had, let's face it, we've been diluted, absorbed on a superficial level, leveled and made superficial. Our explorations of our inner space are the subject matter of the come-on lead articles of the San Francisco *Chronicle*. If someone smokes banana peels on Haight Street, you can hear a joke about it on the Dick Van Dyke show the next week, and for the next recipe, consult *Time* magazine, and you know the kind of world they want to give you, or you did, didn't you?

Well, the Wizard has found his coven on commercial radio, roach clips support much of California's smaller enterprises, Allen Ginsberg in paper top hat will next appear on paper party napkins to be given a big build up in advertising. Want to show the neighbors how in you are, then give a way out party, Trip Special—the latest thing for bon voyage entertaining, Allen Ginsberg Psychedelic Paper Party Mates, come in six delicious colors, Burroughs' Bile Blue, Fugs Fuchsia, Underground Umber, Karma Kiss Pink, Tarot Tangerine, Lysergic Lime . . . and so on.

Someone has got their hand in our soul pockets, beware! In the effort to give America back to the Indians, we may be helping to give the Indians back to America, and you know where we are at, baby, Psychedelia!

May 5, 1967

Round Trip

The army caravan moved viscously along the road opposite us, separated from us by the brown grass of the divider, the black marks of tire screechings, the caution signs. Every two miles or so, another lump of the army appeared, its headlights shining in the afternoon light, sour-looking color, vehicles and men, dust- and canvas-colored trailers, slowly up the road toward where we had just been, up from the coastal cool, to the hot inside sun of the dry middle of the southern part of this state. I think they must have been going to Camp Roberts where, before, the barracks had always looked deserted, ready to become some kind of camp for-what? But today when we drove past, on our way home from the fragrance of the redwoods of Ben Lomond and Bonnie Doon, we had seen activity in the compound, little toy figures past the wire, all in drab, against the drab of the buildings and the drab of the heat, moving between the barracks, slowly in and out. Now we saw more of them, all the way home we saw them, jeeps and trailers, trucks and cars, passing with their lights on like omnivorous beetles afraid of the day.

So many versions of the War. The army moving, the other army, the ones with bells, also moving. We drove up to Mendocino and Lagunitas looking for a farmhouse. Stopped along the way to ask in grocery shops, standing there being customers drinking chocolate milk, patting our hair down, trying to look suitable for the area, indistinguishable. Nothing around here for rent, the people said. The real estate people glared, don't bother to look around here. (The first time I asked I had a bell on my shoulderbag that blinked sound as I walked. I left it in the car the next time.) Houses for rent? Do chicken have teeth? He laughed and, turning to his companion behind the bar, laughed again. Well, the San Francisco *Chronicle* is read in the mountains, we forgot, and the *Chronicle* tells all about the dopefiendhippiefreelovefreakdropouts every day, and warnings: "Hippies Arming." (Say Frank, see here it says "Hippies Arming," better go out and get a knife, gun, poison dart, it's the thing to do.) Or—the editor was sitting in his booth one day and a man from the U-Needa Knife Company came in, hot news for you, Mr. Editor, he said, the hippies are arming (this was his fantasy of sales chart upswings). Oh, says the editor, THAT's a story. I made all that up in my head as I saw the faces in the country around Mendocino and Lagunitas, but they are worried up there, for the Haight-Ashbury dam is bust and the hippies are spilling out all over the countryside.

I can't remember anyone wanting country fifteen years ago; it was a whiskey culture then, and whiskey is a bar culture and the permanent evening of bars and the limbo time of bars and all those black clothes of the existentialists would have looked pretty unpretty out on the farm. Now it's a grass culture.

Stopped by at a community that had a large sign by the road in multipurpose psychedelic/color/style with the word "OM" in the middle. Stopped at the visitor's parking lot. A man in sheep's clothing, furside to his skin, came at us out of the bushes with a small smile. Hello, hello, can I help you, yes, just a looking for a home, full up here, people sent us, yeah, who? People up the road at 1000, oh, well, come on down and look around, if you want to, if you want to. We went down, past a pen full of puppies toward the sound of a band rehearsing in a large wooden house. The man split, we stood, up to our indecision in weeds. Another man, wearing a toy badge—help you? The other man said we could look around, OK, look around. So, what do you look at, the people? Can't go up and look at people. Could see cabins in the trees, God's eyes on branches, hear bells. Can't go and look in windows. Scuffled dirt, stood, waited. Nothing to wait for, how do you visit a community when you don't know anyone? So we left, the puppies barking at us as we went back up the hill.

We had driven down to Santa Cruz along the Cabrillo Highway, neat thin quick road from the desolation of Point Lobos style gaiety. Fog, drifting across the road, wind, bending acres of trees toward the mountains, trees looking like people with hair blowing in the wind. But there was no wind then, just fog and the marks of wind on the trees. Artichokes and cabbage, maybe, or some other kind of munchy dark green-leafed vegetable in plots along the road, farmhouses bleached by the fog, soft silvery wood buildings in the midst, bits of Victorian dado work sagging off the porches, stables and barns, rolling ground and fog. Plenty of room there if you want to live in that gray Kleenex climate.

While we were in San Francisco we drove along Haight Street. It has become a story in serial form for me, first visit: love, flowers, what's underneath to hold it together? (But perhaps I am cynical, over thirty-five.) Second visit: the shops all going curlicue and poster, the pavement parade of costume, the sitting on the curb, the flutes in the street thing, nice, almost nice. Third visit: rumors of gangbang activities on little girls pumped full of dope, strangers in the street staring, still some bells, LSD hamburgers, the rot setting in. This last visit: talk about Superspade who was found in a bag, about the man whose arm was taken for a souvenir (hung from the dashboard mirror?), talk that it's the Mafia moving in, lots of kids pan-handling on the street, gimmie a quarter, looking like the Bowery gone psychedelic, derelict kids with no new place to go having joined the expected influx on the advice of the media, Haight is where it's at this summer, it isn't, not that way.

We are back in Santa Barbara now, reading letters from people who answered our cry for help, going to look for a home, somewhere where it's not happening, sort of guerrilla tactic for a better world, take to the hills, especially the ones NBC doesn't have on the map yet.

August 18, 1967

In the Guru-oove

In 1948 the conversation was cars. It was new chrome jobs and piston rings, special camshafts and tachometers on the walnut pan-eled dashboard. It was channeling, chopping, lowering, raking; it was bore and stroke, transmission ratio and special fuel. It was twelve coats of lacquer and pin-striping by Von Dutch. It was street slicks and quick stops, away at the light and who's-chicken-off the cliff, and most of all it was a man someone knew who could fix anything.

In 1958 the conversation was Hi-Fi. It was woofer and tweeter and input. It was components and hook-ups, amps and ohms. It was spe-cial assemblages and a hand-rubbed Philippine mahogany cabinet. It was a Garrard turntable and a pair of Altec speakers in just the right corners of the room. It was a Fisher amplifier, acoustical paneling, di-amond needles, and most of all, it was a man someone knew who had the parts to fix anything.

In 1968 the conversation is all Karma. It's who's got it smoother, who's got the purer sound of bliss. It's whose soul is best tuned up and whose mind is in harmony. It's heaven-on-earth in low gear and a resonance in the heart. It's shifting to a higher plane and play-it-again-Sam with the mantra. It's beads, Khurtas, and Indian accesso-ries suitable for the cosmic trip, it's a roomful of incense for just the right sound to your inner peace. And most of all, it's a man someone knows who can choose a mantra to fix any soul.

If the cars paralleled the new technology of speed, airplanes and rockets thrusting miles into oblivion, and Hi-Fi was the reflection of the micro-technology of TV tubes, radar sets, and all the mysterious electronic devices of James Bond and Cape Kennedy, then the Guru-oove we are now in must reflect something. Despair, perhaps, withdrawal from the race of engines and turntables, from the sonic boom and the strontium bomb. It's into the tomb womb of it's not happening to us on the skin side outside, or if it is, it doesn't count because where it's at, is in. It's hard to tell history while it's happening, no one in a riot sees anything but the man chasing him and the distance before him to safety. So there is mystery in the day to day combat with Now; but there are also parallels that are striking, for the chatter is reminiscent and the sound is the same. It's a smoother running engine, turntable or soul, and we all have our favorite brand-name.

Hare Krishna, Krishnamurti, Meher Baba, Maharishi, Parmahansa Yogananda, Satchidananda: it's just a list of current available parts; and someone is sure to know a man who can get it for you whole soul.

May 10, 1968

Hark Hark!

Good morning, mother.
Good morning, son.
What's for breakfast?
Puffa Puffa Rice.
But I don't like Puffa Puffa Rice.
Listen son, eat it, don't you want to grow up to be a big strong man like your father?
Yes mother, I do, I want to grow up to be a policeman.
Now you listen to me, no son of mine is going to walk around in drag; you just eat your cereal, and I'll worry about what you're going to be when you grow up.
Here cum de nark in special-issue clothing, six months out of style, still clutching flowers, wearing police-issue Mexican serape and short hair. At the Faire the narks rode horses and wore cowboy boots, or

strolled in pairs dragging their Indian bedspread costumes through the dust almost hiding their plastic go-aheads. The nark, the nark, the Southern California vulture, hark hark the nark is on the wing and we are keeping cool.

The rent-a-hoods (guards hired by the Faire wearing yellow Robin Hood hats) got into the spirit of the uniform. They barked at us, very un-renaissance: "Where's your pass, show me your pass!" Not one of them said, "Prithee sire, may we please see your pass," or other pleasantries. The parking lot attendants were lethal in their day-glo vests. There is, as the saying goes, something about clothes that make the Man.

Underground movie-script: the police are patrolling the Strip dressed as "hippies," ankh, bell and long wig, or as "fags," leather, chain, and tight crotch pants. (How do they choose assignments?) The hippies are dressed as policemen; they wear helmets and clubs and badges. They rush the police and beat on their wigs or choke them with their thonged ankhs. Channel Two is there, confused. The sports announcer is the reporter. In Grand Rapids, Michigan, people, looking at their TV sets, over TV dinners, watch the bust and curse the "hippies." End of film.

You get so you can drive the car very efficiently with one eye looking out the front window and one through the rear-view mirror. It's double distance and hindsight and here cum de nark all over town.

The police in San Francisco walk the beat and therefore are able to relate (in some degree) to the inhabitants. In England, they don't carry guns, in France they wear magicians' capes, but in political/economic action, they are all brutal. Police serve and protect. What/who do they serve and protect?

There is a movement to withhold that portion of the income tax that goes toward the war effort. What about the local tax that goes toward the local war effort? For no one I know thinks the police serve and protect them. At Love-Ins the police serve and protect the city fathers from the city children. On the Strip they serve and protect the real estate at the expense of those in a state of reality. They are not very efficient at recovering stolen property, but this protects the merchants' sales. They are very efficient at serving parking tickets; this protects their bank balance. The kids don't contribute to the economy, neither does peace, it's all quite simple, very disgusting, and commonly accepted.

It is wrong for us to accept harassment, for this city to be dangerous to nonconformists, for us to think this brutality is the natural order. We should think about it every day, because it creeps up on us bit by bit. It is a disaster that the best flowering and fruitful and peaceful minds are forced to flee to Canada, so as not to kill in an insane non-war, and just as devastating to our society that good people must withdraw from civic involvement. We are living like a walled city within a city; it is schizoid and exhausting.

I love America, I don't want all the good and righteous people to withdraw, to have to live like aliens in their own land. I want an America enriched with the products of the minds and hands of honest people, or, is there no America anymore, but just an occupied territory with its best citizens living like expatriates in their own hometown. Maybe the idea of a nation is obsolete, and there is only a quantity of like people, scattered geographically, forming their own nationality of man.

May 24, 1968

Going Straight

They were on their way to Mexico. Nowhere specific, "near the bottom, down where the hippies don't hang out, with lots of ruins to explore, and quiet, I want to finish my book," he said, "and Judy is on a grant, hey, you people have got to come visit us, we are going to have three bedrooms and a horse, two horses and a boat maybe and . . ." But they hadn't been able to get their tourist visa in San Francisco. Tom was worried; he twisted the curling ends of his strawberry hair around his fingers. "They told us to get the visa at the border." "Other people got their visas," Judy said. "It's your hair," I said, "your long hair, Mexico wouldn't let you in, neither will Disneyland." "Yeah," he said. "I know," she said. We sat silently over our food.

We were stringing beads and playing records while they told us about things in San Francisco. They had driven down earlier in the day in their white ambulance, packed with clothing and papers, a typewriter and beads and posters and just junk, of the kind that goes along unnoticed until it has to be packed, and then is too precious to be thrown/given away. "I'm going to cut the fucking stuff off," he said, "that's the answer." We agreed, after all, it was really only a kind of third-stage ploy, putting one over on the Mexican government, making them feel safe on the scalp front. If you looked at it that way, it wasn't so bad, was it? Judy got the scissors and a towel, and I watched. She snipped a little off the front. Tom was silent. She snipped a little more, going gingerly in the direction of an up-to-now-hidden ear. "I'm going to save it," she said, looking at the pile of hair on the table, "and paste it on a portrait of you." She continued to cut, Tom focused on nothing, I watched. It didn't look so bad.

"It was raining when we went to the consulate in San Francisco," Judy said, "and we didn't have umbrellas, so we stood there dripping, and they ignored us and finally some man who was just sitting at a desk doing nothing came up and asked what we wanted and we told him we wanted a tourist visa. He asked us for proof of money, so I showed him my gold seal letter from the Boston Museum Art School, but he said it was no good because it was dated 1967. I explained it took time to get here from Boston, and that the letter was still good, and that it showed I would have money for a year, but he wouldn't listen. Finally Tom asked him if he cut his hair off would it be OK with Mexico. He said, sort of offhandishly, it would be easier, but that we should get an updated letter, and anyway the rules had been changed and we should apply at the border. All the while the people next to us were getting visas and stuff with no trouble."

Tom was shorn; he looked healthy and short haired. "It's a trip," he said, looking in the mirror, "it's a whole new thing." He made serious faces at himself in the glass, turned a little, trying to see himself sideways; he smiled at himself. We went into the other room to watch the news, but not Judy, she disappeared. "Where's Judy?" I asked. But he didn't answer; he was discussing basketball with Robert, who is a compulsive fan, glued mind and soul to the net and the ball.

"I was in the other room, crying," she said the next morning on our way down to the Mexican Consulate in Los Angeles. "I couldn't help it, I loved his hair, he liked it, I felt so awful, cutting it was all right, but afterward, I just started to cry."

In the consulate everyone called Tom "sir." He was wearing Robert's jacket and a Swiss Red Cross in the lapel, and Robert's tie, and his white shirt and had on his one pair of old but "real" shoes, and, of course, new short hair. No one asked to see Judy's gold seal letter; they were so happy to have them visit, six months? With pleasure!

When we left the consulate we stopped at the Bank of America to cash Tom's tax refund. "May I see your identification, sir?" the manager asked, then looking at the passport picture of Tom taken two years before when he was working for the Post Office, said, "Nice picture, looks just like you, sir." And it did.

We came back, Tom took off the polite clothes with the Swiss Red Cross pin, Judy made some supper, and we sat down to get stoned. Mexico was just a day away, and they were going straight there.

March, 1968

Social Notes from All Over

Owen and Jill are going to get married in Muir Woods, Paul told us. We decided to drive up to the wedding together. We picked Paul up in Santa Monica early on a Thursday morning, started up the coast, got as far as Malibu when we had to stop for food. Paul was a mouth-traveler, so we ate all the way up. The car carpet crunched under foot with cherry pits and potato chips; crumbs from McDonald's hamburgers slimed the dashboard; we had three flavors of yogurt and two of diet pills; Hostess Suzy Q's which are my best thing (all smooth and white and creamy in the middle) melted in their wrappers; and a collection of empty soda cans rattled on the back seat. Paul shared his pastrami sandwiches with us (his mother had sent them to him for the trip), and Robert ate a whole container of beef dip even though he said it was lousy. We stopped to get food so often that it was late afternoon when we reached the coast highway.

Hearst Castle looked pale and remote as we drove past in the evening mist, just visible on its hill, lonely and ridiculous. Paul kept saying that we were coming to the place that was the lowest place on earth that pine trees grew, but all I could see was the hillside to my right and the sea on my left, way below us, cool and moving in the shaded light. Robert stopped the car where there was drinking water and a trash can. We got out to stretch and drink. This is it, Paul said, this is the spot! We heard a loud meoooooow. It's a wildcat, Robert said and dropped to one knee reaching for his holster, his trusty Buick by his side. Here pussypussypussy, I said. A gigantic black and white cat, his green eyes ablaze with love and purring furiously, leaped at us from the lowest pine tree in the world (which was about 40 feet tall). Since there weren't any visible means of support around, no cars/trailers/tents/houses people, we took him with us. He curled up on the backseat between the soda cans and went to sleep.

We stopped for coffee in Big Sur at a café that had a sign on the door: NO LONGHAIR HIPPIES. We went inside, broke up a few tables and chairs, and while Paul set fire to the cash register, I used the diversion to grab some American flags (that were sticking out of plastic vases) which I thought would make nice souvenirs. We left as the smoke began to blot out the sunset, drove off to Carmel Valley under a cloak of darkness. It was night, but there were lights on at Ccctmczk's home. They were glad to see us, C was in San Francisco, so we visited with Ccctmczk. They put on costumes and sang for us and we lay around there for two days talking. In the middle of the second night, C came home with a funny man in checkered trousers, who had a new San Francisco drug called H.O.G. and told us wondrous stories about the recording industry.

Left for San Francisco Saturday morning, driving up the starkly beautiful coast road from Santa Cruz. Stopped at the amusement zone on the Great Highway to have our pictures taken (same machine we had used for our wedding photos a year before). I played pitch penny and won a cardboard eyepatch that didn't fit and a harmonica that didn't work.

The apartment in San Francisco was full of people come for the wedding. We introduced the cat and sat around for hours, then went to eat noodles in a thin three-story restaurant in Chinatown, where the food comes up from the kitchen in dumbwaiters and the proprietor shouts continually. We had cappuccino in North Beach and looked at the photos of topless dancers; they had silver stars pasted on their nipples. We went back to the apartment; Big Sur had crapped in the bathtub right over the drain hole, everyone admired his cool.

People arrived all night (the wedding was scheduled for 8 A.M. the next morning). The groom showed us his green brocade jacket, bought at San Francisco's leading fag shop; we showed our wedding clothes, designed by Felicia Michel, made out of Union Jacks and red cloth. Robert's shirt had stars all over the front and red sleeves. My gown was full-length, low-cut stars with a red apron. I fell asleep on the floor. Five A.M., we put on our Betsy Ross and Dave got into an orange nylon jumpsuit, an orange straw waste basket on his head, a belt of bells, and flowers sticking out of all the zipper pockets. He stuffed a pillow in the suit to fill it out. Beverly wore my lace table-cloth dress and red stockings, the stockbroker friend wore a suit, so did his wife, the groom was still in green brocade, two girls were in see-through minis, and Dennis wore his best War Surplus. We were in the street sorting ourselves into cars when the police drove by; they didn't even slow down (San Francisco!).

Muir Woods at 7 A.M. The bride was in the parking lot making garlands out of various leaves and flowers. She wore a dark-brown Chinese dress. Her mother was there in suit and gloves and hat, her uncle, the minister (wearing a black gown), and his four kids and wife were there. We had to climb over a chain, as the park hadn't opened yet. I walked with the bride's mother who was very polite and said it was nice to see so many different kinds of clothing. I agreed. It was still half-dark, greeny black trees, filters of light like veiling fell on the path; we walked silently to the circle of trees called Cathedral Grove, for the ceremony.

During the wedding, while the uncle-minister made a long speech about God and how marriage was a series of forgivings, Dave, his bells ringing, took pictures of the couple, while Robert, dazzling in red, white, and blue, took pictures of Dave's orange jumpsuit, and Mike took pictures of Robert's patriotic shirt. The park ranger stood behind me looking puzzled, so I gave him a reassuring smile. When the ceremony was over he whispered to me that the garland with the big rose (worn by one of the men) was made of poison oak.

The wedding breakfast of champagne and Eggs Benedict was at the Alta Mira Hotel in Sausalito, a dignified place overlooking the bay. The parking attendant was wearing a Kennedy button. I asked him if it was the official endorsement of the hotel. No, he said, it just represented the kitchen staff and the parking lot boys. The people at the hotel were amazed by our clothes but very polite. After the food the bride and groom and some of the guests went to Muir Beach to hear a rock band. Robert and I went back to the apartment to sleep and feed the cat.

June 14, 1968

Holding Time

He lifts his arms up above his head and holds it there for a moment. He is wearing one of those nubby not quite white, creamy colored bouclé knit men's shirts that come from Italy, originally, and are now in the Akron with suspiciously Oriental-looking labels. His mouth is slightly open, not really open in a droolish, like village idiot, open or asthmatic open or even astonishment open, just tender open, tender everything. Eyes squidged shut, letting in a little glow light, a slit of light, but not enough to see his partner's face clearly, just this haze slit of soft glow psychedelic strobed light. Down comes the arm, stillness, though the music plays on, still but stiffly still, poised for the next flutter of fingers, or knee twitch, palms clacking together, head shaking suddenly, hair, soft longish golden hair twirling about his head, he is singing with the band, or almost, his lovely lips mouth the words, almost, almost knows all the words, he moves, a star, he is a rock'n'roll star below the stage, on the little floor, dancing, at the Whisk a Go Go. But he has troubles, terrible troubles, because his dance, all thirty-seven of its calculated movements, goes smoothly with four/four, goes divinely with four/four, only this band is playing nine/four, whatever that is, whatever the steps are supposed to be, no one had told him. Paralysis!

The street seems strange at night, all those people hanging around outside the door, just leaning into space, blank-faced, waiting for, waiting. It's a style, waiting, like coolness, the waiting, spun out on nothing at all but the anticipation of apparently lots more of nothing at all until, the amazing moment when something incredibly meaningful, something significant, a turning point, Absolute, like Leary was, and Acid, like Acid, a big thing, like Peace might have been if it had fallen from the sky two years ago to land, like the chutists at a Love-In, in a nest of flowers and hair. Something like that, something. It's not boredom; it goes beyond boredom; boredom is tired of, fed up with, dragged by, turned off of; this isn't that, not positive, not ennui, not lassitude, not surfeiture, it's not that. It's holding time. Like holding dope. Hanging on, for who knows when the earthquake and the California slide into the sea and the fissure might begin, right there, right near that curb maybe, slender at first, a trembling of the cement, a virgin rending of the concrete, and then, Boom Bang Slither and Slish, all watery grave, all over, no more time. NO TIME LEFT.

So there's a thing to time, to hanging onto nothingness, to filling up with waiting, to eyeing the scene like some immortal engraver who will rend his images of How It Was for Who Survives, maybe on stone or in sand or with smoke against the ashy sky, dressed in skins, furs and skins, with just a touch of rescued silk around the neck perhaps, and a pair of those soft leather boots with little hidden brass zippers, oh those boots are so gorgeous, little heels that raise your ass up, up just a little bit, tighten the thigh muscle, sexy, s-e-x-y, just right for the apocalypse, and they all have them on.

Bang, Boom, Miss Cass Elliot sings about the earthquake on the Smothers Brothers Show, but what, them worry? No, they sign *Hair* for a year where Kaleidoscopes and Queens for a Day and Hullaba-loos used to set the trend, and if the Wizard knows, he isn't telling and if they know they aren't saying, but waiting, on that corner, where the glamorous people go by, because if we have to go, let's all go together.

October 18, 1968

Bullshit Revolution

The Bullshit Revolution is on every channel, tune in, drop one, and let them take you over.

I know a group of people who are by their own evaluation, Drop Outs. Here is what they do. They run about avoiding warrants for traffic violations; they never have money for their rent, are always moving, leaving letters that cannot be forwarded, phone bills unpaid, pregnant girls, piles of dirty laundry, and boxes of junk which they ask you to keep until they get settled. They take a lot of uppers and let their lips flap blabitty blabitty, or they slouch around in a stuporous dope charm mixed with animosity and grins. They travel a lot in a limited circle and fall in love weekly, they let their hair grow and chop it off, they hardly read anything but sometimes go to movies or rock concerts where they sweat a lot and look at the teenyboppers. They come from upper-middle-class homes and had good minds which occasionally surface; they all have old rotten cars and a lot of anxiety.

Well, what have they dropped out of? Nothing. Everything they do is in opposition to the system, which means that they are captives of the system; they are about as free as prisoners who rattle their bars and write slogans on cell walls. Their whole time is spent in avoidance of things, landlords, cops, tax men, bills, warrants, girls who love them, anything, anything which would make them pause for a moment and evaluate their position. I'm not going to take a fucking job in a fucking office, they say, crumbling about in their despair, but what are they going to do? They crash their cars and burn their sleeves and look for dope and swallow any pill you leave around and vanish for weeks and reappear, as dreary and captive as ever. What is the answer? I don't know, except that there is something more to life than just saying no.

If you want out of a repressive system, you have to pay a price, and one part of that price is to play it cool. If you refuse their dance, you better get out of their dance hall, or at least hide behind the curtains, because you don't survive long without cover. Castro didn't advertise his headquarters with banners. If we are the dropouts, the underground, or the revolutionaries, we should examine our methods. Just how underground are we anyway? Look at us, we are fully visible, full of success, our leaders famous and published and photographed in funny funk clothing for the amusement of the great omnivorous masses (you've seen Krassner's rat nest in *Life* and Abby Hoffman on TV in baby battle dress). Our styles are big business, our slogans sell cosmetics, our newspapers carry huge amounts of establishment advertising (LA's KMET "underground" radio station advertises Cadillacs to the tune of Canned Heat's "On The Road Again"), our movies are shown in theaters that charge three dollars to let us see films about revolution, we buy psychedelic clothes from department store quick-quack fad boutiques and decorate our cars with expensive manufactured paste-ons.

We are bullshit revolutionaries, that's what we are. We do our fighting in front of TV cameras; what kind of security is that for a revolutionary, your face on every channel? Look at the Panthers, in case no one would recognize them they wear a uniform! Bullshit, they are walking targets for every cop and rival Black Power gang that covets their fame! "They" are helping Us Kill Ourselves off! Who is going to be safe when every dumb fuck tells anyone who will listen that he has a houseful of guns? What kind of revolutionaries are we when we defeat ourselves by stupid disorganized demonstrations in the face of highly organized troops with mace and clubs and guns? We cry about our mutilated forces but do nothing to protect ourselves, that's not how you take over! Suppose they decide to fill those concentration camps? Who will be left outside, who is working quietly, steadily and organizedly? Look what has happened to the Black leadership: jail, exile, murdered, is that a way to protect leaders?

I haven't gotten away from the point I started with, those friends of mine who "dropped out" are on the same sinking ship, doing the same public half-assed gestures of defiance. They are as uncool and self-victimizing as everyone else. It's advertising that has captured us, advertised revolution, advertised drop-outism. It is the Guise that has fucked us up, the Great American Guise that starts out with MY COUNTRY TIS OF THEE SWEET LAND OF LIBERTY and continues with dyes to make gray hair black and creams to make old skin young and names cars Mustang and Cheetah and crummy blocks of apartments Châteaux and last year put beads and peace ankhs on every instant hippie and this year will sell a billion Western style shirts, that last year sold acid and this year sells THC and feeds you the latest political slogan with the seven o'clock news . . . Hi there folks, tired of the same old We Shall Overcome? Try our bright new Free Huey or Black Power or Pigs Pigs Pigs.

What is the answer? Voltaire suggested that we should cultivate our own garden. It's too late for that, we don't own our gardens anymore, the bank does, and wants cash, and we are told by the latest electronic age sage that it's all one Global Village anyway, so what now? Thinking might help, thinking instead of gobbling up everything that is spewed at us, the Muzak of our times is what's killing us. For most people Vietnam is geographically on the front page of the newspaper or TV set, so what's real? Biafra was last month, so what's new? Everything is dished out, it's one glorious twenty-four-hour show, even the revolutions are sponsored, specials on revolution courtesy of your friendly computer monopoly, and on to detergents and here come de Beatles and here come de news and here come de late night war movie (or is that still the news?).

So my friends drop pills and years like there is nothing out there, drop their own minds like used Kleenex, drop anything that might make them pause and think. Maybe I'm left over from another age, maybe this is the way it's going to be from now on, just a porridge of bodies and slogans and bombs. And when you read this, if you read this, if you haven't turned to the classified for your dose of sexual feelings and the front page for news of this week's voluntary victims to give you your little thrill of paper anarchy, and turned on the TV, and smoked another cigarette to keep your hands busy, what will you do? What will any of us do?

February 7, 1969

Dead Daisy

Talking about the old times, where did they go? She had been in the Haight in '67 or at least it seemed to her now that it was '67 but, as she said, "all that time fused out of accounting" so that it was hard now to remember the exact times. She had been there about two and a half months, something like that, and she had arrived from New York with a hundred dollars. "I spent the hundred the first week and after that," she said, smiling shyly, "it was all ecstasy." Now she was traveling by car for a month across the states with her husband; they had sleeping bags and a tent and a dog with them.

Had she learned any particular thing when she was in the Haight? "Yes," she said, "I learned that I didn't want to live on the streets and I learned that I didn't want to be poor and I learned that it is necessary to love people." They had been picking up hitchhikers on their way across the country, "they all talked to us about politics, only there is so much hate in it, all those SDS people and the other kids talking about killing the pigs. It's funny," she added, not smiling though, "it's funny that I can't talk to a nineteen-year-old, I mean I'm only twenty-one but I just can't understand them."

The changes from love to hate, from the soft sound to the hard sound, from acoustical guitars to amplifiers, from firebombs, from Love Brother to Up Against The Wall Mother Fucker. "What happened?" she asked, but we had no answers. We talked experimentally about the Mafia and about how the life-style had turned profitable. I told them about the store in Century City (funny—I always think of that as the name of a battleground). I had gone into this dress shop and inside it was freaky everywhere. Mirrors and silver shining areas and sales people with long hair and the clothes were all "groovy," fancy with gimmicks in imitation of our spontaneous fantasy of dress. The place was loud with earblast rock and I stood there feeling paranoid watching the rich kids from Brentwood and Beverly Hills buy "our" clothes for $40 a dress. I got out of there fast. But, I added, that wasn't what had happened to it either, I mean true they took our guise of love and made it something pornographic, but that wasn't what had done it; it just didn't have a chance from the beginning because it was unrealistic, there wasn't the supportive structure.

Lovely girl, she was so open faced, long hair, and no makeup and a round still young girl plump body easy in its movements. Her husband had a seriousness that smiled, a droopy mustache; he taught elementary school in a Brooklyn ghetto area. "Lots of young people are becoming teachers now," he said. We sat there, refugees from our various dreams, trying to understand the now/future. "I guess," he said, "most people have decided to draw into themselves, that's what seems to be the answer now, just to do your own thing by yourself." We didn't comment on that, I suppose because we were all thinking that it was a saddening conclusion to what had started out as a movement of universal family.

Earlier in the day I had seen a girl on the six o'clock news; she was speaking before a Senate investigating committee on drugs. She said how they had health classes in her school and how everyone went to them, and most other classes, stoned. She said she used to sit there stoned and listen to the lectures on drugs and think that it was all a bunch of, and she paused a moment remembering her environment, and then giggling said, "all a bunch of nothing. What I want to know," she asked, "is that they tell you that drugs are bad for your body but we know that, we take drugs to make us FEEL good and so if we stop what are the alternatives, I mean what can we do to make us feel good inside?" She was a senior in high school.

There is no grass around now; what are the kids doing I ask people. It's pills now, and smack, pills, speed, downers, anything they can get. In New York I hear there is hardly anything around but heroin so they are using that. Well, Senators, the government is doing something about drugs; they are turning a nation of benign grass dopers onto hard drugs, bully for America.

Another question is what's happening when a high school girl has to ask what she can do to feel good inside if she doesn't smoke dope. It seems to me that sixteen or seventeen should be a time of sprung leaf fresh blooming discovery of the joys of self, freed of the tyranny of childhood, newly on dancing feet, everything possible. Or is it an age when nothing is possible, when the future is the draft, the indefensible war, and no national morality that makes any ethical sense and everybody is wired to the great computer. Maybe nothing is possible, is that what it is like now?

So we were talking about old times, old times, three years ago, or is it that three years is now a generation ago? It is truly a day in the life of . . .

August 29, 1969

Mansonalia

And so perhaps this marks the end of an era. The gravestone—a face straight from central casting, long hair, wild hypnotically staring eyes, the king of "love" called Jesus and Satan and God. And what can we say, we look at that picture, we read the pathetic details of the murder, the senseless, useless, misdirected antagonism toward a world that they know, somehow, has cheated them of reason. Or My Lai, and *Life* magazine with pictures of the dead and the about to die, the eyes again, terror, despair, I want to cry.

What we started out to do and what has happened are connected by the distortion of our times. The war that should never have been, the murders that should never have happened. Pointless, both clothed in jargon. The essential pain is that we are encouraged to accept that individual life is dispensable, destruction of flesh a way of change. The trees defoliated, the land poisoned, bodies torn by metal; the times are, if viewed with some perspective, indicative of the end of men.

We are so small, feel so unable to make our voices heard, so alone in the crowd and even the crowd is ignored. What matter that the young people who may have killed in Hollywood spoke of love, freedom, doing their thing, or that the soldiers who may have slaughtered in Vietnam say they were following orders, they were all following orders, following a madman or an army officer, what difference?

I am sick, made sick, sickened, nauseated, helpless, and almost without hope. Yesterday while shopping for a gift I glanced at the bare arm of the saleslady who was wrapping it for me. On her arm was a tattooed number. I am sick, we are all sick.

Yet sick means not in normal health, and when a nation is not in normal health it is sick, or is sickness its normality, as cancer could be said to be healthily malignant? Death and despair. The sun, which hangs there, faded behind the polluted sky, is still warm, and the tides keep to their basin for the most part, and children laugh and paintings are beautiful and love is warming and . . .

I wanted to save the photograph of the man allegedly the master mind of the killings, to hang it on my wall, it was so exaggerated. What did I find in that photograph, that grotesque conclusion to our voyage of discovery? Our voyage? No, not our voyage, but the merchandised voyage, the voyage made popular by the misinterpretations of the press, TV, the magazines. It bears as little resemblance to our initial purpose as our being in Vietnam has to our claims of making the world safe for democracy.

And so, it must be the end of an era. For the outward semblance of our life-style is the same outward semblance worn by those who slaughtered. Our language is the same language they use as their rationale. The power of the flower has turned into a funeral wreath. We are sick as a nation, and the sickness is contagious and I am tired and want to stay at home with the doors and windows closed and I don't want to hear any more death, and that in itself is sickness.

December 12, 1969

Crumpled Maps

Stranded among a pile of paper cups, torn newspapers, crumbled hamburger wrappings red with the blood of catsup, the beautiful kids sit on the sidewalk at Telegraph next to the Bakta Vedanta chanters isolated on a Persian carpet. The street is a mass of hassled bodies selling dope in the open; first I saw the baggie and then the dope in an open hand. Faces, no radiance, it was the death of Haight transposed to Berkeley, complete with leather shrouds and nowhere to go. Cody's, Moe's, The Print Mint, looking drab and ill used; the Indian Import shop full of imported junk from the exploited areas of the world, but little of India.

Down by the shore the ghosts of beach sculpture fade against the bay mist. Further along the once-gleaming pile of junked cars are reduced now to a flattened pile of rusted metal, squeezed of their shining colors as are the kids in the street.

In Santa Cruz the local department store has handmade bags and belts from some leatherman up in the redwooded hills. "He makes them all by hand," said the gray-haired berouged saleslady somewhat confused by that concept. The roadsides are populated by hitchhikers holding signs—Seattle-San Francisco-Big Sur. Sur is awash with tourists, and at Esalen an engineer's wife regretted her seminar. "The last time I was here we had these hostility encounters, I could yell and scream, but this one I am in now is all gentle and love, how will I ever get to know anybody?" She turns to reassure her husband that the Stroganoff and brown rice is edible, and then to me, "He'd rather eat spam sandwiches!"

After food, lying stoned in the hot sulfurous baths, the water a new atmosphere, I move my limbs languorously and watch the moon make shambles of the ocean. There are three of us in the darkness floating in the warm water; we do not speak. A little later, as we get dressed, one of the people who work at Esalen comes in and starts to light candles; he is a young man and performs his job as though it were a ritual, and indeed it is, for there is something otherwise about this spot overlooking the ocean, it seems to have its own life force. Later still, the regular guests at their evening encounters, we lie on the grass and watch the staff sitting on the porch singing and talking. They see us there and move silently away, we do not belong, are caught between two worlds with no recognizable sign language. We leave; I think it would be nice to come back there, and stay longer next time.

Sausalito is packed with people wearing Sears vacation clothes; a woman in a green dress rests her belly against the table as she eats her morning eggs. Through the window I watch the clean-faced long-haired girls go by wearing faded blue work shirts and sandals. Alan Watts lives on a houseboat near here, and from the San Raphael bridge you can see the lighted windows of San Quentin at night.

The people at Muir Beach protect their integrity by having impossible drinking water, building their houses of weathered wood and glass and refusing to call the cops to chase nude people off their private beach. From one of the hillside houses I could look over the curve of beach, past the monumental rock that rose out of the sea and blocked off part of the lights of San Francisco which delineated the horizon. Muir Woods are not far away and you can buy a postcard in the souvenir shop of a gigantic log house built by a Mr. Schmock. The greenness is everywhere, the flowers and bushes sprout bloom and leaf; it isn't at all like Southern California.

Back down the coast, pushing through the holiday traffic, trying to beat the Labor Day statistics, glad to see the smog of LA establishing the fact that we made it home, alive.

September 12, 1969

Across the Red Bridge

Miss me? Secrets to share. Once again on the way to the red bridge into the mist and green. Flying UP, across the aisle from us a man read a newspaper with the headline, DELLA REESE ABLE TO WALK. No one we asked afterward could tell us why—the San Francisco papers had other news—Mother identifies as daughter girl who jumped from the red bridge. But it turned out to be someone else's daughter; did the mother expect this when the daughter left home? We didn't check out the Haight Ashbury at all, and no one mentioned it the seven days we were up north.

Three days later, sitting in the clearing between the house and the redwoods, someone walked across the green and quiet to tell us Jimi Hendrix was dead. The news was at that time two days old—we were on vacation.

Going for a walk along the dry road bordered by trees and dark charred stumps from which second growth rose fifty feet or more, that on our left, and on our right roll away hills of sun clipped brown, stalk and dirt lumps with stump and twig and fence. Picking up scrap metal (will there be another war?) starting with the foot prodding it along, then the bend over and retrieval and the close eye scrutiny, a piece of door handle from a Volkswagen, part of a ballpoint pen—the pearlescent tube a little torn at the edges and hollow—and in the ditch below, the several head of a deer. Look at that; it's a deer's head, isn't it? Yes, yes, my dear. . . . The hair's matted down to the skin, the skin drying against the bone, the blood a brown glaze over the place where suddenly the body wasn't. Had it been ready for mounting? Started to smell, or the eyes weeping, or the gaze too sad suddenly and the project abandoned in that ditch, with the head left there next to the bulging brown burlap bag which so ungracefully contained what? The body? At least together, the head and the body, a superstition against separation.

Dick Waters makes musical instruments from car parts. A tree grows through his kitchen, and his wife hangs pots and things from the hooks in its bark. We sat on his porch listening to the wind make the car parts sing and mutter. Overhead a flock-crew-scam of vultures swirled and churned the space above us, dipped and disappeared into the trees, crest and swing upwards. Notification of doomsday, perhaps. I contemplated attaching a note to my chair, "Here sat a lady fully prepared to vanish by the warning of birds. Do not look further; I am become feather."

Back over the red bridge and into the white city, houses decorated, stores I have never visited, street names I can't remember; the pleasures of travel. We buy the San Francisco *Good Times* and read a letter supposedly from Tim Leary (and Rosemary—and the Weathermen). It doesn't sound exactly right to me, all the words and the part at the end about being armed and to be considered dangerous. Sounds like it was written by someone (Them?) who wanted an excuse to shoot at sight. Well, I don't know. I just hope wherever they are (Tim and Rosemary) they are hugging and kissing and getting high and putting their smile muscles back into working order. It's nice to think of him as free, of them together, perhaps under as clear a sky as we saw reflected in the bay where on the islands the Indians keep company with time.

In North Beach, walking the streets. Went to City Lights Bookstore. I wanted to find a book of poetry by Sylvia Plath (it had been recommended to me with the suggestion that I would find an affinity there). Where will I find . . . I asked the man behind the counter upstairs, look downstairs on the poetry shelf, he said. Downstairs I faced row upon row of poetry books, not in alphabetical order, the message: you must *really* want to find the book. Or was it; perhaps you are a poet, then beware; for here before you are hundreds of poetry books and who cares, do you care? Do you stop and examine them? I made it through two rows and became nauseated, gave up.

Somewhere behind the cardboard walls the owner might be hiding, the famous Lawrence Ferlinghetti, writing poems, publishing books, running this West Coast pit stop for visiting writers. Two shelves and I had paid my dues, fuck the literary life. I'd try the Free Press Book Stores when I got back to Los Angeles.

Another part of North Beach and the women who dance without their tops or bottoms were being hawked by middle-aged sharks in fringed leather jackets, a hip Mafia! They are careful experts at whom to tout, gave us the uncurious eye, spared us the details of tit and ass but splurted all over the man behind us (suit, a nervous smile) who almost stopped to listen. Around the corner and up the hill, up Grant Avenue, past the Condor (tits) and the Alpine Shop (skis) and the bar (Italian dinners, family style) and the street freaks (got any spare change?) and into Trieste for a frothy cappuccino and a table by the window from which to watch the people. The vacation was almost over and we still didn't know what happened to Della Reese.

October 2, 1970

This Week on Earth
(and the Moon)

NOT so out of it that I can't get into it on the what's happening level. Though on the level of what's happening, things seem pretty out of it! This section deals with realities, or unrealities, and includes the Great Mustache Escapade and Put On which, as R. G. pointed out to me, would reach its ultimate goal when I myself was forced to wear the very mustache I was attempting to paste on Miss America. And of course he was right, for wear it I did, to a local liquor store, to buy Tampax, to work (Capitol Records, Inc.) where the president of the company said, "Say, Liza, that looks nice on you," and to an opening night at the Bitter End West where three girls congratulated me on behalf of Women's Lib and the lead singer of a rock group kissed me, saying, "I always wanted to kiss a girl with a mustache"!

Further developments of the mustache were that Blair Sabol reprinted some of it straight-faced in the *Village Voice, Time* magazine called me, the Steve Allen Show booked me and then chickened out a few hours before the taping, I got photographed for a poster to advertise *Blood Rock,* was a poster, then a Sunset Strip Billboard, and finally, got to like the way it looked! Ultimately I cut my hair and shaved the damn thing off.

Some of the pieces are more serious, dealing with injustices and vanishing cultures, buildings burning, earth quaking, and astronauts landing on the moon. Well, it's all part of everything and everything has its part, and maybe some of it means something cosmic, and maybe it's just a collection of snapshots taken from a fast-moving vehicle of flesh.

Read a little, have a cup of coffee; ah, that's better, it's all just you and me anyway.

Yellow Pages List Sages

There are ten (count them, 10) metaphysicians listed in the Lo
Angeles Yellow Pages; stick that in your infinity and see if it van
ishes! Four (4) of them have Wilshire addresses, so it must be a prof
itable business, or profession, and two live (?) on Cherokee. Ther
is one on Leimert, one on Compton, and one on Stocker. Metaphys
ics is available to all, wherever you are. Out in Compton there is
whole institute to serve you; it is called the Science of Desired Livin
Institute Headquarters, and whether it be rented desk space in an in
surance office or marble-clad cement tower doesn't matter, if you ar
truly metaphysical.

I think the Yellow Pages offer a good indication of the tempo o
this city, take, for instance, Noise Control Consultants. There is onl
one. They hang out on Gindle, which is, I assume, some quiet stree
where no freeway goes. But if it is scalp treatments you want (hai
falling out from too much noise perhaps), you can choose from up
ward of ninety, among which MacTombo Beauty Salon and Silve
Dome Beauty Parlour are memorable for the beauty of their names,
nothing else.

Time of Day Service is monopolized by the Pacific Telephone an
Telegraph Service, but in Bags—Burlap & Cotton the field is wid
open. You might like to try the Shalon Bag and Drum Company o
Mission Road, who advise you to also "see our ad Barrels and Drum
Used," or the Baron Bag Company who will buy, sell, pick up, an
deliver. There are two Cemetery Lot Brokers. One has a display ad
vertisement showing some trees that look like New England maples i
full leaf and the motto "We Buy More—We Sell More." They have
twenty-four-hour phone service and are, no doubt, the last people t
consult about the menace of the population explosion.

On the opposite page (452 of the August, 1967, Yellow Pages
the Inglewood Park Cemetery provides a picture of what looks to m
like downtown Cairo. They are out in Inglewood doing their thing
promising that "one call arranges everything."

For those of you who remember the pleasures of picture books, recommend the yellow pages, for they have pictures, some of which are almost art! Art in the Yellow Pages? But isn't Los Angeles in the midst of a cultural renaissance?! Examine page 777 (of the issue mentioned above); see the vestiges of Pop Art, a jet-propelled Colonel Sanders Bucket whizzing off toward the left margin with some mechanical extrusion hanging out, the whole thing labeled as "Cosmic Engine Rebuilders U.S.A." Turn to page 1001 for a definitive Santa Claus wearing a crown and carrying a load of Hose King Hydraulic Hose (the outré gift suggestion of the era for the man who has everything). Poole, John D., Investigator, is pictured as a post-Sherlock Holmesian type, tilted fedora, sideburns sliding behind an upraised collar, strange Egyptian eyes with the pupil in the middle though the face is in profile. I presume (Dr. Watson) that it indicates that he misses nothing, though if I saw him hanging out in front of my house, I'd know what he was up to immediately. (He is on page 1075, upper-left-hand corner.) Across from him on page 1074 is a fellow in the employ of Shadowing Specialists Cal-Metro Investigators. This man is wearing an eye-patch, presumably to make him as distinguishedly inconspicuous as the side-burned fedora type who works for Poole, John D.

Lest the reader of the Yellow Pages feel that the personal touch is missing, that the world is become large and faceless, that between those we deal with and ourselves stretch miles of tiny print, some firms offer photographs of those who serve. On page 1320 (at the bottom of the page) the Associated Van Lines, Inc., after assuring you of "Worry-free moving . . . free estimates with personal supervision," displays a photograph of their president, Lola Rader. Lola Rader is quite attractive, with a beehive sort of hairdo (which I guess she will change for next year's edition of the Y.P.). She certainly inspires more confidence than the two flying ducks that illustrate the Republic Van Lines advertisement above her on the same page. On pages 622 and 623, there are seven (7) cheerful dentists to choose from though E. N. Porter, D.M.D., looks a little less cheerful than say Dr. Howard L. Mamlet or Dr. R. J. Rothchild. But it's Dr. H. Clemen who wins for happiness; he is positively laughing—maybe it's because he speaks both Spanish and German, while Rothchild only lists Spanish, and Porter has to be content with Bank-Americard as his specialty. Some photos are discouraging to the customer. Take Vince of the Western Scale Company (page 1807). It's not that he doesn't have a good honest face. It's just that he looks a little young (to me) for such responsibility. On the other hand, Sir John Bedford (page 1912) is just the man I'd go to for Plastic Slip Covers. Imagine my pride as I answer friends' admiring comments about my new plastic-covered sofa with a nonchalant "Glad you like it; it's just a little something Sir John whipped up for me."

All things considered, the Yellow Pages are the biggest entertainment bargain in town. They are free, they are exciting, they are friendly (containing such mottoes as "every hello is a goodbuy" —page 478) and they are illustrated, and what's more, folks, they don't clog the drain.

April 12, 1968

San Pedro Harbor

Boats, unmanned at the dockside, are ghost ships; their fleck paint and coiled rope sad in the brilliant sun, they squeak and moan in the oily water. At the docks in San Pedro, where once the Italian fishermen hauled in their silver catch and the town behind them glistened with fishscale prosperity, the boats lay idle these past months, the fishermen on strike against the boat owners, but in reality against the foreign fisheries that have frozen-fished them out of business. Now they are working again, though hopelessly; each year fewer boats ply the coast from California down to the South American seas, for the fishing industry of California is blighted and the young men look landward for their future.

There are other boats that are still prosperous, the trade ships in the harbor and the ships at Long Beach bristling with guns, the warrior vessels of the Navy; and from their decks at night, the oil refineries along the beach look like giant modern cities on the shore. Time was when San Pedro was the center for the Seaman's Hiring Hall, with flourishing supply stores, hotels, and chandlers, and the gay ladies of the night were all new and bright. But the Union moved to Long Beach and the fish ran out, and now the street sags toward the sea with only the hopeless clinging to its hilly curbside. Second-hand shops and more second-hand shops sell the very old and the very useless things to which no amount of age can add art. Between them the steamy stew restaurants and pawnshops and near the bottom of the road the boarded windows of the shoeshine parlor. The street women are still there, the very same women perhaps, whose rutted skin and lusterless eyes match the graying aspect of the old town.

Once there was a ferryboat to take you from San Pedro to Long Beach; now the terminal building is partially used for offices, and there is no way to get across the harbor by boat. The only way across is by car, high on the fine suspension bridge, over the wharves and docks of the passenger and freight ships. Between the major commerce of the large oceangoing steamers and the dying docks of the fishermen is Ports O' Call, a tourist miasma of quaintness and paintings on velvet. Done in "Spanish" architecture, with cobble streets and courtyards paved in tile, wrought-iron grillwork from behind which chiliburgers and Pepsi Colas are dispensed, while inside the imitation adobe are Polynesian mu mu shops, ha-ha postcard vendors, a fancy imported cheese store, Mexican curios, and sometimes in the summer the sound of a strolling band. Ports O' Call has recently been enlarged: built in Hollywood set designers' New England, more shops, selling more expensive decorator junk, only at this end, from under shingle and weathered board. If the conglomerate East/West fishing village looks unreal, it manages to be less unreal than the actual fishing village, where few fish are caught and fewer fishermen fish.

But the harbor is always romantic if for nothing else than its billboard signs with names of places neatly lettered and the invitation to sail away from this port to the other ports of the world, where lying dockside, there are still other ports to go to, for the seas circle the land and if it is true that we are risen from the sea, then that explains our always longing to go back. There is the rhythm of the ocean and the space of a curved horizon, and even for those who have not stood on the deck at night and watched the sky swirl above with the rocking of the ship, there is the bone dream of sea travel.

For me the things that make a city are the docks and markets and railway stations, the feeling of flow, from the world around, and the sound of trains and ship horns. But the sea is becoming old-fashioned for travel, and although there is the International Airport, the sound of jet engines is no substitute for foghorns in the mist. The fishing industry is dying along the coast, the Navy ships are gray and foreboding, and the *Queen Mary,* anchored off the Long Beach coast, wallows at her mooring like a dancer with her legs cut off. Old San

Pedro is a sad place, is a forgotten place. There is a new part of town
with houses that ride the hillside for the view, and the usual town life
of neon signs and dress shops that straddle the high coast road, but i
is unrelated to the sea. And just below the new town is the old town
a ghost town, the hotels now shut, the tawdry bars and food cafés
deserted and sad, and only the remnants of the former inhabitants
with their prosperity memories believe it is still alive.

Come to San Pedro and visit the romantic Ports O' Call, but come
carefully, and don't look around you for the romantic reality of this
former fishing harbor. Just eat your frozen fish sticks and smile, and
when you breathe in, smell the sea, faintly, over the odor of oil and
smog and frying onions.

January 5, 1968

A Day at the Los Angeles Zoo

We parked our car at *E* for elephant and meandered across the
footbridge toward the flying banners with their appliquéd animal designs which wave over the entrance to the new Los Angeles Zoo,
passing our first barricade of ten-cent cold drink and ice cream machines, edging our way through the families zigzagging along the
paths to the erratic push-pull of children's hands and grownup refu-
sals—after all we came here to please you, we are going to take you to
see the giraffe, so forget that silly-looking bird cage, you can see plenty
of birds at home, can't you? Overhead the airborne tragedies, balloons floating off into the smog with little echoes of crying still tied to
their dangling strings.

We went to the children's zoo, I kept my knees bent, we didn't
have a child with us and I was afraid we would be exposed as freaks,
bent on sheep-touching, goat-feeding, rabbit-cooing, when we should
be old enough to know better. But it was OK because the kids didn't
see us; they were busy rabbit-cooing, goat-feeding, sheep-stroking,
that is, when they could get to them through the crowd of parents
proffering celery and corn, saying—See Herbie, you feed them like
this—but I understood, and forgave, and besides I was busy tickling
a goat behind the ears.

The turtle pond was thick and dirty with paper and refuse, and the little ones looking in it for turtles were getting a good view of ice cream wrappers; however, over by the red-painted barn the sheep were getting touched and at the rabbit-hutch, also painted to look like a little red barn, the rabbits had dug a tunnel underneath in the dirt and stared back at us with sleepy pink eyes from the depths of their sand holes. The baby elephant lay down on his side, it was a very hot day, he curled his trunk under his front leg and went to sleep, his tiny eyelashes thick on his wrinkled cheek. Two girl attendants were exercising two little chimpanzees on a chained-off lawn. One girl held the larger chimp by the hand and walked it around, the smaller chimp, clinging to the bare pink ass in front of it, toddled behind. Why does he do that? we asked. She's very dependent—the girl said—wouldn't walk unless we hold her, or she can cling to the other one. The little chimp looked at us with terrible sadness and grabbed at her white security blanket that was lying on the lawn. Oh cute, the mothers said, the children looked worried.

We left the children's zoo and started the ten-mile trek to the grownup part, which means you can look but don't touch, a complete reversal of the usual situation grownup-childwise. For God's sake, I said to Robert, let's take the tram, this place is enormous. We got in line and off we went on the little tram; only, unlike the old zoo where the tram driver told you funny stories about the animals and stopped outside the bear's cage so he could wave and you saw everything from your seat, this tram only covers the outside perimeter and a tape-recorded voice keeps telling you to get off at any one of the five continental stops, the zoo being organized to match the earth's geography. The tram is OK, only it's not worth fifty cents unless you want to see a lot of cold drink machines and a few obsolete horses with enormous pricks and the tail of a cheetah, the rest of which is invisible behind a rock.

But it was hot, so we stayed on till Africa, which is stop four out of five, and after hearing the tape announce that membership in the zoo society was considered a prestige thing, anyone could join, we took to foot, past the sleeping jungle animals fending off the heat and noise of the eager families going woof-woof and grr through the cage bars. Who's on the inside? said a man to the monkeys. But the monkeys didn't answer; they'd heard that one before and they knew.

The drinking fountains were strange; they trickled close to the outlet so that you could get a nostril-full, but not much more. I want a cold drink—I whined, pulling at Robert's hand. The woman in front of me had just put her dime in and pressed Dr. Pepper. The Dr. didn't answer, neither did orange or ginger ale, and the money return slot didn't. Her kids were beginning to pinch her arm. Shove it up your ass, you lousy son of a bitch—the mother said, kicking at the mute machine, and hauled the kids away. She said it very loudly. I looked around thinking the animals would hear, but nobody cared, and we didn't want to risk a dime, so we went off and filled up our noses some more.

There was a large crowd at the tiger tank; the keeper was washing tiger shit off the side of the moat, and the tigers were sploshing and growling and the people were ahing and ohing and envying them the cool and the grandeur and the power. The tigers slopped in the water and paraded around the great cement hill and stared at us with indifference as we roared back at them. The giraffes were busy eating the bottom leaves off a palm that grew on a ledge above their pit, their heads looking like snail heads, their strange bodies suspended between spindle legs and the heavenheight of their sweet little faces. But the sloth bear, ah the sloth bear. He was dancing in the water spray from the keeper's hose; his big flabby mouth sagging off his ecstatic face, his great shag of fur sending off spray, he stood in the water and did the watusi and the frug, and shook and shimmied, and let the water tickle his tummy and his back and leaped for joy and flung himself along his ledge just keeping near enough to the edge to satisfy us all, and his keeper, who smiled at him with understanding. Do you two do this often? I asked; as often as I can, he said. He's beautiful, I said; you should see him when he's dry, he said, his fur really shines. I like these cement mountains, I said. I wish, said the zoo attendant, that Salvador Dali would come and paint all over them.

We got back on the tram and heard the tape again, and got off at the end and walked back to Australia, where we saw a lot of kangaroos lying down and some strange birds and lots more balloons floating in the sky. My feet hurt, said Robert, so we sat down and people-watched, which was almost as interesting as the rest of the zoo. We saw rabbit-people and ape-people and pig-people and peacock-people and parrot-people and people-people.

When we left, we saw a man in the parking lot near the exit with a St. Bernard on a chain surrounded by a crowd of dog-patters. He was having his own zoo show.

February 25, 1968

Panther Beach

We got into the car. Eyes amazed with luster, water, and the white rocks, and the yellow truck with lights that blink splat splat golden glow, we follow numbed by light. I see disaster in the curving road, the bends which reveal trucks as large as Hannibal's elephants and as unexpected, the driver asleep at the wheel and I am shortly to be a statistic. How will they describe me, a middle-aged woman crushed on the curbside and all my friends will wonder what was I doing on that strange road at the seaside in the mid-morning with my feet crusted with sand. Simple.

They had stayed up all night while I slept, and at four A.M. I woke and drank a lot of coffee, three cups, black, no milk in the house, perils of visitation, rituals broken, no milk, a strange place for the light switch in the blur of nighttime bathroom going, now this discomfort of confusion over black coffee. They are still awake, continuity complete, full of pills and beer and cigarettes and playing the same record over and over because the arm on the automatic machine has become exactly that, the same song over and over—fly, blackbird, fly.

That beach, in the early morning, or I guess at any time, that beach just nine miles above Santa Cruz, which in itself is only eleven miles below Ben Lomand's redwood sanctuaries, that beach is a wonder of the world, really, number four, number eight, or, why not, number one. Its walls of rock slashed with color, red and yellow, blue and strangely, like an official warning, white. Inset within the wind-carved sandstone, bones of granite stack upwards, nodules, faces, forms better than can be made, yet surely made, existing, hanging there above the wide stretch of sand which can only be reached by running across a spruit as the wash recedes. Dennis calls it Panther Beach, I only know it is below a brussels-sprout patch whose stalks, crusted with their vegetable nobbles, look hideous. Those are artichokes, says Susan, no, not artichokes, no silvery fronds of leaf, no flowering head of thistle, just gnurled nobbles, clinging like warts to the fibrous stems.

There is a little cave on Panther Beach, small, two tiny chambers and a place carved out of the swirling wall where you could place a

candle. View, only of sky, sand, and water. We sit and watch the sky
lighten, smoking good fragrant grass, the sky lightening, our eyes wid-
ening, sea sounds soothing, the wall above us swirling and jutting;
there are hanging succulents draped down from some protrusions, the
hanging gardens of Babylon, blossoms opening to the rising sun. I sit
in this tiny cave and think, says Susan, of the Indians who sat here,
why not here, so many years, sat here and . . . She does not finish
the sentence. The Indians descended the rocks above us laden with
wild roots and smelling of leather and bayberry and whatever Indians
smell of—all fragrances of the fields and perhaps of the resinous sap
of the forests above.

Dennis is far away along the beach, a small figure growing smaller,
his footprint-tracks silent in the sand, away on the rocks, will he wander off beyond our vision, among the anemones and swordfish and
sharks and killer whales and skeletons of whalers, for not far away is
Davenport where Captain John Davenport fished for whale in the
first half of the nineteenth century, that is, before he moved to Santa
Cruz and became Justice of the Peace and a real estate agent in 1888.
This information is courtesy of Gregory's Country Store, where we
stopped to buy bad coffee and good doughnuts, to play "Circle of Fire"
on the jukebox and use the toilet.

On the beach, three of us, close together under the wall of revolving stone, the tide is coming up as is the sun, it is late, six A.M., late
in a day that started yesterday morning. I want to tell you about those
rocks, ceramic perhaps, the blues so amazingly blue, almost lapis la-
zuli, no, but ultramarine and the red, oxides, I don't know perhaps
oxides are yellow, iron I guess (iron as is the soil of Pennsylvania all
red suddenly after the brown of New York) but red nevertheless in
streaks and circles, in patterns, and again yellow, deep sun-filled yellows and all shades of brown, from the mauve-like brown called
mushroom to the cool grays of brown, and cleft by something, the
wind, most likely that, rising in endless variety of form. It is a
panorama, each pinnacle and scale different: it is a horde of prehis-
toric beasts turned to stone! eyes! backbones! skin! everything
scroonched by time into this hardened towering surface and below it
the sea, moving in double breakers, and the sand, very pale, cool in
the early no heat of the sun, and, above all this, those strangely dis-
eased-looking stalks of Brussels-sprouts.

Time to go, a note to Dennis left in the cave under his can of beer
—Gone Home. He will be all right, take his car and go on to wher-

ever, we will walk back along the sand and around the precipice as the waves retreat and up the hill and to our car and back past Captain Davenport's Davenport. But, the tide is in, IN! Great thunderous waves, enlarging before our eyes, shipwreck and disaster! marooned and deserted on Panther Beach! our bones to bleach in the saline waters, our bodies to become one with the beasts lurking in the stone of the cliffs, what will we do? Nothing, no way out but to climb the green sea-slime-splattered rocks, up over the ledge, bypass the surging churning whirlpool waves, the grinding waters, the eternity of drowning; we climb. I go last, watch Susan and Harvey disappear over the ledge, onto the safe sand of the way out. I crouch, the waves rise and fall, somewhere I have heard that every seventh wave is large; I will wait, crouched on that rock till the natural regression of the water frees me. A woman, Susan, running through the water, tide to her knees, reaching for me, screaming—come down at once, grabbing me, pulling me into the raging sea, gone mad, she has gone entirely mad.

Why did you do that, why did you pull me into the sea, why? I thought, I looked back, you were crouched on the rock, your eyeballs popping, your lips curled back, your hackles rising, your fur on end, your ears pointed, I thought you had freaked out. I was watching the waves, I said. We are calm now, wandering up the beach, behind us the vanquished tides, the mountainous wall of sculpture, the small cave now inhabited by a can of beer and a note, before us the little path up the cliff, gentle and easy, past the plastic rubble of picnickers, up past the driftwood, up past the stalks of cancer, up to where the car is waiting to take us, in our dreaming, back into the morning of San Francisco. We got into the car, feet crusted with sand.

March 28, 1969

Flea Market at Universal City

I love junk stores, I ooze over second-hand stores, I get little shivers of pleasure just reading the words "Goodwill" or "Salvation Army" or "Veteran's Thrift." If I am a junk addict, then you can imagine how mainline it is for me to go to a flea market, the Marché aux

Puces in Paris, Portobello Road in London, Second Avenue in old New York—you name it, I've thrilled to it, touched ratty tatty torn and crumpled all over the world, seeing potential in everything lovely and abandoned, coveting the glass and silk and wood and porcelain and copper, hauling quantities of stuff after me in my travels, weighted down and sinking in a collection of miscellaneous treasure too lovely, too marvelous to jettison.

It was, therefore, with little heaves and sighs that I made my way on Saturday to Universal City, where there was advertised: "Flea Market comes to Universal Studios every Sat. and Sun. 10 to 6—Free admission—everything for sale: fruits, vegetables, men's and women's clothing, antiques, oil paintings, hodgepodge, statuary, Spanish wrought iron, Mexican assortments and clothing—Indian handicraft, Hippie handicraft." I admit to some misgivings prompted by the words "Hippie handicraft." What could They mean? Still, perhaps this was a term They used to tell the general public that there would be handmade objects there; I hoped so.

Universal City, the parking lot and tour part, is perched on top of a reconstituted hill. It is the same hill that is amputated a little lower down to provide a base for the Universal Hilton/Sheraton or whatever that is being constructed there at the moment. What used to be background for the Ponderosa Ranch, scrub and scruff of California vegetation, is now swerving cement road and planted palm and lights! camera! action!

It cost fifty cents to park. "Have a good time visiting Universal City," the young attendant in the ticket booth said. We consulted our map. The flea market is in the Mexican Village—that is, a "village" that did a "Mexican" thing during the summer tourist season, complete with giant electric sombrero. We walked into the "old" plaza, past some "Indians" (?)—either they were Indians selling plastic imitation Indian junk, or they were imitation Indians selling plastic imitation Indian junk. I didn't have the stomach to find out.

Inside it's tawdry—that's the exact word: Tawdry. There are wooden booths, without any style, but that's OK; they might be market stalls, I suppose. And there is merchandise. That is the name for it: giant icky colored glass lamps on gilt chains, the kind they sell in those buy-on-time furniture shops—gaudy, perhaps, Italian, sleazy, ugly, definitely Decorator! The Mexican Wrought Iron Shop has hand-lettered signs about "Wet Backs" and "Welcome Gringos." The wrought iron itself is typical Tijuana tourist curlicue. There are a number of antique stalls, all rather high-priced, I thought, with the usual "precious" tat, silver smelling salts containers, old postcards, little demitasse cups and some dolls. One Shirley Temple doll was very pleasant; it cost $23 and had no political opinion.

The vegetable stalls were reasonable; I bought five pounds of tomatoes for fifty cents—but I had to add onto that the cost of parking. There were no "Hippies" that I could find, much less evidence of their Handicraft, whatever that would be. The oil paintings are of sailing ships, dogs, toreadors, waifs, the kind sold by the roadside next to a large orange sign that proclaims OIL PAINTINGS, FIVE DOLLARS AND UP, ARTIST STARVING (deservedly so, I think). About the only really handmade stuff were hook rugs, one jewelry maker, and the African clothing from the stall run by Operation Bootstrap. The latter had an attractive assortment of Afro-style clothing, shirts and long robe things, etc. The clothing at the other stalls consisted mostly of out-of-style capris and blouses, odds and ends and general low-quality schlock. A couple of stalls sell yard goods—nothing much, though, in quality or price. All together it is a grim affair, what with the obvious tie-in to the tours, the lack of aesthetic governing the operation, the types of people manning some of the stalls, the whole thing reminiscent of the shuck boardwalk entrepreneurs near a dying funland.

It is doubly grim when you think of the money that must be behind it, and the resources. Can you imagine how it could have been if it had been run with the same care as the Pleasure Faire? I don't mean that it had to be renaissance—but just a little charm, just a little quality control, just a little taste, a little eye for design, a little gift to the public of a pleasant place to come to shop or browse, and perhaps eat, a sidewalk café serving French food, a pushcart selling flowers, the stalls decorated, even some craftsmen selling their own wares, perhaps potters potting, sandalmakers making sandals, weavers, jewelers, for there is electricity there, and water, and everything necessary to enable these various activities to take place.

As we left we saw groups of Brownies and Cub Scouts led in, presumably to see, among other things, Hippie Handicrafts. Ho hum; ah well; oh, shit. If Nixon does get elected, I suggest he starts his clean-up at Universal City: It's really blighted.

November 1, 1968

In the City

Just another day in Los Angeles waking up to sun around eleven and wondering what all the other folks are doing. Eating ham, because ham is cheap and protein, eating eggs for the same reason, drinking three cups of blah instant coffee because the electric percolator was left on for days weeks or hours and burned out, all black and thick on the inside coil, reading the advertising in the throw-away paper, whole households of furniture going cheap, phone after five P.M. Well, I'm out of work and out of funds to buy amusements, like fashionable clothing, twenty pairs of patent leather thigh-high boots, a fur hat, and it's Wednesday already and there's only Baxter Ward's news at four thirty and eleven to count on, oh hell.

Robert bought me a round wooden table for Christmas which arrived yesterday because the man who was refinishing it didn't get it done in time, but that's the way it is with people who refinish things or make sandals or are supposed to come over and paint your kitchen or repair your watch. It is always too trips, maybe three, and various reasons for the delay and all that courtesy and all that schlepping and it's a drag except that something done by hand always in the end looks better than some mechanical execration which usually arrives on time, or even five months early, like Christmas decorations in August.

So I have a table but nothing to sit on except folding bridge chairs, really ugly things with plastic covered plastic foam on anodized aluminum or tin or alloy or God knows what, but exactly what I don't like to look at. Since furniture is house sculpture anyway, I think I should live surrounded by only what pleases me, like oak, and bent wood, and iron, and leather, and Oriental rugs. But I have to settle for reality, so we drove off to search for some cheap wooden chairs. First we went to the Goodwill on San Fernando Road because there is a lot of free parking there and I keep remembering the days when it was an inexpensive place to shop, lots of velvet coats and strange lamps and big cooking pots with just little holes in them and chairs and tables that would look pretty good with a coat of paint. It's not the same there anymore though, all the prices are up and the stuff looks worse.

Maybe it looks less desirable as the price rises, I don't know, but it's all gray drab tat, or sloppily cream painted wood, and they want eight dollars for a chair which is ridiculous.

There are still some good buys to be had, but you have to go out of town for them. In Ventura there is the Retarded Children's Thrift Shop which arranges all the clothes by color and size just like the May Company, and even has a loudspeaker that announces, "Welcome to the Retarded Children's Thrift Shop, have you visited all our departments? Ladies' special today, all twenty-cent hats are half-price and for the next hour all coats and suits are also half-price." It's a big cavernous place and I once managed to find six Indian bedspreads for sixty cents each so now my bedroom is all draped and tented with them and it's nice to wake up and see the patterns flow.

Anyway, if we went to Ventura for our cheap goodies we would spend more on gas than on the chairs, so when we left the Goodwill we headed for Pasadena. There are a lot of tat shops there, and they too have upped their prices, but not the Salvation Army "As Is" yard. Now there is a place where the game goes on. It's shove and grab, hassle and bargain but also there is a lot of junk around and only the dealers who half break your arm to get it off something they are after are dangerous. I lost the battle for two carved wooden wallshelves and a big blue enamel stew pot. We got two old oak chairs though, for a dollar each, and were about to blow three on a cherry-wood chair when the big fat man who had done me out of the stew pot rushed up to the cashier and grabbed the chair and said it was his, said it was marked "sold," wondered who took the "sold" ticket off (there wasn't a ticket on it, though tearing them off is an efficacious and fair technique in the junk hunt game). Well we lost that three-dollar chair too, but we have the two oak ones, and the four plastic ones in case somebody comes to visit us and wants to sit down.

On the way home we stopped at the market to pick up our lucky bingo envelope (no luck) and some eggs which are protein and cheap. A woman grabbed us and gave us two tickets to Preview House where she invited us to see and judge upcoming TV shows. There are door prizes, she chortled at us, real door prizes, sometimes even a color TV set. We went, but that's another story, which I will tell you sometime soon, but I wanted to let you know that I won a year's supply of soap. (If I rub it over my TV screen will it make the picture look colored?) After the TV Preview we went to a radio station where I guested on a talk-show and spoke to a lot of loquacious

assholes over the air. But what the hell, it's a lonely town Los Angeles, and when you're out of work everything helps to pass the time.

January 24, 1968

Fourth of July at Westlake

Life, making a grand generalization, is absurd. Well, it is, and its
absurdities comfort me, make me feel secure; I'm not crazy, the world
is. It was, for instance, absurd of me to be riding a horse in a Fourth of
July parade in Westlake surrounded by millions of kids all dressed in
redwhiteandblue. It was absurd of me to be riding a horse at all, the
bones at the bottom of my buttocks, or the tops of my thighs, told me
so. But, there I was, grandiose and poised astride this quiescent horse
midway in a parade celebrating the joys of communal living in a
high-cost tract development where the choice of color scheme went
from puce to puke.

It started out innocently enough (old-time radio introduction) with
my going for a trail ride on the third. A trail ride is a euphemism for
sitting while the horse resignedly walks into the sunset and out again.
I sat, and sang a little, good old-fashioned cowboy laments about
beans and bacon, tried to make like Gabby Hayes, leaning back,
nonchalant, at ease with the range. Fine, said the "character" who
sells horses, you better join the parade tomorrow, gonna' be a
rip-snortin' good time thing. OK, I said, if the horse is willing, I am.

Balmy Fourth, hot skys, lots of sun up thar, no fountain on the
horse but a saddle calculated to rub the strangest places. Kids, five
hundred of them aged five, a like amount age six, age seven, age
eight, all in redwhiteandblue, bicycles in similar color scheme,
streamers in the tines, and one group of kids in red cylinders,
firecrackers?, just their vitamin-boosted arms and legs protruding. We
line up, and like all well-organized community events, wait for the
start (two hours late). Better to sit on that horse and wait rather than
try to remember which side is the one for mounting. Feeling kinda'
stupid, hot in the sun, all those people looking at me, knowing full
well that I don't look like I live on Lake View Terrace or Loma Love-
sick Walk or any other of those charmingly named streets which

have sent delegations with banners wishing everyone a happy Fourth. Glories of suburbia in the desert, how many color TV's per family? Suddenly, pierce-eye vision is mine, the dapple stucco crumbles before my eyes leaving exposed acres of wall to wall carpeting, megamasses of electronic gadgetry, a continent of Spanish style coffee tables, a ream of *Life* magazines with pictures of the astronauts' wives (WASP's every one), a tundra of flower-bordered paper towels, a zillion tubes of fluoride toothpaste with MFP (Mother Fucking Peppermint?).

It was a transformation of roles; no longer was I the object of scrutiny, but THEY were on display for me. An army of hard-faced women and soft-faced men, curlers, Bermuda shorts, flowered cotton dresses, round plastic sunglasses, straw bags from Italy, all the unvariety of middle-class consumerism. It was a populated May Company advertisement, it was *West* magazine come alive, it was, it was America, ah!

Eventually the show got on the road. The kids dressed as Mexicans (no real Mexican-Americans in Westlake, no colored folk either) rode side by side with kids dressed like Attila's Huns. The spokes of the redwhiteandblue bicycles revolved into a smear of color, the ponies with beribboned manes wobbled, the two burros wearing nylon stockings, hula skirts, and lipstick drew cheers, the people waved tiny American flags. I hummed a merry tune and oggled along with the rest, along the tarred streets where once tumbleweed grew, where now well-clipped lawns and picture windows and streetsigns bloomed. I rode past, a veritable queen on horseback reviewing the peasantry. Finally it was over, bowlegged and parched, I dismounted, at least I thought I did, though my bottom, or thigh tops, felt the thrill of the saddle for days.

Ah me, so much for the Fourth, and now only Labor Day to look forward to, and maybe, if I'm lucky, hunting for Easter eggs next year with Julie.

August 1, 1969

Astronauts

> *Late, late yestreen I saw the new moon*
> *Wi' the auld moon in her arms.*
>
> —OLD BALLAD

Crusted with diamond eyes, lovers' wishes ten miles thick, the moans of lust, the reflections of crushed grass, the silver powder of sighs, how lightly they walk on that blanket of dreams.

To dance there gives reason for that flight. To dance in one-sixth gravity, to rise in lunar leap, there where the mark holes of meteorites leave an eternity of history that only man evaluates.

Look upwards, love, the moon of this landscape is blue covered with cloud and holds no mystery except that man is destroying his home.

On the way up I looked out from the protective window and saw Icarus weeping waxen tears.

I dreamed of escape, of flying free of my home earth, of unchaining my feet from the eternal pull, of lollygagging around the universe. I am a Tiepolo angel piercing the plaster and soaring. Now I am here, standing on this new earth, look ma, that's me next to the crater.

Walter spent years following the development, scanned the scanners and talked with the men. Walter, the voice of history, saw this achievement as the vindication of his generation. That is why he was so disturbed by the two young people who spoke of the money being better spent on Biafra or to control pollution. Didn't they understand? They understood too well, saw the earth as the moon's reflection. Warnings warnings, the stars are growing closer.

For the children it was all rather boring, a tedious affair like most of the things parents insist upon. The view was, once observed, not worth further attention. The telescope in the garden was more exciting, showing a glow ball of light pockmarked, and you could, if you wished, just for fun, adjust the sights to make the vision fuzz. It is the real moon, we insisted, and man walking there, didn't they understand what this meant? Bereft of historical perspective and deluged with visual synthetics, they bemoaned the fact that *Mission Impossible* was preempted for this dull show.

Nixon in half screen mouthing platitudes. A man without honor, chosen by the blindness of his times, seeking immortality through the courage of others.

There should have been a payload of poets and lovers; they hold prior claim to the moon. They would have brought flowers and best wishes from the nations of man. There would have been dancing and rejoicing, and a moment of silence for the beginning of this new cycle in the history of humanity.

"The last temptation is the greatest treason: To do the right thing for the wrong reason."—T. S. Eliot

August 8, 1969

Entropy

And it came to pass, and it came to pass, and the earth shook beneath them and the space opened up and the walls fell away and seven or so million people looked at themselves at six o'clock in the morning poised on the brink of eternity.

I remember 1967, acid, and the inward journey, the revolution of the spirit. A revolution which touched minds in middle-class chains, and the intellectuals, and the artists and the free-flying souls in search. We changed, and whirled away on cosmic journeys, finding the elasticity of space, recognizing the vortexural patterns of things, the intricacies of design. We became a drug culture, somnambulists in a world at war, looking for landscapes of inner peace.

But we spend a third of our life in dreams, a third of our expeience is in that time where dreams rule, for however short their span. We rest between the mind's exertion, between the tie to our inner selves, rest from the flash and crash of the reality of self. Toward whose dream does the somnambulist walk; what landscape lies beyond the walls?

At six o'clock in the morning most folks lie in bed, returning. At six o'clock in the morning the fearful death hour of four is past, the hump of the night is crossed, the "silent boatman" has rowed on by, and we will get up soon and see the sun. Safe. Six o'clock is a beginning time, a new day yawning.

We crouched under the lintel, here-here, he said, holding us close under the crossbeam—here is the safest place. The floor rocked and I longed, for the walls to fall away, fall away and leave for my eyes a landscape of suspended people each in his box, each in his moment. And we would look at each other across this encapsulated city and recognize each other. Fall! Fall! I cried, and the floor rippled. From above our heads the plaster drifted down, powdery and gentle, the scar looked as though a slash of lightning had struck where the wall was split by a rivulet of energy, split there the only place in the apartment where it came apart, just over our heads, in the safest place!

The earth rocked me and groaned. Groaned like the sea, the tides of the earth searched the walls of their containment, rough equilibrium and settled down, small heavings, little rumbles. It comforted me. I had flown over the earth and marveled at the effluvial scars, the places where the mountains melted down, places which we, with our vision limited, called valleys, but great places of melting really. And I have wondered at what is the true top of the earth, was it the plateaus and peaks beneath which everything was pitted and scarred, or are those protuberant snow-capped sculptures just that, the moldings and knobbery of action and distress, the exuberance of creation.

We felt the ground move and seek its natural shape, and we felt ourselves carried along the wave and thrust, and knew, every one of us knew, at exactly the same moment we knew, that we were poised on this rippling ball in transition between then and later, with only now for certainty.

I'm all shook up, he's all shook up, we are all shook up, it's a shook-up world, it's jive time, it's run on down the road time, it's look at me time, me look at me time, and we stare at each other, a city of survivors.

And so change, for all of us, change, each seeking his equilibrium, each holding onto the now of things, stripped of future time, freed of the shackles of what must be, free of the hold of what was, free and surging along filling in our spaces. The great acid rock split of 1971, more revolutionary than you think, and its leader was——?

March 19, 1971

Doing the Five Thirty Dance

The neighbor's boy has been into Hollywood to get a job, but they don't pay him in money, only horsemeat catfood. He has come over to tell me this, sliding in while I scrape cigarettes off dishes. He stands there; he wants me to look at his bun. It has pineapple custard on it, only it looks opaque so you can't tell for sure whether it is pineapple or maybe lemon. He talks while chewing on the bun, telling me how many he bought for 50 cents. It's not clear. I see the sweet-potato leaves that are growing over the window slats, little glass slats coated with grease, that move on a pinned axis. But now, with the leaves' exuberant climb, they stay open, immobile, and all the leaves face away from me, toward the sun. I keep looking at the leaves, how all this curl and climb comes out of the potato, a mute hard lump wedged in a jar. The boy still talks about his buns, he got fifty for fifty cents; I can't tell if he got them at the pet shop, or where?

"Where did you get them, those buns?" He got them at the coffee shop up the street; it was at the end of the day and they like to clean out—"Take all the buns and get them out of here quickly before somebody sticks his head in the door and yells STALE"—so he buys all fifty. That seems to me to be a lot of buns to have left over at the end of a day, fifty pineapple custard buns, their sugary edges curling, the syrup sweating the dyed crusts, the congealed stuff laying lump like in the middle. Had they expected a horde of customers, tired commuters to be revived with coffee and sweet rolls? What catastrophe had overcome these hungry wanderers that fifty buns should be abandoned at five thirty on a weekday?

The two men have been here, in my house, all day, having a thing with themselves. They are eating green grapes and yogurt and spinach salad. I hate washing these goddamn dishes while they sit there, under my lamp, eating grapes and spinning out. I lugged a big bag of groceries up the stairs, watermelon and anchovies and sweet butter, a whole feast in a bag.

I was standing behind my cart in the market, looking for a shorter line at the checkout, and a woman called out to me. I couldn't tell who she was, behind all that food, but she took her sunglasses off, and I saw her eyes smiling, her mouth moving. I started telling her about the supermarket; I hate the supermarket, the TRAP it is, the doors that see you coming, the line at the checkout; imagine the horror of waiting to checkout your greed before you, materialized in a metal chariot. I have often thought of charging out with my pushcart and running away, loaded down with groceries, living somewhere completely untraceable, curled up in the basket, pushing my baby in the basket, keeping my books in the basket, using the basket for everything, absolutely everything, a free $30 duplex cage rod basket on wheels, mine for the taking.

I complained loudly to my good friend, whose face and name were meaningless to me, but who apparently had some tangible connection, perhaps I was her pineapple bun? Then I realized the checkout girl could hear me hate the supermarket, hate her supermarket. I wanted to shut up, but I kept on talking. Perhaps that is why she charged me thirty-nine cents for a can plainly marked three for a dollar; they always get you. Just before this the manager had sent me on a fruitless search for clam juice, all the way across the brightly lit sanitary hole of Calcutta that he so proudly managed, to the red cans of soup. There wasn't any clam juice when I got there, no clam juice anywhere in that hideous crunchy-wunchy kingdom. I was exhausted, the lady I had been shouting my agony at whizzed away with a strange smile, and the rubber belt carried my pickings to the counter girl. It took so long, the line, the waiting, and all the time the checkout stand next to me was empty, a little chain across its entrance. The manager was signing checks and giving false information, the little chain mocked my impatience, the register clicked; I was losing control.

The two men are smoking, they are enjoying their exclamations, "out of sight," one says; "oh yeah," the other says, puff, puff, the great big dragon of fantasy floats around over the table, the sink is slippery with fat and coated with ashes, the boy is still chewing his pineapple bun, only the potato has changed. It has grown ten feet tall, its stalk is golden and carved, the branches tremble with joy, the leaves are velvet and the flowers, oh the flowers . . . soon I shall climb up it and escape.

July, 1966

Geriatrics

Geriatrics, geriatrics, prolongation of life. There are lonely old people in rooms, in rooms with the curtains half drawn, looking out at nothing. There are lonely old people sitting at cafeteria tables, tables of catsup and A-1 sauce, holding onto glasses of free hot water, and the minutes, and the hours. Lonely old people on the boulevards with string bags bulging, bulging with folded editions of yesterdays paper rescued from municipal waste bins. Bending over, their skirts hiking up over age-bulged veins, hoisting dead newspapers from the trash. Lonely, lonely, old people in the city, blowing along the street, gray on gray.

Lonely time, elasticized over nothingness, grayness and damp in the bones. Sure to rain tomorrow, can tell when these bones ache. Old and alone in the lines at the station, waiting for the buses to no-place, waiting for a seat by the window and miles like years and memories withering by in the blur of cataract eyes and the faint syncopation of the heart soon to stop. Lonely at the seafront, crouched on benches, winter coats in June and the eyes on the pavement counting the spittle marks of strangers. What's new, what's today that is new, yesterday's teabags rotting on the kitchen table, yesterday's nights a long memory of awake hours and no dreams that are not of death.

Lonely, old and alone, masses of debris in human form, crumpling along the alleys and streets, filling waiting rooms and parks, filling yellowing rooming houses, sitting in front of the Dorisday television watching the advertisements for the beautiful slenderness of the now generation young and in fast cars and diet drinks and they cross bunioned feet and sit there withering and thin or bulging in strange places, knuckles like ripe fruit, backs like storm-twisted trees, watching the whitetooth laughter of the blurry vision screen.

Old and alone, old now and nobody remembers those times and those tastes of that particular day that was their gem and the way it used to be when those berry knuckles were white swan's necks and the wrists bent in delight and the lips unwrinkled into fruitful kisses moist as morning leaves. Old and alone and no one to talk to who was there, who was in any of those million theres that were their own history and a history now unshared. Alone and old, old and alone and everything falling falling into disrepair. The ears full of year's wax-numbing sound and the eyes covered with a silver curtain straining the light and the teeth wobbling on their plastic gums letting little blobs of spittle dry in the corners of the mouth, and the underarm and belly sagging and the skin falling away in folds and the breasts never kissed again, the nipples curdled and the stomach a bag of wind.

Old and alone and no one to pat and touch and caress the skin whose nerves still sing a little sometimes and wish for tenderness and warmth of flesh. Flesh that is warm and adds its warmth to the cooling skin and the dying of the body and the alone of flesh and the bending bone and the mucus days and the phlegm nights of rattle breath and sob coughs and fears of the earthquakes and wondering about families, where are they now. Tables full of souvenirs, plastic dogs and tired photographs of stiff smiling relatives, babies smiles and gritty views, wedding snaps in fancy cardboard signed love to mother, a dried corsage, a book of Blue Chip stamps half full.

The night-light gleams, the phosphorescent hands of the clock stop turning, it is always four in the morning, the hour of dying, the curtains hanging at the window in shadowy falls with no wind blowing. Stains on the carpet and stains on the sheets, pale yellow of spilled coffee and the gray of ash. The hair matted against the forehead in sleep-made masses, the arms tingling from lack of circulation, the eyes' rheumy gaze into the empty dark of nothingness, old and alone, alone and old, a million recluses in a city of activity, a billion statistics on the nation's charts of health and welfare, a million years of added life, of preservation and doctors' hours and hospital fees and geriatric advances and the bodies pile up, flat at night and upright in the day, the ghosts, old and alone, alone and old.

June 13, 1969

Stzzstzz

The tattoo men of the world are ready, their machines poised, the little blue spark flame leaping from point to point, sizzle sound, stzzstzz its onomatopoetic accompaniment to the pierce pin stab bite of the pointed needled flesh pick color planter. The colors are ready, poured from their plastic mustard dispensers onto little squares of white, clean, sterile disposable cardboard containers. The needle is ready, sitting there on the marble shelf in its sterile packet, the tattooer is ready, everything is ready, waiting, hanging on while you examine the pictures on the walls, note the designs, pick one, pick an intimately you forever, forever your one, never a not you tattoo, there like your navel, like a life mark, you, at this moment, where your head is, engraved into your skin forever, a design, or your name in black three dollars, in black and red, four.

Mark says he wants to be a tattooist. I want to be a tattooist, he says. Why? It fascinates me. He is fascinated. You're some kind of a sex freak nut sadist like advertises in the back of the paper, that's what you are. He smiles at that, not a sinister MEANINGFUL smile, just a smile, HE knows why he is fascinated and it's not sex. I'll accept that; he is a craftsman. Having made the most beautiful wooden pot pipes in the world, sold in their own little hand-sewn leather bag with a numbered ticket, "This is pipe number thirty-one" and information "Made of Brazilian feather duster wood," "Made of pineapple grained cheekwood," all exotic woods, all exquisitely carved, honed, that's the word, honed, smoothed and HONED to a sleek satiny sensuous sheen, with His mark inset with brass, he has made that, and now he wants to tattoo.

The man he is hoping will tell him a secret of the art, maybe two secrets, is in the parlor on the corner down the steps from the main road at Long Beach. It's squalid there, puke in the doors and piss on the streets and slit-eyed abductors in Navy clothes with drunken slithering about the corners and the ghost of the roller coaster with the memory of its tortured-to-joy screamers and the shut fronts of the hotdog on a stick stands and all the smells, the whiffs from the oilfields like massive natural indigestion, and the lights of the parlor, and the pictures in the window of marvelous people embroidered with colored lines, whole galaxies of art on their backs and God knows what under their pants, and he wants to be a tattoo man too.

So we lean on the wooden partition inside the place and stare at the reddened pimpled skin of some has-to-be-over-eighteen-years-old-by-law kid from the Navy yards getting his back captioned with a panther whose claw marks are neatly scratched in red, right there over the muscle, as though this small stretching mockery of an animal had ACTUALLY SCRATCHED HIM. He winces, this kid turned canvas, he gasps for mouthfuls of the hideous oil belch air, he is in pain, he is in distress, his eyes widen, it's his fantasy scene from a sex magazine, from a torture film, from a masturbatory dream, and he's getting it right there in Long Beach, he is going to withstand the torture, he will have the tattoo as proof, a hero, a self-imposed hero.

It's an ancient art tattooing, a craft maybe, artisans of the flesh; this man we watch tells us he is a painter, but you can't make money as an artist so he tattoos. I don't believe him, I don't think that's it at all; he feels shamed by Mark's beard and our arty appearance, he has pretensions, that's all, he doesn't think it a craft. But Mark does and he is watching it all happen, and longing to do it, to do a really beautiful tattoo, a true work of art, none of those black and crude outlines, but all shading, a butterfly, a flower, no Burt and Mimi forever or hearts full of mother (favorite the world over) or a dagger dripping blood and the legend, "This man deserves to go to heaven, he's been in hell on earth," none of that common stuff, but psychedelic, dainty, swirling, worthy of skin.

The tattoo parlor is crowded, the girlfriends look as though they were auditioning for an American International film called *Bike Orgy Kitten* and the men, well, the men are, surprisingly, strangely, perhaps only coincidentally, small, slight, and tender.

October 11, 1968

The Squares Light Up

Clink, thawat, clink thawat, the succulently glowing machines swallow coins. Balanced between two bandits, with arms extended, Miss Crucifix drops in the dimes, splat, a return of two hits the metal cup and is retrieved and inserted. The motion hardly breaks, the arms work on, her eyes gaze above the red glowing device at the next row where her image sister also inserts in rhythm. Reno.

Edgar—the old lady is slopped in all directions over a high stool—Edgar, I got a five. The Keno balls bounce like popcorn in their wire basket—twen-tee-two—the man says—four-te-five. The squares light up in random but urgently meaningful pattern; the old lady rearranges her thighs and squints in the permanent twilight, her woven sac bag swings against her dropping thighs. Edgar, I got a five—he looks through his round glasses at her piece of marked paper. The Keno marks are thick and black and like the bird tracks in comic book illustrations. I'm goin' home now, Edgar, I got a date this evening with a lady friend—she is resignedly coy—a lady friend, not a gentleman. She peers at him over the tops of his lenses. The thick exaggeration of the glass swims his thin eyes to pale gray. I'm broke—she says, and giggles, fishing with her clotted fingers deep into the woven bag. Edgar has thirteen pieces of marked paper; he counts them carefully, holds them under the punch-holed check sheet. You got nothing, the old woman says, turns toward me, and smiles.

I'm waiting to see the manager, rehearsing my story . . . I came here because I like excitement, no, that doesn't sound too good, I came here because my boyfriend lives here, do I look like I did that? I came here because California is too crowded. The important thing is that he should think I'm here to stay, here in the biggest little city in the world, why not? I need the job; if I get it I will be a change girl, wear a white blouse and black skirt and forty pounds of coins around my waist. I'll get $13 a day for eight hours on my feet and maybe back trouble. Outside this room, where would that be, the Bank of America, the Mint, outside this room the casinos bind two blocks of the street in electric-bulb opulence.

Above the Primadonna Casino four chorus girls made of fiber glass, gigantic and half-nude, swivel and smile twenty-four hours a day. Once each time around they could see, if they could see, above the electrically glittering roofs, the white stillness of the snow-draped mountains in the distance. Down the street the wedding chapel has a sign in the window ONE HOUR FREE PARKING FOR BRIDE AND GROOM. Along the side streets are ROOMS FOR RENT—DIVORCEES WELCOME; the landlady will testify that you have lived there the required time when the time comes, the witness fee is five dollars, statutory. Also offered are "fun house" in the TV room, perhaps consoling to sit with the bereft and watch domestic comedy from the imaginary suburbs of the Hollywood mind where the only divorces are on Peyton Place.

Edgar has left, he carried the pieces of paper in his hand with him, maybe he will go home and reexamine them, perhaps. . . . The old lady stares at me—any luck honey? I finger the warm dime in my pocket, should I put it into one of the machines, would I win seven fifty, and then what, would I walk away, would I? You the girl looking for a job? He's standing in front of me wearing a red vest; his name plate says SKIP. I wish I could. Yes, I stand up; he looks at my ankles. Ever worked in a Casino before? No—I say it with what I hope will look like an eager, but not too eager, a sort of honest but not too honest, a charming but not too refined, smile. OK—he says— go over to personnel and fill out a form and see me tomorrow; you can go through the alley—he points the way. It's on the next street— he says. I walk through the Casino, and out under the revolving plastic women and past the ubiquitous sixty-five-cent-ham-and-eggs sign, down the alley and to the back street where the pawnshops are. PERSONNEL, it says on a glass door. Skip sent me, I say to the girl inside. OK—she says and hands me an application form. I leave out my college education, my previous experience, sales I write, $85 a week. I can't remember my social security number, I say; she looks up from her typing. Oh well, she says, you can add it later if we need it. How's things? I ask, hoping to impress her with my existence in this city of anonymous distress and mechanical luck. Slow, she says, real slow; it's the snow that's hurting us—soon as it stops they'll come pouring in. Where do they come from? I ask with sincere interest, a smile, I want to get ahead even though she can see I am going (maybe if they will have me) to start from the bottom. Oh, California, San Francisco mostly, Oregon too, it's mad on weekends, Saturday and Sunday, she explains, in case I'm confused. Sometimes there are more California license plates than Nevada, you'll see, wait till the snow stops. I hope I get the job, I say. Yeah, she says and starts typing; my application is in a basket with all the others.

I walked back to the clinking womb of the club. Robert is waiting; he's been trying for a job as a shill at another club. How did it go? I ask him. They're all shits, he says. Earlier, on our first try, a man told us not to apply as a couple, not even as friends, they never hire couples, too easy for you to steal. We walk out, past the old lady who looks at us. Take it easy, she says, still rummaging in her cloth bag, her body lopsided on the high chair. If we don't get the jobs, we will hang out in the library. It's very beautiful and modern and full of green growing plants. I thought them plastic until I stuck out my hand to touch one and felt the moist tenderness of a real leaf. Their bulletin board announces daily classical record concerts in the library auditorium, and next week a woman is coming to play the flute.

April, 1967

Zip Zap

In and out of the New York Hilton in twenty-four hours of crush, Spanish screams in the hallway in the A.M., broken B & W TV and no Mr. Fix-it, check-in-check-out, might as well try and stay in the airport waiting room, ugly, depressing, visions of things to come? I hope not.

Moved to the Dorset, just around the corner, but thick Oriental carpets and hush-hush service. New York all different this time, opulence coats the pill, but pill it remains. Tried to get to Brooklyn in a thunderstorm, thrown out of three taxis before nice old driver said, OK, Lady, somebody has to take you there. But then he was over thirty-five and remembered what a service job entails. Money, it's all money, lady, he said, you try and get a cab from Kennedy to Brooklyn—hah! Or the Bronx! It's Manhattan or nowhere from the airport, 'cause all they want is money these days. I gave him a big tip when we finally got there, over the Brooklyn Bridge—dear iron relic, sold, they say, to every hick that hits town since it was built.

But then I'm a hick now, face craning up at the skyscrapers (at least you can see the sky), and the air is autumnal and greets the lungs and quickens the blood. Inside everywhere, it's too warm, stores, restaurants, office buildings, my lips evaporate in the steam heat, and I've used half a chapstick in six days. Saw *Trash* produced by Warhol, starring the usual unbelievables who symbolize all the alienation and people are meat syndrome of this decaying gotham. I found it poignant, moving me to a sighing sorrow, hanging inside my head along with his other masterpieces (I use the word precisely—works by a master). I think they will, in years to come, be reevaluated as the most relevant of our current films.

I spoke on the phone to Viva! My agent (yes—I have an agent now, and an editor, and a publisher for a book of my columns) is Viva's agent. Here, talk to Viva, she said! I did, it was, for me, a big moment. I imagine it was rather dull for Viva as I was over-awed and therefore tongue-tied. I will tell you that it wasn't at all like the conversation I reported two weeks ago, which as you no doubt suspected, was all made up. It never pays, I find out, to meet your idols, always

more cosmic to create it after the lights go out, you—your idol—
bowing and scraping into the Sunset. Went to the Whitney Museum
to see the Georgia O'Keefe retrospective. Amazing luminosity, giant
purple black iris, "looks to me like she's a lesbian" my mother had
said to me years ago, pointing to those same vaginal flowers. It was a
Wednesday morning and the museum was tea shoppe full of ladies
killing time until the matinee. Looked at the isolated landscapes with
my ears full of recipes and gossip. Also on show were Jackson Pol-
lock's drawings done for his psychoanalyst (who sold them recently
to a dealer). A distasteful ripoff of his privacy as well as his money as
he no doubt paid his fees as well. "Hum," said a lady, "well I always
knew he was an alcoholic." The Whitney is housed in a marvelously
textural cement building full of shape and shadow, for me one of the
best buildings I've been in.

Apart from that, most of the week has been spent in dodging cars
(they stop for no one), signaling taxis (likewise), and asking directions from policemen (polite but unhelpful). It's weird to be a stranger in your own hometown; I'm homesick for Los Angeles! (That last
statement amazes me too!)

November 13, 1970

What's That on Your Upper Lip?

Back in California I find it something of a relief not to have to see
another matron in maxi fake fur and Dynel mustache waddling toward
me through the omnipresent crowds of a New York street. The first
time I saw the mustache, and in this instance, worn with a contrasting
curly Van Dyke, I thought (it turned out incorrectly) that I was in
the presence of a true eccentric or, perhaps, a mocker of Women's
Liberation. No such thing for, I am advised by Paul (Paul d'Aldez of
Chez d'Aldez), mustaches for women are *le dernier cri,* the *absolu-
ment* up to the minute, mark of the now look.

I was taken to Chez d'Aldez by Violet Twing (fashion writer,
model, scene-maker) who said if I wanted to meet somebody outra-
geously creative and very with it, I should hop into her taxi and she'd

take me to meet Paul. OK, I said, New York by its totally debilitating effect having made me game for anything (more or less). We careened across town to East Fifty-fourth Street (where his salon is conveniently located amidst rows of Boutiques and Shoppes all featuring high-priced garments that make you look as though you had been dressed by the Kansas City Salvation Army). After Violet and Paul had pronounced each other's corporeal beings as splendid and marvelous, I was introduced as "someone you will love from Hollywood"!

I chatted a bit and then got up my courage to ask him about the hundred or so mustaches and beards of every color and texture that were suspended from the rococo ceiling by golden threads and twirling in the scant breeze from the electrified peacock fan over the Chinese sofa covered in uncut puce velvet and bordered with gold tassles of silk. Ah yes, he said, patting his softly powdered hairless cheeks, these are my gift to women. You see, said Violet, Paul is not just a creator of Face Pieces; he thinks of himself as a social commentator, a sociologist, maybe even a philosopher. Paul nodded modestly.

What gave you the idea of making beards and mustaches for women? I asked. Face Pieces, he said, I call them Face Pieces. Well —he crossed his leather-sheathed loins—well, you know all this brouhaha about Women's Liberation, well, I mean pants suits and unisex and little cigars; it's all part of the sexual revolution, isn't it? Besides with these new fibers, they don't itch at all and you can wash them and they dry right away over a toaster or the radiator; it isn't as though I were suggesting you wear one of those scratch-pasted Charlie Chaplins, Brillo, but Dynel, it's so silky, nice, nicer than real hair really and the color possibilities are enormous and worn right they hide those awful laugh lines and sagging chins. I mean not everyone wants to get a face-lift, do they, and as you can see—he gestured toward the twirling Face Pieces—the possibilities are absolutely endless. I've even made a tie-dye one for Enger Dilpe; it matches her Kaftan and when she wore it last week, it was a minor sensation, and there aren't too many sensations left these days, are there?

I asked if I could try one on. Of course, he said, they are practically indestructible; of course if you are serious you have to let me design one especially for your face—contours differ and the bone structure and all that—I try and make them fit naturally, match your skin tone, here try this amber one. The amber one had little jewels of yellow glass on the tips of the mustache which was splayed out like a cat's whiskers and came with a matching fuzzy "chin piece." You see, he said, pushing it against my upper lip, each hair is individually placed, this model is called Pussykat, and notice how the "chin piece" is cut away so you could wear a choker or even a cat's collar if you wanted to carry the design out to its fullest. He was busy dotting the thing with glue. Same stuff, he said, as you use for eyelashes, I stared past him into the mirror and must admit I sort of liked it, was I a victim of penis envy?

Everyone feels a little self-conscious at first, he said, but there is really no reason to feel self-conscious, I mean all fashion is artifice, high heels, wigs, rouge, whatever, why draw the sex line? Why indeed, I said. I think, he said, that it is the ultimate compliment to a man for a woman to wear a face piece. Perhaps it doesn't suit everyone, but what style does? He laughed. He could afford to laugh, for everyone that counts (in the fashion game) in New York is wearing them. What is this little red beard doing here? I asked (it was hanging almost hidden on the end of one hair of the mustache and beard). Ah, he said, that's my signature, I mean you could go to a man's hairpiece shop and buy just any old beard and mustache, and I've heard some people do, but that always happens, people will settle for cheap copies of anything—look at those plaster statues everywhere painted that awful gold, but it never looks right. If you want the real thing you have to come to Paul. That's true, said Violet, why I know someone, I wouldn't mention names, who bought one at that men's wig store on Forty-second Street and wears it everywhere and every time I see her I absolutely crack up; she even put a red bead on it somehow to try and make it look like she bought it from you, gets her clothes at Ohrbach's.

It's not the money, he said, it's the artistry. I asked him to peel off my mustache; it was beginning to tickle and I was afraid I would sneeze on it. Just tug away, he said, you can't hurt it—only thing you can't do in it is shower, but for making love . . . His eyebrow shot up.

Genuine Paul d'Aldez Face Pieces cost from $100 up, depending on the style, color, jewels, etc. He has one set made out of peacock feathers (for gala occasions) and others, rather more simple, for daytime wear. They all have the tiny red bead signature and no matter what price model you buy you get a personal fitting and a carrying case of clear plastic molded like a face so you can see (more or less) what it looks like on even when it is off. Thank you, I said, as we got ready to leave. It was my pleasure, he said. I'd love to do one especially for you, a little curly at the edges, I think, in graduated shades of blue. . . .

What do you think of that? asked Violet as we waited for a taxi. I think it's time I got back to the reality of Plain Old Hollywood, I said.

December 4, 1970